I0797426

Christianity and the Qur'an

Christianity and the Qur'an

The Rise of Islam in Christian Arabia

GABRIEL SAID REYNOLDS

Yale UNIVERSITY PRESS/NEW HAVEN & LONDON

Published with assistance from the foundation established in memory of Calvin Chapin of the Class of 1788, Yale College.

Yale University Press books may be purchased in quantity for educational, business, or promotional use. For information, please e-mail sales.press@yale.edu (U.S. office) or sales@yaleup.co.uk (U.K. office).

Set in Minion Pro type by Westchester Publishing Services.
Printed in the United States of America.

Library of Congress Control Number: 2024950831
ISBN 978-0-300-28175-0 (hardcover)

A catalogue record for this book is available from the British Library.

Authorized Representative in the EU: Easy Access System Europe, Mustamäe tee 50, 10621 Tallinn, Estonia, gpsr.requests@easproject.com

10 9 8 7 6 5 4 3 2 1

To my family

Contents

Preface and Acknowledgments

During my time as a student, and later as a faculty member at the University of Notre Dame, I have often read descriptions of Muhammad's Mecca as a city that was as rich as it was pagan. The riches and the paganism often go together in such descriptions, since the key to Mecca's wealth is imagined to be the attraction of its pagan shrine. Mecca in the seventh century CE, we are told, was a city of merchants and pagans, but it was not a city of Christians. Perhaps a few lone Christians passed through the city, but they were strangers, and out of place. This description has always felt off to me, above all because the Qur'an seems to engage, almost everywhere, with Christian traditions, Christian arguments, and indeed with Christians themselves. In the past few years I took the time to address the tension between the dominant story about Muhammad's Mecca and what the Qur'an itself suggests. The present work is the result.

This book has four chapters. In Chapter 1 I survey and assess earlier scholarship on Christianity and the Qur'an. Chapter 2 is a study of the Qur'an's biblical material. Chapter 3 addresses recent work on the linguistic context of the Qur'an and on pre-Islamic Arabian inscriptions (as the first part of this chapter is a bit technical, readers might want to take only a quick look at it to get a sense of its data, before moving on to its second part, beginning with the section "Qur'anic Evidence for Christianity").

In Chapter 4 I argue that the Qur'an, even when it does not explicitly mention Christianity, is concerned throughout with Christian ideas.

In a way, the immediate impetus for making this argument was the recent work done by scholars on Ancient North Arabian and Paleo-Arabic inscriptions. Among these scholars I owe a particular debt to Ahmad Al-Jallad and Hythem Sidky, who are both first-rate scholars and people. I am also in debt to the exceptional community in the International Qur'anic Studies Association, who have dealt with many (probably too many) of my talks on the Qur'an. I am grateful for the friendship of Emran El-Badawi, who was a pioneer in establishing the learned society. I am also in the debt of Nicolai Sinai and Jack Tannous, not only for their feedback on this particular book, but for the work they have done that has demonstrated how the Qur'an engages with biblical traditions. Nicolai and Jack have both produced works that will be seen as the landmark studies of our generation. I am also grateful to Marianna Klar and my colleague at Notre Dame Mun'im Sirry, both terrific scholars and also friends who have patiently put up with me and my various requests. Finally I must mention two more dear friends, Mehdi Azaiez and Martino Diez, who through the years have guided me, encouraged me, and forgiven me for my many faults. Many more colleagues and friends in academia have supported me as I worked on this project, and I beg their forgiveness for not mentioning every name.

The initial work on this book was done during the fall semester of 2022 at the University of Notre Dame. I am grateful to the university and to the Theology Department for that semester of leave, and to my colleagues in the department for their friendship through the years. John Cavadini was chair when I was hired and somehow found a reason to trust in my potential. Khaled Anatolios was chair as I was working through the final version of this text and has continued to support me.

I am grateful to David Bertaina, Emran El-Badawi, and Nicolai Sinai for carefully reading and critiquing an earlier version of this book. I express sincere gratitude to the team at Yale University Press, especially Jennifer Banks, Eva Skewes, and Mary Pasti, for their exceptional work on this text and support generally, and to Jessie Dolch for her exceptional copyediting. I am also grateful to the two anonymous reviewers for Yale University Press. All errors are my own responsibility.

Finally I thank my wife, Lourdes, and our five children. If there is something that I am proud of, it is not this book, or anything that I have ever written. It is my family.

Christianity and the Qur'an

O • N • E

Traditional Ideas About Christianity in Muhammad's Arabia

Islamic tradition makes Abū Bakr, ʿAlī, Khadīja, or Zayd b. Ḥāritha the first professed Muslim, but the standard account of Muhammad's first revelation makes someone named Waraqa b. Nawfal the first person to recognize him as a prophet. Muhammad, according to most traditional biographies, would spend a month each year on a mountain above Mecca known as Ḥirā' in a sort of spiritual retreat usually referred to as *taḥannuth* by the sources.[1] It was during one of these retreats on the mountain that the angel Gabriel appeared to Muhammad and communicated to him the first five verses of the Qur'an:

> Recite: In the Name of thy Lord who created
> Created Man of a blood-clot
> Recite: And thy Lord is the Most Generous,
> Who taught by the Pen,
> Taught Man that he knew not.[2]

In the version reported by Muhammad's biographer Ibn Isḥāq (d. 151 AH/767 CE), Muhammad later hears a voice as he makes his way down from the mountain: "O Muhammad! Thou art the apostle of God and I am Gabriel."[3] Yet despite hearing these words, and despite subsequently having a vision of the angel that appeared to him on the horizon,

Muhammad still doubted the authenticity of his experience. Reaching the bottom of the mountain he confided in his wife Khadīja, who told to him, with a touch of affection: "This cannot be, my dear. Perhaps you did see something."[4] When Muhammad explained what he had seen, Khadīja replied to him, "I have hope that thou wilt be the prophet of this people." Ibn Isḥāq continues:

> Then she rose and gathered her garments about her and set forth to her cousin Waraqa . . . , who had become a Christian and read the scriptures and learned from those that follow the Torah and the Gospel. And when she related to him what the apostle of God told her he had seen and heard, Waraqa cried, "Holy! Holy! Verily by Him in whose hand is Waraqa's soul, if thou hast spoken to me the truth, O Khadija, there hath come unto him the greatest Nāmūs who came to Moses aforetime, and lo, he is the prophet of this people. Bid him be of good heart."[5]

This account of Ibn Isḥāq is surprising not only for the way in which it places a Christian in Muhammad's Mecca (which is otherwise described as a pagan city), but indeed for the way in which it has a Christian so closely related to Muhammad (Waraqa also appears in the version of the account recorded by the traditionist Bukhārī [d. 256 AH/870 CE].[6] And Waraqa, as Henri Lammens points out, in the Islamic sources is not only a Christian, but a careful student of the scriptures.[7] This has led a number of scholars to speculate that Waraqa, who in fact is barely heard from again in the biography of the Prophet, could have played a particular role in communicating biblical traditions and ideas to Muhammad.[8]

In 1979 an argument to this effect was published in Arabic under the title *Qass wa-nabīy* ("The Priest and the Prophet") in a book series titled *al-Ḥaqīqa al-ṣaʿba*, "The Difficult Truth." The author, named in the Arabic edition only under the pseudonym Abū Mūsā al-Ḥarīrī,[9] argues that Waraqa not only was a key informant of Muhammad, but in fact was a priest of a community of Christians known as Nazoreans.[10] The historical existence of this community is suggested (to the author at least) by the Qur'an's use of a unique term for Christians. The Qur'an does not refer to Christians as *masīḥiyyūn,* as Arabic-speaking Christians refer to themselves, and as one would expect on the basis of the Greek name for Christians, *kristianoi,* and the Syriac name for Christians, *mshīḥāyē* or *krīstyānē.* Instead, it refers to them as *naṣārā,* a name that seems to be related to the city of Jesus, Nazareth (in Arabic *al-nāṣira*), and that is used (in a hostile way) to refer to the followers of Jesus in the Book of Acts.[11] Tellingly (for "al-Ḥarīrī"), certain late antique authors refer to a heretical sect of Christians known as the Nazoreans.[12]

The author, who in fact is named Joseph Azzi, argues that this community represented a form of "Jewish-Christianity" that had long before disappeared elsewhere but had continued on in Mecca. Indeed Azzi holds that our contemporary knowledge of the origins of Islam is clouded by the inability of Muslim scholars to see past the later Islamic biographies of Muhammad to the actual historical situation in his time and place, and the inability of Christian scholars to recognize the possibility that "Jewish-Christianity" had survived in Mecca and had a role in the rise of Islam. By Azzi's telling, Nazoreanism disappeared in Mecca only when Islam took its place, and Islam's rise, according to Azzi, was the collective work of Waraqa and Muhammad. They were concerned with divisions in the Nazorean community and sought to unify it under Muhammad. And yet Waraqa was definitely the brains of the operation.[13] It was Waraqa who took the word of God from Aramaic (the language of the Nazorean community, as Azzi sees it) and translated it into "clear Arabic" for Muhammad to recite. Nevertheless, the "priest" would disappear from history, while the "prophet" would rise and be remembered as the leader of a new religion.

Now, for his part Ibn Isḥāq names Waraqa among four men who, in pre-Islamic times, sought out the "Ḥanīfiyya, the religion of Abraham."[14] The other three include two who became Christians, like Waraqa. One of these is ʿUbaydallāh b. Jaḥsh, who became a Christian only after first converting to Islam. He joined fellow Muslims on the first emigration, to the Christian country of Ethiopia, and there embraced Christianity.[15] The other is ʿUthmān b. al-Ḥuwayrith, who became a Christian after emigrating to the Byzantine Empire; he converted after meeting the emperor. Finally Ibn Isḥāq mentions Zayd b. ʿAmr, to whom he gives the most attention by far. Zayd, Ibn Iṣḥāq tells us, accepted neither Judaism nor Christianity. He simply insisted that he worshipped the God of Abraham, and he set off on a quest looking for a new prophet. His quest took him as far as Iraq, where he learned that the new prophet was to come from his hometown: Mecca.[16]

Scholars, including Richard Bell, have long wondered why Ibn Isḥāq speaks of these four men seeking out the "Ḥanīfiyya," and where, after all, this term comes from. Ḥanīfiyya seems to be related to the Syriac word *ḥanpā*, the primary meaning of which is "pagan."[17] How could the two terms be related, when Ibn Isḥāq uses *ḥanīfiyya* precisely to refer to those men who were *not* pagan? I have argued that the close association of this term *ḥanīf* with Abraham in the Qur'an (eight of the ten uses of *ḥanīf* in the Qur'an are related to Abraham),[18] and the Qur'an's insistence that Abraham lived and taught before the Torah and the Gospel, suggests that, in the Qur'an at least, *ḥanīf* is used to indicate that Abraham was neither a Jew nor a Christian. In other words, in these qur'anic passages *ḥanīf* means "gentile" (in the sense of neither Jew *nor* Christian) or one of the "nations."[19] Tellingly, *ḥanpā* is used at least once to translate *ethnikos* ("gentile") in the Syriac New Testament (Matt 18:17). Accordingly there is an important precedent for the Qur'an's use of this Semitic root with the meaning of "gentile."

For his part, however, Bell holds that the term simply comes from the Arabic root *ḥ-n-f*, meaning "to leave" (since these four men "left" paganism). It thus would be roughly parallel to another term in the Qur'an that has confused commentators: *ṣābi'ūn*. While the Qur'an (Q 2:62, 5:69) seems to use this term to refer to an unknown group of monotheists alongside Jews and Christians, the classical Arabic lexicographers suggest that its root (*ṣ-b-'*) also means "to leave" and specifically "to leave" one religion for another.[20] Still, Ibn Isḥāq is up to something different than the Qur'an with his account of the four "*ḥanīf*s." While the Qur'an uses this term principally to make an argument against Jewish and Christian claims to represent the religion of Abraham,[21] Ibn Isḥāq means to show, through his story of these men, that there were people in Muhammad's context, right at the time that Muhammad emerged, who rejected paganism. The four *ḥanīf*s serve as a sort of preparation for the coming of Muhammad in his biography, not unlike the manner in which John the Baptist "makes straight the way" for Jesus in the Gospels.

And yet scholars like Bell tended to see these reports not as an element of the apologetic strategy of Ibn Isḥāq or other Muslim scholars, but rather as more or less reliable accounts of "what really happened." Thus Bell wonders what these *ḥanīfs* were doing in Arabia and what role they had in Muhammad's own religious development. To Bell the sudden appearance of *ḥanīfs* in Mecca must mean that some cultural or social phenomenon was occurring. The Arabs were now yearning for monotheism.[22] Perhaps, Bell speculates, Muhammad was the ultimate product of this cultural phenomenon. Bell writes: "Some memory of the existence of such a movement [a movement searching 'for a more satisfying faith'] in Arabia, and particularly in the neighbourhood of Mecca at and before Muhammad's time, is probably preserved in the Moslem traditions as to the Ḥanīfs who were more or less associated with the Prophet."[23] Bell argues ultimately that Muhammad was indebted to the religious movements around him: "He is not the originator of monotheism in Arabia. In a sense he is not even the preacher of monotheism. For with him that there is one God is an axiom rather than a truth to be argued for."[24] But what sort of monotheism was actually surrounding Muhammad in early seventh-century Arabia? Was there only a vague sort of notion around about the worship of one God represented by *ḥanīfs*?

Or did the *ḥanīfs* exist at all? The Belgian scholar Henri Lammens argued in 1918, several years before Bell published his *Origin of Islam,* that there is good reason to think the *ḥanīfs* are simply the creation of Islamic tradition, invented "in order to fill the gaps of pre-Islamic history, to create groups and believers in the supposed *dīn* of Abraham, that is precursors of Muhammad."[25] Bell, however, insists that they were real.[26]

A "Degenerate" Christianity

If Bell saw the *ḥanīfs* as representing a movement among the Arabs toward monotheism that had a role in Muhammad's religious awakening, he also told another story about the role of Christianity in Islam's rise. This story—related to but different from the story told by Joseph Azzi—begins with the principle that the Christianity which Muhammad encountered in the seventh-century Middle East was only a disfigured vestige of the pure faith that the apostles of Christ had preached and practiced. Bell develops this idea, alongside his ideas about the *ḥanīfs*, in *The Origin of Islam in Its Christian Environment*, an edited version of a series of lectures delivered in 1925 at the University of Edinburgh (presumably before a largely Protestant audience) where he had recently been appointed. Bell, who was himself a minister of the Church of Scotland, opens the first lecture with the following reflection:

> From one point of view the triumph of Islam in the East in the seventh century AD may be regarded as the judgement of history upon a degenerate Christianity. The degeneration of the Church may be said to have begun in the fourth century. The seeds of it were present earlier, but they could not well develop in a persecuted Church. When the Church was freed from the danger of persecution by the accession of Constantine, they began to develop rapidly.[27]

To Bell and many other, principally Protestant, observers of Islam, it is not so much Muhammad's fault that he rejected Christianity and decided instead to start his own religion. The Christianity he encountered was "degenerate" and would have repulsed him, not attracted him.[28] And yet (Bell imagines), Muhammad nevertheless found things that he liked about the Christianity of his day and borrowed them. For example, Muhammad (from Bell's perspective) discovered the idea of combining religious and political authority from the imperial Christianity of his day: "If we sometimes feel ourselves brought up with a shock against the fact that Islam is apparently incurably political, is, as we say, not only a religion but a state, we must remember that that was what Muhammad saw in Christianity, and also what he gathered from the Old Testament."[29] Later in Bell's work we read that he is also interested in the possibility that a particular strain of a particularly unorthodox Christian group, namely the Elkesaites, somehow played a role in the rise of Islam. Now, Bell thinks that the "El" in the name of this group and that of its eponymous founder, Elkesai, implies that he was an Arab (since, in fact, El or Al is the definite article in Classical Arabic). Thus Bell speculates, rather unfortunately, that the Elkesaites might "illustrate the effect of mingled

Jewish and Christian ideas upon the Arab mind."[30] Setting aside this simplistic view of culture and "the Arab mind," we might nevertheless note with Bell that Elkesai claimed, according to patristic reports, to have received a book from God, to have emphasized the last judgment, and to have instructed his followers to pray toward Jerusalem.[31] All of this seems close to our reports regarding Muhammad (who by tradition had his followers for some time in Medina pray toward Jerusalem). Finally Bell allows himself to speculate that the Qur'an actually refers to the Elkesaites, calling them by the name Ṣābi'ūn (a name we've discussed above) and counting them among the monotheists alongside Jews and Christians (Q 2:62, 5:69). And yet in the end Bell also acknowledges that we have no record of Elkesaites beyond the first few Christian centuries, and indeed even then no record of them anywhere near the Hijaz, and thus he calls this an "obscure" matter.[32]

It seems to me that Bell's interest in the Elkesaites, despite the absence of any real evidence placing them in the late antique Hijaz, reflects two convictions: first, that the Hijaz was largely untouched by "orthodox" or mainstream Christians (that is, Melkites, Jacobites, and the Church of the East), and second, that the qur'anic statements on Christ are best explained anyway as echoes of heterodox or heretical Christian teaching. Together these two convictions led him to the conclusion that whatever fragments of Christianity Muhammad encountered were likely to have been corrupted almost beyond recognition from the apostolic faith of the first believers.

Bell's idea of Elkesaite influence on Islam's origins, which incidentally was proposed (putatively) before Bell by the Austrian scholar Aloys Sprenger, is one manifestation of a more general interest in Jewish Christianity and Islam that is particularly important in late nineteenth- and early twentieth-century scholarship (but which has never entirely gone away).[33] The classic articulation of this idea is that of the Protestant theologian Adolf von Harnack in his *Lehrbuch der Dogmengeschichte:* "Islam is a transformation of gnostic Jewish-Christianity, which is itself a transformation of the Jewish religion in Arab soil, through a great prophet."[34] Yet the theory of Jewish Christian influence on Islam had its critics even early on and is largely out of favor in recent scholarship.[35]

Other Protestant observers, while not focusing on Jewish Christianity, were still more insistent on the idea of a "degenerate" Christianity in Muhammad's Hijaz. From January 23 to 28, 1911, a meeting was held in Lucknow, India (at the time under British colonial rule), bringing together missionaries from various Protestant denominations to discuss the "problem" of evangelizing Muslims.[36] This was the second such conference, after a meeting in Cairo in 1906. To my knowledge a third conference, planned for Cairo in 1916, never took place (presumably because of World War I). One of the addresses from Lucknow preserved in the written acts of the conference is that of an American missionary from New York named Robert Speer titled "The Attitude of the Evangelist Toward the Muslim and His Religion." After discussing the need for missionaries to be absolutely fair, and to recognize all that is good in Islam, and after considering some of the teachings of Islam, Speer wrote the following:

> The view of Christianity which lies at the base of Islam and which led Muhammad to repudiate it was a false view. He had never met the Christianity of Christ and the Apostles. The Qur'an shows what a travesty of the Gospel had come to him. When we inquire into Muhammad's rejection of Christianity, we find that he never had anything but the most perverted idea of what Christianity really was. The Christianity which he rejected was of a very debased type, half polytheistic in its theology, superstitious in its worship, and with a sacred history encrusted with puerile legends.[37]

Now, when the missionaries gathered in Lucknow called for a "united front" against Islam, they meant a united Protestant front, and the statement above shows particularly Protestant convictions. In any case, the logic in the statement is interesting because it involves a certain approach that moves backward from the Qur'an to its apparent (decadent) Christian sources. "The Qur'an shows," Speer says, that only a "travesty" of the Gospel had reached Muhammad, by which he may have in mind (although he doesn't give specific examples) a few specific passages. First, one thinks of Q 5:116, which has God ask Jesus, "Didst thou say unto men, 'Take me and my mother as gods, apart from God'?" This statement is often imagined to imply that Muhammad had a mistaken idea of the Trinity: instead of "Father, Son, and Holy Spirit," he thought of "Father, Mother, and Son."[38] Speer (although I am speculating here) might have thought that a "half polytheistic" veneration of Mary in the historic Christian churches of the Near East led to Muhammad's "confusion" about the Trinity.

Second, one imagines that by "puerile legends" Speer has in mind the sorts of miracle stories that the Qur'an tells about Jesus but that are not found in the New Testament, for example, that Jesus formed a bird from clay and brought it to life (Q 3:49, 5:110) or that he spoke as an infant "in the cradle" (Q 3:46, 5:110, 19:29). These stories are found in texts known as the *Infancy Gospel of Thomas* and the *Gospel of Pseudo Matthew*, respectively.[39] Tellingly, they are both, in their Christian context, meant to act as proofs of the divinity of Jesus. It is accordingly not surprising to find that the Qur'an credits these things to "God's permission" each time it mentions them (the exception being Q 19:29–33, but there the infant Jesus declares himself the "servant of God").

Third, it is possible that Speer would say (he would not be alone) that the apparent denial of the crucifixion of Jesus in the Qur'an (Q 4:157–59) is somehow the product of another Christian heresy, this one a sort of docetic Gnosticism.[40]

Protestant apologists were not the only ones who looked for heretics in the context of the Qur'an. Hamilton Gibb, Scottish historian and professor first at Oxford and then at Harvard, found it unlikely that "institutional" Christianity was a significant part of the Qur'an's context. After noting that much of the Qur'an's religious vocabulary is colored with expressions from Aramaic, he continues:

> It is a far cry from this, however, to infer that pre-Islamic monotheism in Arabia was directly connected with the institutionally organized Jewish or Christian communities. Such communities certainly existed in Arabia, but there is considerable evidence both from Muslim texts and from external

> sources that other monotheistic groups were to be found in Arabia, independently of the organized churches and hence "heretical" in their eyes.[41]

In my opinion there are better ways of explaining the qur'anic material on Jesus than hunting for heretics. As I have argued, the most important thing to keep in mind when evaluating qur'anic material on the Bible, and on Jews and Christians, is that the Qur'an does not simply copy or repeat traditions around it.[42] The qur'anic author is an original, active, and creative force. He thoughtfully reshapes, even caricatures, the ideas and traditions of his opponents. For example, in Q 9:31 the Qur'an speaks of Jews and Christians worshipping (literally, "taking as lords") their "rabbis and monks." What if one were to apply the sort of reading seen above for Q 5:116 (which explains the mention of "taking" Mary as a goddess with reference to a sect of "Mary worshippers") to Q 9:31? One would then, presumably, need to hunt for "clergy worshippers" in the Qur'an's context. Perhaps these "clergy worshippers" were pushed out into the Arabian desert by the fanatical Chalcedonian emperors and bishops of Byzantium. After all, Arabia is thought to be (although we will see the saying does not have a clear source) *haeresium ferax*, "the womb of heresies."[43] Perhaps these "clergy worshippers" baked loaves of bread for their priests and rabbis as (according to Epiphanius) other heretics baked loaves of bread for the Virgin Mary (and thus were given the name Collyridians).[44]

This is meant of course as a *reductio ad absurdum* of the idea that one should hunt for heresies in order to explain the qur'anic material on Christianity. In fact, I consider it a much more reasonable position to acknowledge that the Qur'an's author is creative and ingenious and uses rhetoric to build up straw-man opponents or to paint caricatures of other beliefs. Thus, in other words, Q 9:31 would seem to be more about the author's conviction that Jewish and Christian clergy wield too much authority (perhaps the sort that was preventing their followers from acknowledging a new prophet).[45] Similarly, other statements about Christian doctrine in the Qur'an need not be precise reflections of aberrant or heretical Christian currents but might be thoughtful and purposeful (mis)representations of orthodox Christian teaching. Of course, it is also possible (although this idea is barely countenanced any longer in qur'anic studies scholarship) that the qur'anic author had a less-than-perfect understanding of Christian doctrine or practice.

And yet the old suggestion that Muhammad would have embraced Christianity if only he had met apostolic Christians does not always depend on the idea that he encountered strange, exotic groups of Christian heretics in Arabia, Mary worshippers, apocryphal gospel lovers, or otherwise. For Bell the Eastern Church generally, including its traditional communities, was the problem:

> That in spite of its intellectual superiority [the Eastern Church] was weak in moral and religious insight, when called upon to meet the onslaught of Islam the treatment of that religion by John of Damascus furnishes proof. He regards it simply as a kind of bastard Christianity, which is sufficiently refuted by the absurdities contained in the Qur'ān, and the defects of its intellectual conception of God. For the dynamic force and moral passion of this new religion which was conquering the world around him he has no eyes at all.[46]

To Bell the church in the East was overcome by "tradition and fanaticism" and had in fact (despite its intellectual activity on questions such as Christology) lost its ability to see or think clearly. The Eastern Church was in the hands of "worldly, ambitious, and self-proud prelates" who were overcome with internal rivalries, as "the relation of the divine and the human in Jesus Christ, became the shuttlecock of warring parties."[47] One may wonder how Bell knew so much (in 1920s Scotland) about the interior dispositions of the priests and bishops of the late antique Near East. Nevertheless, he goes on, and with no little sympathy for Nestorius, the bishop of Constantinople, to describe the Christological troubles of the fifth century that led to lasting divisions in the church between Melkite, Jacobite, and "Nestorian." All of this leads him to the following declaration: "But if Islam may thus be regarded as a hostile force, whose irruption into the cultured lands of the East was made easy by the pride and unloveliness of a debased Christianity, from another point of view it may be regarded as in part at least the fruit of Christianity itself."[48]

It is here where things really get interesting in Bell's analysis of Islam's "origin." For while Bell laments the description by John of Damascus of Islam as a Christian heresy, and while he finds the Christianity of the East to have been "unlovely," he also thinks that it had something to do with the emergence of Islam after all. Perhaps Eastern Christianity not only had a repulsive force, but also had a positive role in the formation of Islam. And yet Bell conceives of Muhammad only gradually getting to know Christians and Christianity. Following a strict chronological reading of the Qur'an, Bell acknowledges that there is biblical material in the "Meccan" Suras, but he argues that Muhammad did not even know of the difference between Jews and Christians before the halfway mark of his prophetic career. This explains Bell's statement, "The key to a great deal both in the Qur'ān and in the career of Muhammad lies, as I hope to show, just in his gradual acquisition of knowledge of what the Bible contained and of what Jews and Christians believed."[49] As regards Muhammad's acquisition of knowledge about Christianity in particular, Bell sees this largely coming from outside of Arabia, something we will contend with in this book.[50]

Muhammad and Allah

Approximately ninety years after Richard Bell delivered his lectures in Scotland, Aziz Al-Azmeh published *The Emergence of Islam in Late Antiquity* in England. Al-Azmeh agrees with Bell that the religious ideas in the Qur'an are in large part the personal achievement of Muhammad. He disagrees, however, with the notion that Islam was a primitive force that intruded into "cultured" Christian lands. Instead, he holds that Islam itself is the "crystallization" of the late antique period, in part but not only because of its monotheism.[51] Al-Azmeh writes:

> While Barbarian Germanic invaders are most often seen, with the possible exception of the Ostrogoths, as having sapped away the capacity and the constitution of the Roman empire, Barbarian Arab invaders gave it added capacity and vigour, greater geographical extension, and a fresh lease of life, albeit under a novel and unexpected signature. The Arab empires

> were in continuity with Rome in terms of their notion of a monotheistic world religion, in their œcumenical vocations, and in a variety of other senses as well, including culture. All of these were appropriated, selectively, as from an inventory of possibilities "decanted" in Late Antiquity, and instantiated under a new signature, Arabic in language and Muslim in religion.[52]

Thus Al-Azmeh sees Islam as revivifying older Roman culture (a novel perspective that I will not address further here). However, the monotheism brought by Islam was fundamentally new, for from his perspective the pre-Islamic Hijaz was a pagan island in a monotheistic sea:

> Western Arabia of c. 600 was an anachronism. In terms of religious history, it was not contemporary with surrounding territories between which it was wedged. It was a pagan reservation that had been largely passed over by developments occurring elsewhere, and was in a real sense historically retarded with respect to surrounding areas, retardation being understood in terms of the historical dynamics of *Verzeitlichung*, temporalisation, and shorn of its normative connotation.[53]

One discovers later in Al-Azmeh's book how these convictions regarding the paganism of Arabia play out in his view of the origins of Islam as a religion. He insists that the God of Islam was not "borrowed" from the God of Christians—no matter how much Arabic *allāh* resembles Syriac/ Aramaic *alāhā*. For Al-Azmeh it is not right, historically speaking at least, to think of Allah as the God of the Bible. He also denies the popular orientalist idea that Allah was the high god of the pre-Islamic Arabian pantheon before becoming the only God of Islam.[54] Instead, he holds that Allah was an obscure god in pre-Islamic Mecca.[55] The rise of Allah (if we may put it that way) was, simply put, the achievement of Muhammad: "For all its slight incidence in ancient Arabic poetry, on the assumption of integrity and despite the possibility of interpolation, we have seen that Allāh had no significant or durable cult among the late antique

Arabs of the Ḥijāz or elsewhere, but was, as we shall see, invited to inhabit the Meccan Kaʿba during the ministry of Muḥammad."[56] Indeed Al-Azmeh holds that Muhammad associated the figure of Allah, whom he also called al-Raḥmān ("The Merciful"), not only with the Kaʿba but specifically with the mysterious black stone at its corner.[57] Early in Muhammad's career Allah was "the sublime presence residing in the betyl at the Meccan Kaʿba" and so named *rabb al-bayt,* "Lord of the House."[58] Later Allah came to "denote divinity overall."[59] All of these observations, however, are complicated by the presence of Arabic Christian inscriptions (see Chapter 3) that speak of God indeed as *al-ilāh* (plausibly seen as a calque of *ho-theos,* "the god," in Greek). Al-Azmeh is aware of these, but he denies any connection between them and Allah.[60] Since the publication of his book, Christian Robin has offered a convincing reply, showing after a meticulous study of South Arabian Paleo-Arabic inscriptions (and Syriac hagiography) that almost certainly pre-Islamic Christians referred to God not only as *al-ilāh* but also as Allah.[61] Thus this name seems after all not to isolate Islam but to connect it to Arabic-speaking Christianity.

Al-Azmeh's explanation for the presence of biblical material in the Qur'an (which he does not deny) is analogous to his explanation for the origin of the name Allah. The Qur'an's author did not borrow, and was not fundamentally shaped or influenced by, biblical traditions or ideas. Instead, the Qur'an's author shaped those ideas for his own purposes: "The Qur'anic Biblicism did not amount to a Biblisation of the Qur'ān, but rather involved the Qur'ānisation of biblical figures, fragments, and templates."[62]

It is not hard to imagine examples that would seem to vindicate the argument of Al-Azmeh on the point of "Qur'ānisation" of biblical matters. I offer just one. In Qur'an 11 (cf. Q 15:51–60, 51:24–37) three messengers (*rusul*) appear to Abraham and his wife and announce news of a son. The story is close to that of Genesis 18 in which the promise of a son, given earlier to Abraham (Gen 13:16, 15:5), is dramatically fulfilled through the visit of three mysterious men who arrive just after Abraham has fulfilled his responsibility of circumcision. From the midst of these three visitors God speaks. The divine announcement is made even more dramatic by the reaction of Sarah (Gen 18:12), who laughs upon hearing the news (and later lies about laughing). It is all simply unbelievable, since she and her husband are past childbearing age. The laughter is key to the whole episode, as "she laughs" (*tiẓḥaq*) is a play on the name for the son whom she would conceive, "Isaac" (*yiẓḥāq*). In the Qur'an, however, the drama is reduced. Abraham's wife, who is unnamed, does indeed laugh, but it is not clear in the text why she laughs. Qur'an 11:71 reads: "And his wife was standing by; she laughed, therefore We gave her the glad tidings of Isaac, and, after Isaac, of Jacob." The key bit in Arabic is *ḍaḥikat fa-bashsharnāhā,* which suggests that she laughed *before* any announcement of a son. This is translated reasonably by Arberry "she laughed, therefore We gave her the glad tidings." In other words, Arberry, following the qur'anic word order, does not imagine that "Sarah" laughed *because* of the promise of a son, although presumably he knew the connection with Gen 18:12 by which her laughter is a response to (and not a cause of) these glad tidings.

Now, the order of things may be reversed because the Qur'an needed the verse to rhyme in *īC* or *ūC* (*C* representing any consonant). This was achieved by placing the name of Jacob, *ya'qūb,* at the end, after Isaac.[63] Nevertheless, this reordering of things is not really the issue. On the one hand, the play on words between Isaac and laughter cannot be achieved anyway (as Arabic "she laughed," *ḍaḥikat,* is from a different root than the name Isaac, *isḥāq*). On the other hand, the Qur'an is not concerned here with any covenant made earlier by God with Abraham. The whole logic of the pentateuchal narrative, where the election of Abraham anticipates that of Israel, is hardly of interest to the Qur'an. Instead, the Qur'an integrates this story into its larger theme of divine punishment and divine mercy, by having the messengers (angelic or otherwise) both reassure Abraham that they have been sent to destroy Lot's people (11:70) and reprimand Sarah (who declares her shock at the "glad tidings" in v. 72; cf. Q 51:29, where she strikes her face) for doubting God's command (v. 73). She possibly is set up here as a parallel figure to Lot's wife, who is condemned a few verses later (v. 81). All of this does indeed seem to be something like a "Qur'anisation" of biblical figures.

And yet I argue (principally in Chapter 4) that the relationship of the Qur'an to the Bible is not that simple, and indeed that the warp and woof of the qur'anic tapestry is in fact biblical. By this I mean that biblical material is not a mere ornamentation or decoration that adds color or texture to the theological message of the Qur'an. Instead, the Qur'an is in substance, both in its form and its content, related to the Bible and biblical traditions. The Qur'an speaks of one God who created the heavens and earth in six days, who imbued the earth with signs of his existence, who shows mercy to humans through the messages delivered in the ministry of prophets, and who has a certain regard for human freedom to come to valid moral judgments concerning both worship and the ethical treatment of other humans, and who will judge them on the Day of Resurrection. This is a common foundation to both the Bible and the Qur'an. The Qur'an, in other words, is not biblical only in the stories it tells, in its turns of phrase (see Chapter 2), or because its main protagonists are Adam, Noah, Abraham, Moses, Mary, and Jesus (along with demons and angels). The Qur'an is biblical in its fundamental theological and anthropological vision.

Al-Azmeh is not the only scholar to disagree with my perspective. In his book *The Qur'an and Its Biblical Reflexes* Mark Durie holds that the biblical material in the Qur'an is "borrowed" not "inherited." Much like Al-Azmeh, he argues that the Qur'an represents a fundamental disruption with biblical theology. This is more or less what he means by "reflexes" (the title of his book perhaps being a play on my earlier book *The Qur'an and Its Biblical Subtext*). The Qur'an, from his point of view, does not preserve the theological system or the structural relationship of ideas in the Bible. He advances this point toward the end of his work by analyzing a number of the Qur'an's key religious concepts. He argues, for example, that the theology of the Qur'an, unlike that of the Bible, is based principally on Arab understandings of a slave-master relationship: "In the Qur'an the relationship of a believer to Allāh is not covenantal in the Biblical sense, for what is emphasized is divine command and human obedience, rather than a covenantal understanding of mutually binding obligations involving loving loyalty."[64] One sign he points to in order to argue that the qur'anic idea of the divine-human relationship is fundamentally different from that of the Bible is the Qur'an's exceptional interest in the idea of *shirk*, or "association." The Qur'an makes *shirk*, the act of associating something with God, the unforgiveable sin

(Q 4:48, 116), whereas the idea of association (and the Semitic root *sh-r-k*) is of little consequence to the Bible (according to Durie).

Similarly the Qur'an's idea of a prophet (again, according to Durie) has little to do with that of the Bible. Biblical prophets are all unique and respond in particular ways to the certain situations in which God sought to communicate with his people. Qur'anic prophets, on the other hand, are all fundamentally similar (Durie calls this "messenger uniformitarianism"). They are all faced with the opposition and rejection of infidels, and they all prepare the way for divine vengeance (all of which is connected with the idea of *sunnat Allāh*—the "way" or "conduct" of God). Thus Durie argues that the Qur'an generally is not fundamentally related to the Bible: "[The Qur'an] is neither a text subsidiary to the Bible, nor is it to be attached to a genetic 'family tree' alongside it. Instead, it is a work which marches to the beat of its own theological drum. Drawing extensively on other sources, but not theologically beholden to them, it imposes its distinctive theological frame on everything it repurposes."[65] In some ways the works of Al-Azmeh and Durie are quite different. For example, Al-Azmeh imagines (not unlike some of the earlier orientalists) that it is possible to follow the interior developments of Muhammad's mental convictions, for example, his "transition from the receipt of inspiration to the receipt of revelation."[66] By "inspiration" he means a general concept of *waḥy,* which Al-Azmeh, drawing from Montgomery Watt (Bell's student), renders as a "flashing suggestion or prompting," and by "revelation" he means "being the recipient of a readable and verbally transmissible Scripture."[67] Al-Azmeh also emphasizes pagan Mecca as a key element of the Qur'an's historical context, while Durie speculates that Islam might have originated farther to the north of the Hijaz in a monotheistic environment. However, both authors agree on the independence of the Qur'an's religious system and seek to separate it from that of the Bible.

It is interesting to note how far apart Al-Azmeh and Durie are regarding the historical context of the Qur'an. Al-Azmeh's insistence on the pagan nature of the Hijaz more or less falls in line with the perspective of the early orientalists. Bell himself spends much of *The Origin of Islam* in mapping out where he thinks Christians might have been found in early seventh-century Arabia. He starts by describing the Arab Christians of late antique Syria, noting that Arab Christians were found well to the north of the Arabian Peninsula, for example in the region of Antioch, and indeed contends that the most famous saint of the time, St. Simeon the Stylite, was an Arab.[68] He also notes that the Jafnids/Ghassanids, who had varying degrees of sovereignty in the region of modern-day southern Syria/northern Jordan (their center of power was at Jabiya in the Golan Heights), and who played a central role in Byzantium's rivalry with Persia, were Christian Arabs. Bell emphasizes in particular the role of the Jafnid ruler al-Ḥārith (r. 528–569 CE) as an advocate for, and protector of, Jacobite/Miaphysite Christianity.[69] Similarly, Bell describes the spread of Christianity among the Arab Nasrids/Lakhmids, whose rule was centered in the Iraqi city of Hira. Unlike the Jafnids, the Nasrids were largely members of the Church of the East (Bell uses the misnomer "Nestorian"), and they had close relationships not with Byzantium but with the Sasanian Persian Empire. Of particular interest is a figure known as Hind bint Nuʿmān, who married a Nasrid ruler named al-Mundhir (not to be confused with a Jafnid ruler from the sixth century of the same name). Hind was herself a daughter of a Jafnid and a Christian; she founded a convent in Hira (according to Islamic sources), and her son ʿAmr, who went on to rule in that city, was a faithful Christian.

Finally Bell turns his attention to the south, describing the importance of Christianity in Abyssinia/Ethiopia in late antiquity and noting the role that Abyssinian Christianity would play in South Arabia in the sixth century, after the invading of Yemen and overthrowing of the Jewish king Dhū Nuwās there in 525 CE. For the next century or so Christian rulers, with the support of the Abyssinians, would rule in South Arabia. Soon after the overthrowing of the Jewish ruler, who presumably was a native of Yemen, a Christian ruler originally from Abyssinia named Abraha (that is, Abraham) would rise to power and extend his influence into Central Arabia. Islamic tradition holds that he also built a great church in Sanʿa and sought (but failed) to destroy the Kaʿba by leading an expedition to Mecca (with an elephant) in the very year of Muhammad's birth. This story is almost certainly a myth, but there is evidence of Abraha's campaigns elsewhere in Central Arabia (see Chapter 3).

The presence of Christians in South Arabia is well attested in pre-Islamic inscriptions, some of which bear crosses. Moreover, certain terms in the Qur'an, most famously the use of "The Merciful" (*al-raḥmān*) to refer to God, are often attributed to linguistic practices attested in these pre-Islamic, Christian (and Jewish), South Arabian inscriptions. Still, Bell questions whether the presence of Christianity in South Arabia is really part of a story of Christianity that might involve also the Hijaz, where Islam will rise. He writes, "In a way the existence of a Christian Church here belongs to the Christian encirclement of Arabia rather than to the history of Christianity in Arabia itself."[70] By this he means that South Arabia, principally because of its geography, had historically been separated from the regions of the Arabian Peninsula to the north. The mountains of Yemen limited the contact (over land, at least) between Central and South Arabia.

In fact South Arabia had its own language family. Ancient South Arabian represents an independent branch of the Semitic language tree and is distinct from Ancient North Arabian languages/dialects, including Classical Arabic. The religious history, including the pantheon, of the diverse South Arabian regions before Islam is also generally held to be distinct. Now, Islamic tradition tells the story of a Christian deputation from the South Arabian city (in the south of modern-day Saudi Arabia) of Najran to Muhammad's Medina. However, this story might be seen as just that and no more. It appears to be a convenient way of explaining a passage of Sura 3 (*āl 'Imrān*) and especially the reference in it to a "trial" or "ordeal" (*mubāhala*) that would decide whether Muhammad's view of Jesus, or that of some anonymous group of Christians, is the truth (Q 3:61).[71]

In any case, Bell's description of Christianity "encircling" Arabia, reflected years later in Al-Azmeh's idea of western Arabia as a "pagan reservation," brings us closer to the theme of this book. It raises the question of whether Christianity was also found in the interior, and possibly in Muhammad's own environment, the Hijaz. On this question Bell is notably agnostic.[72] The orientalists long speculated about the possibility that individual Christians wandered into the Hijaz either to trade or to evangelize, or both; Bell is no exception.[73] Still, they generally hold that Christianity had only a modest presence in the interior of

Arabia and no real impact on the culture and thinking of the pre-Islamic Arabs. That is, they held that there were Christians here and there in Muhammad's environment but no real settled Christian community. Bell, after analyzing various passages of poems attributed to pre-Islamic authors, writes the following: "Had Christianity produced a deep impression upon Arabia, it would no doubt have burst through the convention which confined poetry to the subject and temper of the old desert life, or at least have produced a religious literature of its own. But it was left to Islam to bring that impulse."[74] There are (at least) two problems with these comments. First, among the "pre-Islamic" poems are many attributed to Christians, a topic examined extensively by the Syrian Jesuit Louis Cheikho in his book *Shuʿarāʾ al-naṣrāniyya qabl al-Islām*.[75] Second, this poetry might be the way it is (with few references to Christian themes even by "Christian" authors) because it is in fact principally the product of later Muslim authors imagining what poets from pagan times might have written. The "pre-Islamic" poems that Bell discusses, and which before him Cheikho had examined extensively, are all (without exception) from Islamic works (from the Abbasid era, as a rule) that claim to be quoting something said by a pagan hundreds of years earlier. For example, Imrūʾ al-Qays is said to have died around 550 CE, yet the earliest of his poems dates from the time of Aṣmāʿī (d. 213 AH/828 CE) or that of the *Kitāb al-Aghanī* attributed to Abū l-Faraj al-Iṣfahānī (d. 356 AH/967 CE). In addition, the poetry shows no particular indication of regional registers of Arabic, as one would expect in light of the various tribal backgrounds of the authors to whom the poems are attributed, but instead is written in the Classical Arabic typical of Abbasid-era writings, heavily influenced by the Qur'an.[76] Indeed these poems not infrequently contain references to material in the Qur'an, which led Clément Huart to imagine that the works of Umayya b. Abī l-Ṣalt offered us a "new source" of the Qur'an.[77] To his credit Bell recognizes that at least not all of the so-called pre-Islamic poetry is genuine.[78]

Although referring to "pre-Islamic" poetry is back in vogue, it is worth remembering some old-school observations.[79] Lammens notes, for example, how the pre-Islamic Christian poet ʿAdī b. Zayd (from Hira, modern-day Iraq) is improbably made to testify to the "god of Mecca."[80]

More recently Franz-Christoph Muth has shown that the "pre-Islamic" poetry cited to explain the *hapax* phrase *ṭayr abābīl* in Qur'an 105 presumes knowledge of Islamic traditions about that Sura.[81] Nöldeke made a similar observation regarding the pre-Islamic poetry used to explain why the Qur'an calls the mountain on which Noah's ark landed al-Jūdī.[82] Classical medieval commentators cite poetry extensively to justify their understandings of qur'anic vocabulary. In his biographical dictionary *Mīzān al-iʿtidāl,* al-Dhahabī (d. 748 AH/1348 CE) speaks of an exegete who insists that he cited fifty thousand verses of poetry in his commentary on the Qur'an (to which Dhahabī adds, *allāhu aʿlam,* "God only knows").[83] However, the earliest *tafsīr*s, such as that of Muqātil v. Sulaymān (d. 150 AH/767 CE), do *not* cite poetry. Finally, it is worth emphasizing that what is at stake in the debate is not whether poetry was a part of pre-Islamic Arabian culture; the Qur'an itself (e.g., in Qur'an 26, "The Poets") refers to poets and responds to accusations that Muhammad was a poet (e.g., Q 69:41). The question is only whether the lines recorded in medieval Islamic works are indeed citations of poems composed centuries earlier by pagan, or "Jāhilī," poets. Indeed, it is quite possible that the fascination of medieval Muslims with citing (or imagining) pre-Islamic poetry is (in part) a reflection of qur'anic references to poets. Perhaps even certain ideas about these "Jāhilī" poets (e.g., their wandering around but not really finding anything) reflect lines from the Qur'an ("hast thou not seen how they wander in every valley"; Q 26:225).

Now, Bell is certainly right to point out that there is no pre-Islamic Arabic Christian literature, but then there is no pre-Islamic Arabic literature of any kind.[84] Meanwhile, there is reason to believe that the rise of the Arabic script is related to the spread of Christianity among the Arabs, a theme to which we will return.

Moreover, we do know more than ever about the inscriptions that pre-Islamic Arabs left us, and it is certainly relevant that at least a century before Islam the pagan inscriptions disappear entirely, while Arabic-language Christian inscriptions begin to appear.[85] It seems peculiar that for the period when pagan inscriptions disappear we are meant to trust that pagan poetry and culture generally were thriving.

In addition we now have a more nuanced idea about biblical material in the Qur'an. Whereas some earlier orientalists seemed to imagine that all of this (or at least the Christian material) could be accounted for with reference to a few outsiders who wandered into the Hijaz and left some stories behind them,[86] we now have a sense that the Qur'an was engaging with an audience for whom these stories—about Mary and Jesus, or the Companions of the Cave—were both familiar and meaningful. Indeed in this book I make the case that Christians were a significant part, perhaps the predominant part, of the Qur'an's audience. However, I do so without relying on the traditional reports of medieval Islamic literature.[87]

Qur'anic Pagans

As we have seen, the dominant narrative in works on the emergence of Islam is that Christianity "surrounded" or "encircled" the Hijaz where Muhammad preached, but it was more or less nowhere to be found in the Hijaz itself. In effect, and despite the considerable amount of new evidence regarding the presence of Christians in Arabia, scholarly consensus remains essentially that of Richard Bell, as we have seen with Aziz Al-Azmeh.[88] Bell argued that Muhammad was preaching in a pagan world in which the traditional religion was fading away in the face of "the creeping in of a dim unmoralised idea of a superior deity." This "creeping in" was leading to "a search for a more satisfying faith."[89] Bell thus offers a rather vague, social (and indeed psychological, at times) explanation for Islam's origins.[90] This nicely exemplifies what Gerald Hawting would later call the "evolutionary" model for explaining the imagined situation by which the Arabs of Muhammad's time acknowledged one "high God" but maintained polytheistic practices, even idols.[91] The pre-Islamic Arabs are often seen to be on the "evolutionary" path from polytheism to monotheism, generally assumed to be a superior form of theism and the one toward which all polytheistic societies inevitably progressed.[92] As Hawting points out, this perspective reflects the monotheistic "suppositions and premises" of modern-day scholars (even the atheists among them), namely that polytheism is a mark of primitive societies and that such societies inevitably proceed toward monotheism.[93]

In reading the qur'anic material that has the opponents of Muhammad, the *mushrikūn* or "associators," declare their faith in Allah, one can see how Bell arrived at his convictions. The picture the Qur'an paints of his opponents seems to be one whereby they accept in principle the sovereignty of Allah, whom they name creator and master of nature: "If thou askest them, 'Who created the heavens and the earth and subjected the sun and the moon?' they will say, 'God.' How then are they perverted?" (Q 29:61; cf. 29:63, 31:15, 39:38, 43:87). These *mushrikūn* are said to be "perverted" (*yu'fikūn*) in part (one deduces) because of their immorality and in part because they deny things about Allah that they should accept, above all his power to raise the dead: "That is their recompense because they disbelieved in Our signs and said, 'What, when we are bones and broken bits, shall we really be raised up again in a new creation?'" (Q 17:98, 13:5, 17:49, 23:82, 37:12–17, 56:47).

These sorts of verses arguably gave birth to later Islamic traditions that paint in vivid colors the paganism of Muhammad's Arabia. Muslim authors imagined that the "associators" worshipped idols (perhaps in part because an analogy was made with the stories of Abraham's idol-worshipping opponents). Indeed one learns from these later traditions of the zealotry that the Quraysh in Mecca supposedly held for their idols in the Kaʿba. In Ibn Isḥāq we read of how Muhammad, after the conquest of Mecca, entered into the Kaʿba and destroyed the pagan idols that were kept there: "He summoned ʿUthmān b. Ṭalḥa and took the key of the Kaʿba from him, and when the door was opened for him he went in. There he found a dove made of wood [*ḥamāma min ʿīdān*]. He broke it in his hands and threw it away."[94] In a lucid essay titled "The Empty Ḥijāz," James Montgomery discusses the way that the Qur'an itself "emptied" the Hijaz of its culture by insisting on its absolute uniqueness and denigrating all religious and cultural competitors.[95] Later Muslims followed the Qur'an's signal and transmitted very little about the society and culture of the Hijaz: "If the notion of early 'Islam' suffers from conceptual vagueness, the Ḥijāz, its topographical birthplace, is so indeterminate and so open to meanings as to be empty of meaning."[96]

There are, of course, a few verses in the Qur'an that offer names of pre-Islamic pagan Arabian deities. Of these the most famous by far are in Sura 53: "Have you considered El-Lat and El-'Uzza, and Manat the third, the other?" (Q 53:20–21).[97] We know from epigraphic evidence that these three were indeed goddesses venerated before Islam by the northern

Arabians. Together, these various bits—the qur'anic references to "associators," the later traditions about these associators and their idols, and the actual (albeit few) references to pagan deities in the Qur'an—led scholars such as Bell to imagine a pagan world in which Muhammad preached. Yet, strangely, "El-Lat and El-'Uzza, and Manat" do not appear anywhere in sixth-century Arabian inscriptions. What if this idolatrous world had disappeared from Arabia by Muhammad's day? Perhaps pagans appear in the Qur'an as part of a literary motif, a backdrop to the author's monotheistic arguments, but in fact they were long gone.

There are obviously larger questions of textual interpretation and historiography in play here. The conviction, or rather the assumption, of most early orientalists (the great exception being Henri Lammens)[98] is that Islamic reports tell us more or less "what actually happened" around Muhammad. Indeed some of them held that they could tell us what was happening *within* Muhammad. Bell is perhaps a typical example of this sort of psychological speculation.[99] This confidence regarding Muhammad's thoughts and feelings, about the kind of thing that "made a tremendous impression on him," is still found in more recent works.[100] The better way of approaching early Islamic texts, including the Qur'an, is as texts; that is, and as Andrew Rippin repeatedly argued, we should appreciate the literary nature of the Qur'an.[101]

Perhaps the most outstanding challenge to this dominant narrative regarding Muhammad's context is Gerald Hawting's 1999 book *The Idea of Idolatry.* Now, Hawting does not make particular claims about the historical context in which Muhammad preached.[102] Instead, his principal argument is that the accusation of idolatry, in the history of religious literature or the history of religions more generally, does not always correspond to how things truly were. Very often monotheists portray or caricature other monotheists as idolaters as a way to discredit or vilify them. It is this point that Hawting means to communicate when he notes historical examples of how Protestants (including Elizabeth I) accused Catholics of idolatry or Catholics accused Muslims of being idolaters in the Middle Ages.[103] He also points out that certain Muslim thinkers, such as Muḥammad b. 'Abd al-Wahhāb (d. 1792), accused Christians explicitly of *shirk.*[104] If later Muslims thought of Christians, or rather portrayed Christians, as *mushrikūn,* would it not be possible that accusations of *shirk* in the Qur'an could also be directed against monotheists? Perhaps against Christians? In other words, Hawting's point is that the Qur'an is a polemical discourse and that we should be alert to the possibility that this sort of religious literary work may employ the label of "associators" even against fellow monotheists, as a way of discrediting and indeed vilifying them.[105] In this his point is related to that of John Wansbrough in *Qur'anic Studies,* namely that works of literature should be read as just that, and that it is problematic to make historical inferences on the basis of a text that liberally employs motifs and topoi for the sake of particular arguments.[106]

Many of these explanations for the rise of monotheism among the pre-Islamic Arabs involved a sort of zealous denial of any connection with Judaism and Christianity. Long before Aziz Al-Azmeh made his case that Muhammad personally transformed Allah from an obscure Meccan god to the God of the universe, other scholars held that Arabian monotheism underwent an indigenous, isolated process. Carl Brockelmann, in 1922, argued that Allah was an ancient "high god" of the Arabs. In 1962, Hamilton Gibb wrote "Pre-Islamic Monotheism in Arabia," and then, in 1980, M. J. Kister argued that the Islamic records of pre-Islamic devotional practice during the *ḥajj* point to the appearance of an indigenous monotheism in Arabia.[107] All of these scholars saw a movement from paganism to monotheism in Arabia that was essentially isolated from the larger monotheistic traditions of the late antique Near East.

One problem with this approach is the degree to which this entire portrait of pre-Islamic Arabia is itself based on the Qur'an. Hawting sees a vicious circle here; he recognizes that the portrait of Muhammad's life was painted in part to provide a context for qur'anic verses that left early Muslim interpreters asking questions about where, when, and why they were proclaimed.[108] Hawting articulates this point with reference to the exegesis of Q 6:136: "They appoint to God, of the tillage and cattle that He multiplied, a portion, saying, 'This is for God'—so they assert—'and this is for our associates.' So what is for their associates reaches not God; and what is for God reaches their associates. Evil is their judgment!" As Hawting notes, Ibn Isḥāq tells a story in connection with this verse, a story that "identifies" "they" as the Arab tribe of Khawlān and identifies "the associate" as their (pagan) god ʿUmyānis.[109] I might add here two more examples to make the same point.

The first is connected to Q 3:181: "God has heard the saying of those who said, 'Surely God is poor, and we are rich.' We shall write down what they have said, and their slaying the Prophets without right, and We shall say, 'Taste the chastisement of the burning.'" Like Q 6:136, this verse includes anonymous references, namely the pronouns "those" (later, "they" and "their"). Also like Q 6:136 (which refers to "associates," not to one specific "associate"), this verse refers to a group and not a specific individual. Indeed the accusation made against this group of "slaying the Prophets" suggests that the Qur'an has in mind the Jews, as this is a frequent charge that it levels against them.[110] Nevertheless, a common story that is meant to explain this verse identifies one individual who is responsible for the sacrilege:

> Abū Bakr al-Ṣiddīq entered one day into the Jewish place of study [*bayt madrās;* cf. Hebrew *beth midrash*]. He found them gathered around one man whose name was Finḥāṣ. He said to [Finḥāṣ], "Fear God and embrace Islam, for indeed you know that Muhammad is the messenger of God." He replied, "By God O Abu Bakr, how are we poor in respect to God? Rather God is poor in respect to us, for if He were rich in respect to us he would not ask to borrow from us." Abū Bakr grew mad and hit Finḥāṣ hard on the face. He said, "By God, if there were not a pact between us, I would have cut your head off." So Finḥāṣ went and complained to Muhammad. Abū Bakr told him what [Finḥāṣ] had said and Finḥāṣ denied it. Then the verse [Q 3:181] came down.[111]

This story paints a picture, along with many other stories that involve Jews, that is meant to show their impiety and deceit. More importantly for our purposes, it provides meaning and context to a verse that otherwise is without precise references (or indeed any proper nouns at all), something named occasionally *taʿyīn al-mubham* ("specification of what is uncertain"). In light of this last point, it is worth asking whether this meeting between Abū Bakr and Finḥāṣ ever took place. Now, this story is about Muhammad (and Abū Bakr) and the Jews, but the insight about the role of storytelling in creating a stage for the qur'anic drama might apply also to stories that involve pagans. That is the point of Hawting in regard to Q 6:136; it is also the case with a second example, earlier in the same Sura.

Qur'an 6:122 relates: "Why, is he who was dead, and We gave him life, and appointed for him a light to walk by among the people as one whose likeness is in the shadows, and comes not forth from them? So it is decked out fair to the unbelievers the things they have done." The verse itself has no clear reference to pagans (*mushrikūn*) although it does refer to unbelievers (*kāfirūn*) at the end. It also has no clear references to any specific individuals. The final clause, "it is decked out fair to the unbelievers the things they have done" (*zuyyina li-l-kāfirīn mā kānū ya'malūn*), suggests that God adorns (*tazyīn*) the evil works of unbelievers to make them seem good, so that the unbelievers will not repent, believe, and be saved (but rather continue in their unbelief and be condemned). The initial clause is a comparison between the one who has come to life, perhaps spiritually, and now walks in the light, and one who walks in shadows (*ẓulumāt*). This is quite a rich verse theologically, and there is no reason to think that it refers to any particular event or people. And yet the Islamic exegetical tradition still provides specific explanations.

Ibn al-Jawzī writes that there are five (!) different explanations of the context of this verse. The first (attributed to Ibn 'Abbās) is that it was revealed in regard to Ḥamza (uncle of the Prophet) and Abū Jahl (another story that involves hitting):

> Abū Jahl threw the guts of an animal [*farth*] on the Messenger of God. Ḥamza, who was not yet a believer, was told of what Abū Jahl did. He approached and hit Abū Jahl with his bow. [Abū Jahl] told him, "Do you not see what he has brought? He calls us stupid and insults our gods." Ḥamza said to him, "Who is more stupid than you? You worship stones instead of God! I testify that there is no god but God and Muhammad is His servant and messenger." And then this verse was sent down.[112]

This verse thus becomes the occasion of telling a story about the uncle of the Prophet, Ḥamza (who according to the biography of Muhammad would later be martyred at Uḥud). It is Ḥamza who begins to "walk in the light," and who came to spiritual life, when he embraced Islam by his profession of faith. It is Abū Jahl who remained in the shadows with his worship of stone idols (something conspicuously missing from the text of the Qur'an).

Curiously, however, Ibn al-Jawzī goes on to name four other explanations for this verse, with different ideas about its protagonists. Others propose that this verse is rather about a man named ʿAmmār b. Yāsir and Abū Jahl, or about ʿUmar b. al-Khaṭṭāb (the second caliph, whose conversion is dramatically narrated by Ibn Isḥāq) and Abū Jahl, or about Muhammad himself and Abū Jahl, or generally about any believer and any unbeliever.

At this point the critical observer is faced with a decision to make regarding the five stories. One can choose a story that is most likely to be the "right" one. This is the approach of most of the early orientalists, who rely so heavily on the twists and turns of Muhammad's biography as related in such reports. Alternatively one could recognize that all of the stories are just that, stories produced by speculation on the qur'anic text.

One sign that this alternative approach is more prudent is what one finds in the commentaries for passages that do not lend themselves easily to stories or to *taʿyīn al-mubham* accounts. Perhaps the most obvious example of this are the "mysterious" or disconnected letters at the beginning of twenty-nine Suras. I discuss this point in *The Qur'an and Its Biblical Subtext,* noting that Abū Jaʿfar al-Ṭabarī (d. 310 AH/923 CE), for example, offers fourteen different opinions on the disconnected letters, before concluding "the interpreters of the Qur'an differ over its meaning."[113] Why is it that there is no clear historical memory over these letters? Why are they a "mystery"? Does it not seem likely that the author of the Qur'an would have known their meaning when he proclaimed or wrote them? Would his companions not have asked about them?

If observers might be persuaded that the letters are mysterious not because they were intended to be such (as some apologetic scholarship suggests), but rather because their original meaning was not transmitted, then they might also take the next step and consider the importance of this observation. These letters are a very prominent part of the text. They constitute, for the most part, the first verse of twenty-nine different Suras, and yet the explanation of their meaning was not passed down to the first generations of Qur'an commentators. Now, if the meaning of the letters was not transmitted, how much confidence should we have in the stories that the commentators tell us to explain other elements—even relatively obscure elements—of the text? For example, should we trust that Q 6:122 was really about a dispute between Ḥamza (or ʿAmmar, or ʿUmar, or Muhammad, or any believer) and Abū Jahl? In other words, perhaps the question is not so much which of the five options is the "correct one," but rather whether any of them are.

It is this line of thinking that calls into question not simply one narrative (about the god ʿUmyānis or Ḥamza's bow) but instead the very master narrative that shapes the standard approach to the Qur'an and the rise of Islam generally. Perhaps this master narrative, populated with pagans and their gods, is more the work of exegesis than of memory. This proposition might allow space for alternative ideas regarding the historical context of the Qur'an, including those that offer a more prominent space to Christians.

Qur'an and Prayer

In the present book we look at various elements of the Qur'an itself, and at the material record from late antique Arabia, that make such an alternative narrative attractive. Here I turn to a point already raised by Richard Bell which does just that (although Bell does not take the insight to its logical conclusion), namely the significance of two words in the Qur'an. The first of these is the Arabic word *qur'ān* itself. Now, in thinking through this word it is necessary to keep in mind that we know "Qur'an" as the name of the Islamic scripture with its 114 Suras (and this because later Islamic tradition chose "Qur'an" as a name for the believing community's book). However, when the word *qur'ān* appears in the text, it seems to refer to something different, something smaller and discrete. It is a "self-referential" term, but it refers not to the complete scripture (which necessarily did not exist yet when the passages including the word *qur'ān* were composed) but to a smaller packet of proclamations, or to revelation/scripture in a general sense.[114] Bell writes the following:

> In these early passages it does not of course mean the whole collection of prophecies, as it now means when we speak of "the Qur'ān." Each separate deliverance is in fact a *qur'ān*. There has been some discussion as to the meaning of the verb *qara'* and the related word *qur'ān*. But there can be no doubt, and it is now agreed that they belong to that religious vocabulary which Christianity had introduced into Arabia. *Qara'* means to read or solemnly recite sacred texts, while *qur'ān* is the Syriac *qeryānā* used to denote the "reading" or Scripture lesson.[115]

It is worth looking at a few examples of the use of the word *qur'ān* (translated "Koran" below) in the Qur'an, which collectively vindicate Bell's explanation:

> O believers, question not concerning things which, if they were revealed to you, would vex you; yet if you question concerning them when the Koran is being sent down, they will be revealed to you. God has effaced those things; for God is All-forgiving, All-clement. (Q 5:101)

> Say: "God is witness between me and you, and this Koran has been revealed to me that I may warn you thereby, and whomsoever it may reach. Do you indeed testify that there are other gods with God?" Say: "I do not testify." Say: "He is only One God, and I am quit of that you associate." (Q 6:19)

> And when the Koran is recited, give you ear to it and be silent; haply so you will find mercy. (Q 7:204)

> And when Our signs are recited to them, clear signs, those who look not to encounter Us say, "Bring a Koran other than this, or alter it." Say: "It is not for me to alter it of my own accord. I follow nothing, except what is revealed to me. Truly I

> fear, if I should rebel against my Lord, the chastisement of a dreadful day." (Q 10:15)
>
> The unbelievers say, "We will not believe in this Koran, nor in that before it." Ah, if thou couldst see when the evildoers are stationed before their Lord, bandying argument the one against the other! Those that were abased will say to those that waxed proud, "Had it not been for you, we would have been believers." (Q 34:31)
>
> Say: "It has been revealed to me that a company of the jinn gave ear, then they said, 'We have indeed heard a Koran wonderful.'" (Q 72:1)

The term *qur'ān* appears seventy times in the Qur'an, alongside a constellation of terms that are used in a similar manner (*kitāb, dhikr, furqān*). For a comprehensive consideration of this one would need to note those passages where the text swears by *al-qur'ān* (Q 36:2, 38:1, 41:3, 50:1), those passages where the text compares *al-qur'ān* to the Torah and the Gospel (e.g., Q 9:111), and those passages that speak of the descent of *al-qur'ān* as a heavenly book (e.g., Q 2:185). For our purposes, however, it might be a useful exercise to think through the use of *qur'ān* in this set of representative verses above.

All of this leads to the question of why the author of the Islamic scripture would choose to use the word *qur'ān* to refer to his proclamations/revelation. Qur'an 5:101 speaks of asking things when *al-qur'ān* is being sent down; Q 6:19 speaks of "this *qur'ān*"; Q 7:204 (much like 5:101) counsels a certain disposition when *al-qur'ān* is recited (or proclaimed); Q 10:15 speaks of a *qur'ān* as a text or proclamation that was already present; Q 34:31 suggests that there are at least two different *qur'āns*; and Q 72:1 relates how the jinn said that they heard a wonderful *qur'ān*. Although there are likely several different meanings communicated here with the word *qur'ān*, it is clear that it is commonly used for a divine message of this particular prophet. When one keeps in mind that the Qur'an suggests that the Torah (*tawrāh*) is the divine message given to Moses and explicitly names the Gospel (*injīl*) as the divine message given to Jesus, it becomes clear that the *qur'ān* is, or perhaps better the various *qur'āns* are, Muhammad's messages. This is all brought together nicely by Bell when he speaks of Muhammad producing *qeryānē,* using the Syriac plural of *qeryānā.*[116]

Now, the traditional (among orientalists) etymology (followed by Bell) is that the word *qur'ān* is borrowed from the Syriac word *qeryānā.* There are good linguistic reasons to question whether this is a strict borrowing (in part because Arabic has a *y* and so *y* should not drop out if the word were taken into Arabic, and in part because the *ān* ending is found in Arabic nouns, including qur'anic nouns, such as *ghufrān,* "forgiveness," and *'adwān,* "enmity").[117] However, even if *qur'ān* were not a strict borrowing, the use of this term in the Qur'an specifically for divine messages and warnings (and not just anything that could be read or recited) strongly suggests that its intended meaning is shaped by the Syriac *qeryānā,* the lectionary, or compilation of scripture passages, used for public recitation in a liturgical setting.[118] It would then be something like a *Lehnbedeutung,* a semantic loan.

A second word that betrays a particular engagement with (Syriac) Christianity is the qur'anic term for prayer: *ṣalāh.* The term *ṣalāh* is closely related to Syriac *ṣlōtā* (prayer).[119] What is particularly intriguing is the Qur'an's use of the phrase *aqāma al-ṣalāh* to mean "perform prayer" (Q 2:3, 43, 83, 110, 177, passim), which seems to reflect a Syriac use of the verb *q-w-m.*[120] It is even possible that the particular qur'anic orthography for this word, by which a *wāw* appears (orthographically, *ṣ-l-w*), might reflect a Syriac origin of the term (the qur'anic orthography for *zakāt* and *mishkāt* is similar).[121] If this insight is correct regarding *ṣalāh,* then one might ask whether the very notion of prayer in the Qur'an is connected in some way to the observance of Christians at prayer, or at least to a familiarity with Christians speaking about prayer (keeping in mind that Syriac was principally a Christian language in late antiquity). Thus it seems possible that the Qur'an's notion of both scripture and prayer is rooted in a Christian culture.

In *The Idea of Idolatry* Hawting questioned long-held assumptions about the pagan background of Islam by emphasizing the literary qualities of the Qur'an. More recently Ilkka Lindstedt offers a meticulously detailed case for the predominance of monotheism in Muhammad's Hijaz in his work *Muhammad and His Followers in Context.* In the opening chapter he notes the assumption of both medieval Muslim and modern Western scholars that Jews and Christians were not a major element of pre-Islamic Arabian society. He continues: "But they were: in fact, the sixth-century epigraphic evidence attests only Jews, Christians, and perhaps other (gentile) monotheists. Jews and Christians formed in all likelihood the majority in pre-Islamic Arabia."[122] In the present work I largely argue in favor of Lindstedt's perspective, but I also contend that Christians were more important than Jews to the Qur'an and that this particular importance of Christians is evident in the way in which the Qur'an advances its message.

The Newness of the Qur'an

And yet the Qur'an is not a Christian text. Christianity is not the source of the Qur'an. It is rather the rival of the Qur'an, which offers something fundamentally new in the religious landscape of late antique Arabia. The newness of the Qur'an, in my opinion, is connected above all to its Arabic language and to Muhammad himself. In a number of passages the Qur'an identifies itself as a work that confirms earlier revelations:

> And believe in that I have sent down, confirming that which is with you, and be not the first to disbelieve in it. And sell not My signs for a little price; and fear you Me. (Q 2:41)
>
> When there came to them a Book from God, confirming what was with them . . . (Q 2:89)
>
> And when they were told, "Believe in what God has sent down," they said, "We believe in what was sent down on us"; and they disbelieve in what is beyond that, yet it is the truth confirming what is with them. (Q 2:91)
>
> Say: "Whosoever is an enemy to Gabriel—he it was that brought it down upon thy heart by the leave of God, confirming what was before it, and for a guidance and good tidings to the believers." (Q 2:97)

When there has come to them a Messenger from God confirming what was with them, a party of them that were given the Book reject the Book of God behind their backs, as though they knew not. (Q 2:101)

He has sent down upon thee the Book with the truth, confirming what was before it, and He sent down the Torah and the Gospel. (Q 3:3)

And when God took compact with the Prophets: "That I have given you of Book and Wisdom; then there shall come to you a Messenger confirming what is with you—you shall believe in him and you shall help him; do you agree?" (Q 3:81)

You who have been given the Book, believe in what We have sent down, confirming what is with you, before We obliterate faces, and turn them upon their backs, or curse them as We cursed the Sabbath-men, and God's command is done. (Q 4:47)

And We have sent down to thee the Book with the truth, confirming the Book that was before it, and assuring it. So judge between them according to what God has sent down, and do not follow their caprices, to forsake the truth that has come to thee. (Q 5:48)

This is a Book We have sent down, blessed and confirming that which was before it, and for thee to warn the Mother of Cities and those about her; and those who believe in the world to come believe in it, and watch over their prayers. (Q 6:92)

This Koran could not have been forged apart from God; but it is a confirmation of what is before it, and a distinguishing of the Book, wherein is no doubt, from the Lord of all Being. (Q 10:37)

In their stories is surely a lesson to men possessed of minds; it is not a tale forged, but a confirmation of what is before it, and a distinguishing of every thing, and a guidance, and a mercy to a people who believe. (Q 12:111; cf. Q 35:31, 46:12, 46:30)

The Qur'an's author thus presents his scripture as a confirmation of earlier revelations to the prophets. Indeed certain verses above (notably Q 3:3, 4:47, 5:48), especially when seen in context, seem to make a direct connection between this revelation and the revelation given earlier to Jews and Christians. What is new (these passages suggest) is not the nature or content of the "Book" that the Qur'an's prophet is proclaiming. What is new is the prophet himself. The Qur'an is particularly eager to make this point, that God would send a new prophet and that people should accept him in the line of prophets. Qur'an 3:81 illustrates this point, inasmuch as it has God speak to all of the earlier prophets (the context is not clear—is it a primordial moment? a moment after the death of the prophet before Muhammad?) about the new prophet who would come. Thus one can emphatically agree with Gerald Hawting's insistence that the Qur'an's notion of prophethood is fundamentally biblical.[123]

There is also some reason to believe that the Qur'an's author is aware of, and strenuously working against, the notion in late antiquity that prophethood had ceased, something generally agreed upon among Jews and Christians.[124] The zeal (and frequency) with which it makes its point that there is now a new prophet suggests (although it does not prove) that the Qur'an's author is aware of resistance to the idea of a new prophet. In addition at least one verse speaks of a gap or interval in prophecy:[125] "People of the Book, now there has come to you Our Messenger, making things clear to you, upon an interval [*fatra*] between the Messengers lest you should say, 'There has not come to us any bearer of good tidings, neither any warner.' Indeed, there has come to you a bearer of good tidings and a warner; God is powerful over everything" (Q 5:19). The other element that is new is the language of this book. In one of the verses that presents the Qur'an as a confirmation (not quoted above), we find a suggestion that what distinguishes this book from the "book of Moses" is its Arabic language: "Yet before it was the Book of Moses for a model and a mercy; and this is a Book confirming, in Arabic tongue, to warn the evildoers, and good tidings to the good-doers" (Q 46:12). The Qur'an names the people to whom it is speaking *ummiyyūn* and refers to Muhammad as *al-nabīy al-ummī* (Q 7:157, 158).[126] This expression is rendered by Yusuf Ali as "the unlettered prophet" in deference to the Islamic doctrine that Muhammad could not read (and consequently must have learned things directly from God, and not from books). It is rendered by Arberry as "prophet of the common folk." Droge similarly translates this phrase "prophet of the common people" but helpfully comments in a note "or the gentile prophet."[127] In any case the principal point for our purposes is that Muhammad is portrayed as rendering to Arabic speakers, and in Arabic, divine revelation given earlier to the prophets of the Jews and the Christians.[128]

A similar message is advanced in those passages that refer to the Arabic nature of the Prophet's revelation. Qur'an 16:103 emphasizes its Arabic nature as a way to deny that Muhammad was being informed by an outsider: "And We know very well that they say, 'Only a mortal is teaching him.' The speech of him at whom they hint is barbarous; and this is speech Arabic, manifest." This verse, incidentally, suggests that there *were* outsiders around, those who spoke a different language and who had some sort of knowledge of divine revelation or religion generally. It seems almost certain to me (and I will try to prove the point in Chapter 3) that the Qur'an is alluding to Syriac/Aramaic speakers here. Qur'an 42:7 is a bit more precise about the importance of the Qur'an's Arabic language. It explains that the Qur'an is in Arabic for the sake of Arabic speakers, so that they might receive a warning and profit by it: "And so We have revealed to thee an Arabic Koran, that thou mayest warn the Mother of Cities and those who dwell about it, and that thou mayest warn of the Day of Gathering, wherein is no doubt—a party in Paradise, and a party in the Blaze" (Q 42:7). The point for the Qur'an is that now, finally, a revelation had come in Arabic for Arabic speakers. One imagines (although I admit this is speculation) that behind this sentiment was an earlier situation in which Arabic speakers knew the word of God only as it was translated from non-Arabic books, likely the writings of Jews and Christians in Hebrew and Aramaic, or from non-Arabic speakers, perhaps principally Syriac-speaking Christians.

This conclusion seems to match quite well with what we know of the nature of pre-Islamic Arabic speakers (see more in Chapter 3). Here it is worth pointing out simply that while the history of Arabic speakers stretches back centuries before Islam, and indeed centuries before Christianity, there is no documentary evidence of any pre-Islamic Christian (or other) Arabic literature. It is true that later Islamic literature records lines of pre-Islamic Christian poets (most famously ʿAdī b. Zayd, d. ca. 600), but the authenticity of these claims is highly dubious.[129] Otherwise there is no sign of an Arabic Christian book, including the Bible, before Islam. What does this mean for the social-linguistic situation of Christian Arabs at the time? As Jack Tannous explains, there are various signs that many Arabic speakers (or at least people with Arabic names) had become Christians during the first Christian centuries. There are even various reports (in Syriac) of a "Monastery of *ṭayyāyē*" or "Arabs."[130] He says, "More generally, it seems to be the case that before the rise of Islam, there were Arabic speakers who were Christians who wrote in languages other than Arabic"; he mentions John Rufus (d. after 515) and Theodore of Bostra (d. late sixth century) as possible Arabic speakers who wrote in Greek.[131] One might consider here as well the family of John of Damascus (d. ca. 750), who were apparently Arabs (John's grandfather is thought to have been named Manṣūr), but even several generations after the Islamic conquests John continued to write in Greek.[132]

The Qur'an's emphasis on its own Arabic language, which in some ways is quite extraordinary (most scriptures, including the books of the Bible, do not include references to the language in which they are written), is plausibly seen as emerging from just this sort of context. There were many monotheistic Arabic speakers by the early seventh century, and Christians were notable among them; however, they knew both scripture and other religious texts only in non-Arabic languages.[133] It is possible (although our knowledge of liturgy in this context is modest) that they even worshipped in non-Arabic languages, presumably Syriac and Greek above all. Along comes the Qur'an and proudly announces that God has finally spoken in Arabic for Arabic speakers. As Tannous notes, all of this matches closely the declaration of the Qur'an that God sends prophets who speak the language of their own people: "And We have sent no Messenger save with the tongue of his people, that he might make all clear to them; then God leads astray whomsoever He will, and He guides whomsoever He will; and He is the All-mighty, the All-wise" (Q 14:4).[134]

Now, I do not suggest here that the Qur'an was meant only for Arabic speakers or for the *ummiyyūn,* the "unscriptured" or "gentiles." There are other verses of the Qur'an in which the Prophet addresses himself to Jews and Christians, or to "the people" (*al-nās*) generally. Qur'an 4:47 (quoted fully above) begins: "You who have been given the Book, believe in what We have sent down, confirming what is with you." Indeed a number of passages of the Qur'an exhort everyone, without exception, to acknowledge the new revelation and a fortiori the new prophet as well. Qur'an 21:107 famously declares, "We have not sent thee, save as a mercy unto all beings."[135] Nevertheless, it is perfectly coherent to argue that the author of the Qur'an saw it as a scripture for the Arabs especially, but also one that, as a true revelation, is valid for everyone.

The "Very Words" of Muhammad?

Bell's work (for all of his critical ideas about Muhammad's psychological development) is profoundly traditional. In a sense it is not far removed from the classical Muslim scholars who sought to explain references to Christians in the text through stories of Ethiopians or Persians who wandered through the Hijaz. Bell agrees with these scholars that the Qur'an as we have it is essentially the words of Muhammad, and that it can be rearranged chronologically so that one can really know which words Muhammad spoke first. He agrees that the immediate historical context of the Qur'an is essentially that of a pagan culture, one of the last pagan cultures of the Near East.[136] I will argue that the immediate historical context of the Qur'an is essentially that of a Christian culture.

Before moving on to Chapter 2, where we begin to examine the qur'anic basis for this claim, it is important to say something about the other presumption of Bell, namely the notion of the Qur'an as Muhammad's "very words." The present work is not an exercise in structural criticism, and I do not mean here to develop a comprehensive proposal for the historical formation of the qur'anic text. Nevertheless, the reader at some point may wonder why I do not consider, along with Richard Bell, "what Muhammad was thinking," or "what was going on around Muhammad," at the time when he proclaimed this or that verse. As mentioned above, those sorts of considerations rely on the ideas, first, that the Qur'an is a transcript of what Muhammad said at some time, and second (assuming the first point), that scholars are able to reconstruct the order in which he said the things in the Qur'an. From the beginnings of critical research on the Qur'an in the nineteenth century, scholars took for granted the first point, and so the great task of the early orientalists was to address the second. This is essentially the job of the first volume of Theodor Nöldeke's *Geschichte des Qorans,* and not for nothing, since the 1860 work was the German version of an 1856 manuscript that he wrote (in Latin) in response to a competition by the Académie des inscriptions et belles-lettres of Paris that asked precisely this. The guidelines of the contest asked participants "to determine, as far as possible, with the aid of Arab historians and commentators, and subsequent to an examination of the [qur'anic] passages themselves, the moments in the life of Muhammad to which they are related."[137]

I have addressed the problem of "Qur'an as transcript" in a few publications that are meant to show the importance of redaction to the formation of the qur'anic text as we have it.[138] In brief, the critical question is whether one sees the words of the Qur'an as more or less a recording or transcript of Muhammad's very words, albeit recorded out of order, or whether one sees, as I propose, the Qur'an as a literary work formed through significant editing, reformulation, and redaction. For those who take the second option, as I do, this need not negate the real possibility that there was an historical figure, Muhammad, who proclaimed messages about God and about himself. It is quite possible to imagine an initial oral proclamation in a particular *Sitz im Leben,* followed by written redaction (possibly in a different *Sitz im Leben*). It is also important to consider whether redaction of the text was limited to moving around as so many puzzle pieces passages proclaimed by Muhammad (e.g., the "insertion" of Medinan passages into otherwise Meccan material), or whether the redactors had an active role in reformulating material in order, for example, to "improve" the text, develop ideas, or smooth the transition between two blocks of material (something that could lead, if done well enough, to the problem of the "disappearing redactor").

It is true that I am presenting the problem in rather stark terms. Nicolai Sinai has sought to establish more of a middle way by following and defending the "Nöldekian" paradigm but also allowing for possible "improvements" of the text and a few possible post-Muhammadan insertions. I would encourage the reader to consider his arguments as an alternative case to that which I am advancing here.[139] For the sake of contrast, however, I will briefly discuss the ideas of the late Oxford professor Alan Jones on the formation of the qur'anic text.[140] In a concise article Jones considers the way in which Muhammad's opponents accuse him of being possessed by a genie. This is important to Jones because it shows (according to him) that Muhammad in the Qur'an was speaking in a register similar to that of a storyteller or an oracle or priest (*kāhin*) in the pagan world of Mecca, and somewhat close to the register of a poet (*shāʿir*). According to common scholarly ideas about the pre-Islamic period, both *kāhin*s and poets were imagined to be inspired by demons or genies.[141] Jones thus quotes Q 34:8, which includes the question "What, has he forged against God a lie, or is he possessed?" He comments: "Here we have the two most potent objections of Muḥammad's Meccan opponents put together in the form of a question that invites the answer No."[142]

Later in the same article Jones clarifies further his vision of the formation of the qur'anic text. He speaks of Muhammad possibly making changes in the course of his oral proclamations of Suras during his prophetic career. Jones introduces the matter by discussing Q 74:31, a famously long verse with "Medinan" turns of phrase. He notes that this verse might have been inserted by Muhammad himself at some point. Jones goes on to comment:

> The question remains: how did verse 31 get inserted? If one examines such passages in the context of oral tradition, there is no great problem. The text of every *sūra* would have remained open during Muḥammad's lifetime, but closed at his death. Every time Muḥammad recited a *sūra* changes *could* have occurred (Changes might very well occur when another person recited, but only Muḥammad's changes would have had authority).[143]

This model for the formation of the text is of course plausible, but it is also entirely speculative. We have no independent, contemporaneous reports that Muhammad one day (in Medina now) chose to add verse 31 to Sura 74 as he was reciting it for the second (or third, or umpteenth) time, or indeed that he changed the wording of other Suras during various recitations of them (the last version, apparently, becoming the one that was preserved for posterity). Indeed it strikes me as no less plausible that verse 31 was added in the process of the editing of the text (presumably to explain the mysterious reference to "nineteen" in verse 30).

So what is the alternative to the "Qur'an as transcript" approach to the text? In brief, it is to grant the possibility that the Qur'an is the product of significant redactional work. Moreover, it is extremely likely (on the basis of known cases of redaction) that this work involved not so much the "rearranging of pieces" but rather the active reshaping of those pieces. The observations of Robert Fortna on redaction are apropos here: "Redaction is the conscious reworking of older materials in such a way as to meet new needs. It is editing that does not simply compile or retouch but creatively transforms."[144]

In light of the possibility that the qur'anic text has been creatively transformed in the process of redaction, I do not take for granted that qur'anic passages reflect Muhammad's "very words" at one moment of his career with no subsequent reshaping or transformation.[145] Accordingly, and as to avoid my own speculative ideas about the formation of the text, the starting point for my analysis is the canonical Qur'an as text and not Muhammad as person. This means that I am not principally concerned with traditional stories that are often cited as linking Muhammad with Christians or Christianity: whether a childhood journey to Syria or a visiting delegation from South Arabia. Instead, in the following chapters I look at the Qur'an and its own engagement with Christian (and Jewish) tradition; I broadly consider the historical evidence, including inscriptions, for the presence of Christians in Arabia at the time of the Qur'an's origins; and I ask what importance the presence of Christians and Christianity in the Qur'an's milieu had for the articulation of a new theology.

T • W • O

Christian Material in the Qur'an

The Qur'an proclaims that its Prophet is a messenger in a line of earlier prophets, many of whom are known from the Bible. It also claims that the last of these biblical prophets, Jesus, knew of and announced the arrival of the Qur'an's own prophet: "And when Jesus son of Mary said, 'Children of Israel, I am indeed the Messenger of God to you, confirming the Torah that is before me, and giving good tidings of a Messenger who shall come after me, whose name shall be Ahmad.' Then, when he brought them the clear signs, they said, 'This is a manifest sorcery'" (Q 61:6).[1] This passage (which admittedly refers to Ahmad [or *aḥmad*] and not Muhammad) has attracted the significant attention of scholars, in part because of the way Ibn Isḥāq connects it to Jesus's promises of the Paraclete in the Gospel of John.[2] For Ibn Isḥāq, Jesus did not promise his followers that the Holy Spirit would descend upon them after his ascension to heaven. He promised that a new prophet would come after him in Arabia.

The name given by this verse to the promised prophet, Ahmad (or *aḥmad*), and not *muḥammad*, has also been discussed at length. While *aḥmad* could be seen as "Ahmad," a proper noun and another name for Muhammad from the same Arabic root, it might also be seen as an adjective meaning "most praised" and thus a description of the new prophet.[3] Whatever option one chooses, this passage still appears to be part of the larger case that the Qur'an makes for the acceptance of a new prophet. It might be fruitfully read together with Q 3:81:

> And when God took compact with the Prophets: "That I have given you of Book and Wisdom; then there shall come to you a Messenger confirming what is with you—you shall believe in him and you shall help him; do you agree?" He said, "And do you take My load [*iṣr*] on you on that condition?" They said, "We do agree." God said, "Bear witness so, and I shall be with you among the witnesses."

Here Arberry renders the Arabic *iṣr* as "load." The term appears in two other places in the Qur'an: first, Q 2:286, the final verse of al-Baqara, in which the Qur'an seems to be modeling what faithful believers should say: "Our Lord; charge us not with a load such as Thou didst lay upon those before us" (*rabbanā wa-lā taḥmil ʿalaynā iṣran ka-mā ḥamaltahu ʿalā lladhīna min qablinā*). Although it would take too much space to make the case here, in light of the content of Qur'an 2, this prayer seems to allude to God's punishment of the Jews with heavy burdens. The second occurrence is Q 7:157, which speaks of a written prediction of the "gentile prophet" (*al-nabīy al-ummī*) in the "Torah and the Gospel" and then speaks of him as "relieving them of their loads" (*yaḍaʿu ʿanhum iṣrahum*). In these two passages *iṣr* is used in a polemical context, either alluding to the loads, or binds, of Judaism, or announcing Muhammad as the one who makes things easier for believers.[4]

In Q 3:81 God asks a nameless group of prophets (all of them, it would seem) to accept a new prophet or messenger (*rasūl*) who will come and "confirm" earlier messages ("what is with you").[5] Notably, the description of this new messenger as one who "confirms" aligns with the qur'anic description of Jesus. In Q 61:6 (quoted above) Jesus insists that he confirms "the Torah that is before me." Elsewhere in Sura 3 the Qur'an similarly has Jesus declare to the Israelites that he has come "confirming the truth of the Torah that is before me" (Q 3:50; Arberry has inserted "the truth of" into his translation here). Thus the Qur'an describes the new messenger in "Jesus-like" terms. Something similar is seen in Q 7:157: "Those who follow the Messenger, the Prophet of the common folk, whom they find written down with them in the Torah and the Gospel, bidding them to honour, and forbidding them dishonour, making lawful for them the good things and making unlawful for them the corrupt things, and relieving them of their loads [*iṣr*], and the fetters that were upon them." Here the "Prophet of the common folk" (*al-nabīy al-ummī;* I would translate as "the gentile prophet"),[6] who is said to be written about in the Torah and the Gospel, is promised to relieve "them" of "loads" and "fetters" (*iṣrahum wa-l-aghlāla allatī kānat ʿalayhim*). It is difficult to read this passage as anything but an appeal to the Jews and the Christians (those who have the Torah and the Gospel with them) to embrace the teaching of the new prophet.[7] This is similar to Matt 11:29–30, where Jesus declares: "Take my yoke upon you, and learn from me; for I am gentle and lowly in heart, and you will find rest for your souls. For my yoke is easy, and my burden is light" (see also Luke 11:46, with its condemnation of the legal scholars for "burdening" people).

One might compare the way Matthew uses the language of yoke (a common agricultural image in the Hebrew Bible) in his description of how Jesus offers a light burden. The Qur'an, for its part, uses the image of fetters or shackles (*aghlāl*), an image that is not agricultural but rather seems to refer to an instrument used by those in slavery or prison, including those trapped in hellfire (cf. Q 13:5, 34:33, 36:8, 40:71, 76:4).[8] Thus Jesus lightens the "yoke" of the Mosaic law, something he is said to do in the Qur'an as well, and Muhammad removes the shackles of that law.[9]

Also to note in Q 61:6 is the term that the Qur'an has Jesus use to announce the coming of the next prophet. The Qur'an uses (in the active participial form) the verb *bashshara*, meaning "to give good tidings," when it has Jesus allude to Ahmad/Muhammad in the clause "and giving good tidings of a Messenger who shall come after me." The use of the expression "giving good tidings" (*mubashshir*) may possibly reflect, or even be a calque of, Greek *euangelion* (literally, "good tidings," "good news") or "Gospel" (see the discussion in Chapter 4). In other words, it is possible that the Qur'an means to have Jesus suggest that the true "good news" is the message about the new prophet. Even if one is not persuaded by this final point (which is probably impossible to prove), it nevertheless remains important that in this verse the Qur'an has Jesus divulge the knowledge given to him (perhaps in the primordial moment alluded to in Q 3:81) that a new prophet will come.

Another way to think of Q 61:6 is as a counterpart to those verses in which Jesus is made to advocate for the Qur'an's theology. In certain verses the Qur'an has Jesus himself reprimand Christians for their doctrines concerning God and concerning himself. This is prominent, for example, in Q 5:72, which includes a quotation of Jesus: "They are unbelievers who say, 'God is the Messiah, Mary's son.' For the Messiah said, 'Children of Israel, serve God, my Lord and your Lord. Verily whoso associates with God anything, God shall prohibit him entrance to Paradise, and his refuge shall be the Fire; and wrongdoers shall have no helpers.'" Here Jesus insists that God is his lord, implying that he is a servant (cf. Q 19:30) and using language that is close to that of John 20:17 (although it is the risen Christ who declares, "I am ascending to my Father and your Father, to my God and your God"). The verse as a whole is interesting inasmuch as it begins with a declaration, including a quotation of the sort of things Christians might, according to the Qur'an, say ("God is the Messiah, Mary's son"), and continues by quoting Jesus in a way meant to testify to that declaration (God calls them unbelievers, and Jesus explains that they will go to hell). Notably the qur'anic Jesus implies that those who have deified him are thereby guilty of associating (*yushrik*) him with God (cf. Q 9:31). Elsewhere (Q 4:48, 116) the Qur'an makes this "association" (*shirk*) the one sin that God will not forgive, and accordingly it is not surprising to find Jesus explaining (in Q 5:72) that the refuge of those who "associate," apparently Christians, is hellfire.

However, not everywhere is the qur'anic Jesus so severe in his attacks on Christians. Toward the end of the same Sura Jesus seems to have a different religious disposition (Q 5:116–18):

> 116 And when God said, "O Jesus son of Mary, didst thou say unto men, 'Take me and my mother as gods, apart from God'?" He said, "To Thee be glory! It is not mine to say what I have no right to. If I indeed said it, Thou knowest it, knowing what is within my soul, and I know not what is within Thy soul; Thou knowest the things unseen.

> 117 "I only said to them what Thou didst command me: 'Serve God, my Lord and your Lord.' And I was a witness over them, while I remained among them; but when Thou didst take me to Thyself, Thou wast Thyself the watcher over them; Thou Thyself art witness of everything.
>
> 118 "If Thou chastisest them, they are Thy servants; if Thou forgivest them, Thou art the All-mighty, the All-wise."

The setting of the conversation between God and Jesus in this passage (like that of Q 3:81) is nowhere specified, but it is evidently sometime after Jesus's life (note the past-tense statement of Jesus in v. 117: "when Thou didst take me to Thyself [*lammā tawaffaytanī*]").[10] In verse 116 God essentially (without using a word with the root *sh-r-k*) asks Jesus if he told his followers to associate himself and his mother with God. In response, however, we do not see the condemnation of Christians manifested by Jesus in Q 5:72. Instead, he seems to express a certain quietism or agnosticism regarding the fate of Christians (whom the Qur'an evidently is accusing of deifying Jesus). He simply describes himself as a witness in verse 117, and then, in verse 118, he explains that the fate of those who have deified him is in God's hands: "If Thou chastisest them, they are Thy servants; if Thou forgivest them, Thou art the All-mighty, the All-wise."

And yet despite this openness to the possibility that Christians might be saved, Jesus still acts as a spokesman for the Qur'an's theology. Again we find Jesus declaring "Serve God, my Lord and your Lord" (v. 117). Especially notable is the piety that the Qur'an has Jesus manifest in Q 5:116. In response to God's question as to whether he told people to "take" him and Mary as two gods, Jesus does not simply say "no" but instead responds with reverent, and indeed almost zealous, feeling: "To Thee be glory! It is not mine to say what I have no right to. If I indeed said it, Thou knowest it, knowing what is within my soul, and I know not what is within Thy soul; Thou knowest the things unseen." This is a sort of short homily, a mini-lesson for the reader on the proper sort of reverence one should manifest before God.

Moreover, the allusion to "taking" (*ittakhidhū*) Jesus and Mary as gods connects this verse to other verses in which the divine voice of the Qur'an condemns Christians and Jews (Q 9:31) for "taking" their clerics as lords, or those who take "gods out of the earth" (Q 21:21). It is also connected to those passages where the Qur'an denies that God would "take" a son or offspring (*walad;* Q 2:116; 10:68; 17:111; 18:4; 19:35, 88, 92; 21:26; 23:91; 25:2; 39:4; 72:3). In other words, in Q 5:116 Jesus is brought in to speak about a theological concern of the Qur'an.

Thus the Qur'an uses Jesus to articulate its own arguments regarding both God *and* Muhammad. The theological use of Jesus is prominent in passages such as 5:72 and 5:116–18. The prophetological use of Jesus is prominent in Q 61:6 (and obliquely in 7:157). Indeed one might argue that the employment of Jesus for prophetological purposes is not limited to the prediction of Muhammad in Q 61:6 but includes as well Jesus's affirmations that he confirms the earlier revelation, especially the Torah (Q 3:50, 61:6). In the Qur'an Jesus comes to confirm Moses's book and Muhammad comes to confirm Jesus's book (Q 3:3, 46:12). In addition, Jesus is made to play an anti-Israelite role in the Qur'an, something prominent in Q 61:6, where the Israelites respond to his statement and miracles by accusing him of magic, and perhaps implied by Q 3:52 (where the words "when Jesus perceived *their* unbelief" may be read as an allusion to the Israelites in Q 3:49). This role given to Jesus might be intended for the sake of the Qur'an's presentation of Muhammad. The Qur'an's own prophet condemns the Israelites as "greatest in enmity" (Q 5:82) to the believers and people who have been cursed (Q 2:88, 5:13). Jesus is made to anticipate Muhammad's condemnation of Jews (see Chapter 4).

Yet my interest in this book is not the Qur'an's disposition toward Jews, but rather its relationship to Christians and Christianity. Accordingly, we might consider why the Qur'an employs Jesus to make arguments about God and Muhammad.

Indeed the Qur'an's *principal* use for Jesus is as an "argument-maker." The Qur'an does not seem particularly interested in describing Jesus's role in a salvation history, or emphasizing elements of his teaching or the things he did around Palestine. There is very little of the parables, discourses, travels, and deeds of Jesus in the Qur'an.

That the Qur'an chooses to use Jesus to advance its teaching is a first sign that it is working in a Christian environment where an argument articulated by Jesus would be meaningful and, potentially, convincing. We now look at more elements of the Qur'an that suggest the same about its environment: the Qur'an's use of Christian turns of phrase and of Christian legends.

Christian (and Jewish) Turns of Phrase in the Qur'an

In a book chapter from 2019 I discuss biblical turns of phrase in the Qur'an.[11] Here I summarize that research and its conclusions, mention two further examples of biblical turns of phrase in the Qur'an, and speak to the connections of that study with the current book.

In that chapter I identify ten biblical turns of phrase in the Qur'an:

1. Q 7:140: "Those that cry lies to Our signs and wax proud against them the gates of heaven shall not be opened to them, nor shall they enter Paradise until the camel passes through the eye of the needle. Even so We recompense the sinners." (Matt 19:23–26; Mark 10:25; Luke 18:25)
2. Q 2:88, cf. 4:155: "And they say, 'Our hearts are uncircumcised.'" (Lev 26:41; Deut 10:16; Jer 4:4, 9:26; Ezek 44:9; Acts 7:51–53; Rom 2:28–29; Phil 3:3; Col 2:1)
3. Q 21:47, cf. 31:16: "Not one soul shall be wronged anything; even if it be the weight of one grain of mustard-seed We shall produce it." (Matt 13:31–32, 17:20; Mark 4:30–31; Luke 13:18–19)
4. Q 16:77: "And the matter of the Hour is as a twinkling of the eye, or nearer." (1 Cor 15:51–52)
5. Q 16:79, cf. 67:19: "Have they not regarded the birds, that are subjected in the air of heaven? Naught holds them but God." (Matt 6:26; Luke 12:24)
6. Q 49:12: "And do not spy, neither backbite one another; would any of you like to eat the flesh of his brother dead?" (Gal 5:13–15)

7. Q 9:80: "Ask pardon for them, or ask not pardon for them; if thou askest pardon for them seventy times, God will not pardon them." (Matt 18:21–22)
8. Q 2:93, cf. 4:46 (also Q 2:285, 5:7, 24:51): "They said, 'We hear, and rebel'" (*sami'nā wa-'aṣaynā*). (Deut 5:27, *we-shāma'nū wa-'āsīnū;* cf. Exod 24:7, where the order is reversed)
9. Q 21:104: "On the day when We shall roll up heaven as a scroll is rolled for the writings." (Isa 34:4; Rev 6:14)
10. Q 21:105: "The earth shall be the inheritance of My righteous servants." (Ps 37:9, 29; Matt 5:4)

To these ten from the original study I now add two additional turns of phrase:

11. Q 32:17: "No soul knows what comfort is laid up for them secretly, as a recompense for that they were doing." (1 Cor 2:9)
12. Q 5:45: "And therein We prescribed for them: 'A life for a life, an eye for an eye, a nose for a nose, an ear for an ear, a tooth for a tooth, and for wounds retaliation'; but whosoever forgoes it as a freewill offering, that shall be for him an expiation. Whoso judges not according to what God has sent down—they are the evildoers." (Exod 21:23–45; Lev 24:19–20; Matt 5:38)

The most important point about the biblical turns of phrase quoted above is that they exist at all in the Qur'an. The standard biography of Muhammad's life teaches us that the Qur'an was proclaimed in essentially a pagan or completely Islamic context (except for just a few years when there were still Jews in Medina). It comes as somewhat of a surprise, then, to see the Qur'an using biblical turns of phrase. As we will see (and, perhaps, as the reader has already surmised), the Qur'an does not employ these turns of phrase to comment on passages in the Bible. Rather, it employs them to express new points (more on this below). In other words, one has the impression that these biblical turns of phrase are not being introduced for the first time to its audience, but rather that they are used precisely because they were known among Arabic speakers in the Qur'an's environment and were recognizable. They were "in the air."

The second important point, and the one that is most relevant here, about these turns of phrase is that they tend to come from the New Testament and not from the Hebrew Bible. Now, I do not pretend that this list of twelve biblical turns of phrase is comprehensive. No doubt I missed others in the Qur'an, perhaps some that are connected only to the Hebrew Bible. However, to the best of my knowledge this list is fairly representative.

By "turn of phrase" I mean something between an individual qur'anic term that seems to reflect a Hebrew, Greek, or Syriac word and a pericope that engages with a biblical narrative. Turns of phrase are interesting because they are short units that can be lifted from their original biblical context and used in a new qur'anic context. As we see in what follows, they generally do not in themselves have unambiguous theological content. Indeed the Qur'an seems to be using turns of phrase that can be neatly integrated into its own theology. Moreover, the Qur'an presumably uses them because they are familiar to the Qur'an's audience. One might say that this is the principal reason for their use in the Qur'an.

In any case, the key point for our study is the preponderance of turns of phrase from the New Testament, despite the fact that the New Testament is much shorter than the Hebrew Bible. Of these twelve examples of biblical turns of phrase, seven (numbers 1, 3, 4, 5, 6, 7, and 11 above) occur only in the New Testament; four others (numbers 2, 9, 10, and 12) occur in both the Hebrew Bible and the New Testament; and only one (number 8) occurs exclusively in the Hebrew Bible.

Number 8 above is exceptional in another manner as well, for it seems to involve a play with Hebrew. The Hebrew expression *we-shāmaʿnū wa-ʿāsīnū* means "We shall listen and act accordingly," whereas the similar-sounding Arabic expression in the Qur'an (*samiʿnā wa-ʿaṣaynā*)—which is attributed to the Israelites—has more or less the opposite meaning: "We have heard and disobeyed." Meanwhile the *meaning* of *we-shāmaʿnū wa-ʿāsīnū* corresponds roughly with a phrase attributed elsewhere in the Qur'an *to the followers of Muhammad* (and not to the Israelites): "They say, 'We hear, and obey [*samiʿnā wa-aṭaʿnā*]. Our Lord, grant us Thy forgiveness; unto Thee is the homecoming'" (Q 2:285; cf. 5:7, 24:51). In other words, this is a notable case, not to be ignored, where the Qur'an engages specifically with the Hebrew Bible, and with the Hebrew language.[12] It does so, importantly, in a polemical manner (something to which we will return).

Almost all of these turns of phrase are deployed in the Qur'an in a new manner. Number 1 above, in regard to a camel and the eye of a needle, is an important example of this. In the synoptic Gospels this expression is used to explain how difficult it is for a rich person to make it into heaven ("it is easier for a camel to go through the eye of a needle than for a rich man to enter the kingdom of God," Matt 19:24). The Qur'an, however, applies it to the case of a person who denies God's signs ("Those that cry lies to Our signs . . ."). Now, the Qur'an, like the Gospels, is concerned elsewhere with the problem of economic inequality; in other words, there is no prima facie reason why it would not reproduce the larger context of Matt 19:24 (or Mark 10:25 or Luke 18:25). Nevertheless, the Qur'an applies this turn of phrase to a different theme of central importance to its teaching on the divine-human relationship, namely God's merciful provision of signs to humans and humans' consequent responsibility to recognize them. This is exactly the sort of thing we would expect if the Qur'an were *not* commenting on a biblical passage but rather using an expression that was familiar in its context.

Now, it is also possible that the Qur'an is thoughtfully repurposing a biblical passage and seeking to replace the Christian valence of the turn of phrase with something new. We do see a sort of direct engagement, and repurposing, of the Bible in the expression (number 8 above) "We hear, and rebel." However, the logic of the Qur'an in its play on the biblical text with this latter expression is evident. There are no signs of any similar play with the biblical saying involving the camel and the eye of the needle in Sura 7. Accordingly it seems to me likely that the Qur'an is "simply" using an expression that was circulating in its (Christian) context.

The case of the "circumcision of the heart" (number 2 above) is similar. The biblical authors who speak of the circumcision, or the noncircumcision, of hearts are appealing to an important element of Jewish religion. Circumcision (of boys) is not only a requirement of the Mosaic law; it is also prominent in the story of Abraham and God in Genesis. Indeed it is central to that story. In Genesis 17 God makes the circumcision of Abraham and the males in his family a necessary condition of their covenant with God: "This is my covenant, which you shall keep, between me and you and your descendants after you: Every male among you shall be circumcised" (Gen 17:10). Again, a few verses later, God declares, "Any uncircumcised male who is not circumcised in the flesh of his foreskin shall be cut off from his people; he has broken my covenant" (Gen 17:14). It is thus meaningful when the biblical authors develop the idea of the circumcision of the heart. Thereby they appeal to the Israelites to develop an interior disposition of obedience that matches their exterior acts of obedience. In Deut 10:16 the author has God himself speak of the circumcision of the heart: "Circumcise therefore the foreskin of your heart, and be no longer stubborn." Jeremiah 4:4 is similar to Exod 10:16, and later in Jeremiah we find this image employed in a different way, for the sake of a reprimand of Israel: "Egypt, Judah, Edom, the sons of Ammon, Moab, and all who dwell in the desert that cut the corners of their hair; for all these nations are uncircumcised, and all the house of Israel is uncircumcised in heart" (*ʿarlē lēb;* Jer 9:26). With this expression the prophet seeks to awaken the religious conscience of the people: The gentiles are uncircumcised in the flesh, but how are Israelites better if they are uncircumcised in their hearts?

The prophet's exhortation to his own people in Jeremiah is taken up in a number of passages in the New Testament and integrated into a larger argument regarding the repeated failure of the Jews to obey God, a tendency that culminated in the rejection and death of Christ.[13] This is perhaps best exemplified in Stephen's speech in front of the Sanhedrin in Acts, which comes to a climax with an appeal to this image:

> You stiff-necked people, *uncircumcised in heart and ears,* you always resist the Holy Spirit. As your fathers did, so do you. Which of the prophets did not your fathers persecute? And

> they killed those who announced beforehand the coming of the Righteous One, whom you have now betrayed and murdered, you who received the law as delivered by angels and did not keep it. (Acts 7:51–53, italics added)

The turn of phrase continued to be a popular way for church fathers, and notably Syriac church fathers, to develop arguments against Jews.[14]

The Qur'an, however, does not use this expression in order to develop an argument about the relative values of circumcising the flesh and the heart. Indeed, it shows no particular interest in circumcision anywhere. On both occasions where this expression appears in the Qur'an it is put into the mouths of the Israelites themselves:

> And they say, "Our hearts are uncircumcised [*qulūbunā ghulf*]." Nay, but God has cursed them for their unbelief; little will they believe. (Q 2:88)

> . . . and for their saying, "Our hearts are uncircumcised [*qulūbunā ghulf*]"—nay, but God sealed them for their unbelief, so they believe not, except a few. (Q 4:155)

The statement of the Israelites here, *qulūbunā ghulf*, is generally taken by the commentators as their way of saying, "Our hearts are covered," meaning, "We will not listen to the message of Muhammad."[15] It seems to me that the commentators read this turn of phrase in the Qur'an correctly, and indeed that Arberry might have translated it as "Our hearts are covered" instead of as "Our hearts are uncircumcised." There is none of the layered biblical meaning in the Qur'an surrounding uncircumcision of the heart, and no comparison between two different sorts of circumcision. The expression in these two verses might be fruitfully compared with Q 41:5: "They say, 'Our hearts are veiled [*fī akinna*] from what thou callest us to, and in our ears is a heaviness, and between us and thee there is a veil [*ḥijāb*]; so act; we are acting!'" (cf. Q 6:25, 17:46, 18:57). Although Q 2:88 and 4:155 involve Jews and Q 41:5 does not (at least not explicitly so), the mise-en-scène is the same. The reference to "covered" or "veiled" hearts does not appear as an accusation against the opponents or adversaries (say, in the way that Acts has Stephen make this accusation against the Sanhedrin). Instead, the opponents themselves are made to say this in direct speech. They almost boast of having closed hearts. Their boast is ironic in Q 2:88 and 4:155, as the Qur'an has God clarify in both cases that their unwillingness to believe is actually the effect of God's curse (Q 2:88), or God's own sealing of their hearts (Q 4:155). Thus it shows how God outwits those who seek to outwit him.

In both instances where the Qur'an speaks of a mustard seed (number 3) it does so to speak of the microscopic reach of God's knowledge of humanity and their deeds. Qur'an 21:47 has God declare, "even if it be the weight of one grain of mustard-seed We shall produce it"; Q 31:16 expresses the same idea, although in this case the speaker is not God but the sage Luqmān, who counsels his son, "If it should be but the weight of one grain of mustard-seed, and though it be in a rock, or in the heavens, or in the earth, God shall bring it forth; surely God is All-subtle, All-aware." Two applications of this phrase are found in the biblical subtext. Matthew 13:31–32, Mark 4:30–31, and Luke 13:18–19 are parallel passages in which Jesus compares the kingdom of God to a mustard seed: "Another parable he put before them, saying, 'The kingdom of heaven is like a grain of mustard seed which a man took and sowed in his field; it is the smallest of all seeds, but when it has grown it is the greatest of shrubs and becomes a tree, so that the birds of the air come and make nests in its branches'" (Matt 13:31–32). Matthew 17:20 is different: "He said to them, 'Because of your little faith. For truly, I say to you, if you have faith as a grain of mustard seed, you will say to this mountain, "Move from here to there," and it will move; and nothing will be impossible to you.'" Here the image of the mustard seed is not used to describe the kingdom of God but rather the small amount of faith that is needed to have one's prayers answered. Notably, however, the qur'anic use of "mustard seed" (*ḥabba min khardal,* the last word being cognate with the Syriac of the Peshitta *ḥardlā*) does not correspond with either of the ways in which this phrase is used in the Jesus sayings of the synoptic Gospels.[16] In the Qur'an it is applied instead to the inability of humans to hide anything from God's judgment, including something as small as a mustard seed. In this the use of "mustard seed" in the Qur'an corresponds to its use of *dharra* ("speck," but often inaccurately translated as "atom"; Q 4:40; 10:61; 34:3, 22; 99:7, 8).[17] Again we see the Qur'an using a distinctive biblical turn of phrase but in a way that is not connected to its biblical use, something that suggests that it had entered into the culture of the Qur'an's context.

One last example of this sort from the list above might be enough to demonstrate the point. Qur'an 9:80 (number 7 above) has God say to the Prophet, "Ask pardon for them, or ask not pardon for them; if thou askest pardon for them seventy times, God will not pardon them." The use of the number seventy here in the context of a religious discourse about forgiveness strongly suggests that there is some relation to Matt 18:21–22: "Then Peter came up and said to him, 'Lord, how often shall my brother sin against me, and I forgive him? As many as seven times?' Jesus said to him, 'I do not say to you seven times, but seventy times seven.'" These two passages even have a certain resemblance in their framing. In Matthew Jesus is speaking to his (arguably) principal apostle, Simon Peter. In the Qur'an God is speaking to his apostle, the Prophet Muhammad. Now, in the qur'anic verses it seems quite clear that the reference to "seventy times" is used to represent a countless number of times. So one might ask, Why use the number seventy? Why not one hundred, or one thousand?[18] There is one other case in which the Qur'an shows an interest in the number seventy, when it speaks of a chain in hell that is seventy units long (Q 69:32). Nevertheless, the use of seventy in a passage such as Q 9:80 that is on the question of forgiveness strongly suggests that there is some connection with Matthew 18.

And yet this is clearly not a quotation of Matthew 18. In the Qur'an the question at stake is how many times one should ask God to forgive an unbeliever, whereas in Matthew the question is how many times someone (Peter, to be specific) should himself forgive a sinner. The sort of counsel in each case is different as well. In the Qur'an God refuses to forgive, whereas in Matthew Jesus demands that Peter forgive. Accordingly, one can see this (as with the other cases discussed above) either as an intentional subversion of the biblical lesson or as a reflection of a biblical (and specifically Christian) habit of speech, whereby people spoke of forgiveness and the number seventy together. Again it seems to me (although, again, it is probably not possible to prove) that the latter option is more likely, in the absence of any other sign in the Sura 9 passage of concern with Matthew 18.

Finally I discuss briefly the case of Q 32:17 (number 11: "No soul knows what comfort [*qurrat aʿyun*] is laid up for them secretly, as a recompense for that they were doing") and 1 Cor 2:9 ("But, as it is written, 'What no eye has seen, nor ear heard, / nor the heart of man conceived, / what God has prepared for those who love him'"). Quite a bit has been written about the relation of 1 Cor 2:9 to the Hebrew Bible, as well as its relation to Q 32:17 and to a hadith *qudsī* that represents it much more closely.[19]

In this case the messages of the qur'anic verse and the biblical verse are quite similar. The Qur'an, like Paul in 1 Corinthians, means to speak of the ineffability of the experience of paradise. Now, the Qur'an speaks of no one or no soul (*nafs*) "knowing," whereas Paul (possibly alluding to Isa 64:4) speaks of the faculties of the eye, ear, and heart (a combination incidentally, favored by the Qur'an as well: see Q 2:7, 17:36, 46:26). There may be some connection between Paul's allusion to the eye and the qur'anic expression rendered above by Arberry as "comfort"; in Arabic it is *qurrat aʿyun*, literally "coolness of the eyes" (cf. Q 28:9, 25:74), that is, something that is refreshing to behold. In any case, the point of both verses is that no one can truly know what God has "laid up" or "prepared" for the blessed (those who do good, according to Q 32:17, or those who love God, according to 1 Cor 2:9). While this parallel is not a case of the Qur'an using a biblical turn of phrase in a new way, it nevertheless confirms what we have seen of the nonverbatim correspondence between the Qur'an and the New Testament.

It is also interesting to note the relative preponderance of turns of phrase from Paul's letters (numbers 2, 4, 6, 11). This may come as a surprise, as the Qur'an never mentions Paul and seems not to have a place for him in its vision of salvation history. That these echoes of Pauline expressions nevertheless find their way into the Qur'an is thus telling. This speaks to a situation in which the Qur'an's author is using turns of phrase from the speech of Christians (for whom Paul is a saint and an apostle), perhaps without awareness that some of these turns of phrase come from Paul, and not from the Gospels.

Christian Legends in the Qur'an

Along with using Christian turns of phrase, the Qur'an also engages with Christian narratives or legends. Here too we are not dealing with direct quotations from the New Testament or other Christian texts. Indeed generally the Qur'an shows no clear awareness of the New Testament or the Hebrew Bible per se. The Qur'an refers to "the Gospel" (*al-injīl*), but it does so in a distinct manner. Whereas Christians in late antiquity used "Gospel" to refer to the proclamation of Jesus's life, death, and resurrection, or to one of the four written texts in their canon which include that proclamation (Matthew, Mark, Luke, and John), the Qur'an uses *injīl* (from the Greek word for Gospel, *euangelion*, perhaps through Ethiopic) to refer to a heavenly book that God sent down (*anzala*) to Jesus.[20] This is seen in Q 3:3 where the divine voice of the Qur'an declares to the Prophet, "He has sent down upon thee the Book with the truth, confirming what was before it, and He sent down the Torah and the Gospel."

The Qur'an never refers to Matthew, Mark, Luke, and John. Although it refers to the apostles (*ḥawāriyyūn*, from Ethiopic) of Jesus, it does so only in general terms (and intriguingly uses neither the Arabic *rusul* nor some form related to Syriac *shlīḥē*).[21] The *ḥawāriyyūn* are those who answer the appeal of Jesus to be his supporters with God (Q 3:52, 61:14), and who witness the descent of a table (*mā'ida*, also from Ethiopic) from heaven upon the request of Jesus (Q 5:112–15).[22] Indeed the Qur'an does not refer to any individual book of the New Testament. The Gospels, the Acts of the Apostles, the letters of Paul, the catholic epistles, and the Revelation of John are not named in the Qur'an. There are also no true quotations from the books of the New Testament, or indeed from any book in the Bible (Ps 21:105, which resembles generally Ps 37:29, and Matt 5:5, notwithstanding). This, of course, is a necessary consequence of the absence of any Arabic Bible at the time of the Qur'an's origins.[23] Notably, the closest thing to a direct quotation in the Qur'an is not of the Bible but of the Mishnah, namely Qur'an 5:32.[24]

It is all the more intriguing, then, that the Qur'an *does* engage robustly with Christian (and, to a lesser extent, Jewish) legends. Here I look particularly at the Qur'an's use of four legends: Adam and the fall of the devil, Abraham in his father's idol shop, Joseph and his sojourn in Egypt, and the Seven Sleepers of Ephesus. There are many more such cases, including examples from the Jesus and Mary material in the Qur'an.[25] These four cases, however, together make the point that the Qur'an engages robustly with Christian legends. It is notable that even many narratives in the Qur'an that are connected to the Hebrew Bible (notably the Adam and Joseph material that I discuss below) bear unmistakable signs that they have been transmitted through Christian communities.

Before turning to the Adam account, however, it is worth saying a word about the Qur'an and legends. Although the Qur'an's engagement with biblical tradition is robust, and includes questions of law, eschatology, and ritual, it shows a particular interest in stories or legends. This much is seen in the sorts of material from the canonical Bible that is alluded to in the Qur'an. As for the Hebrew Bible, the Qur'an includes significant discussions of Adam and the patriarchal figures from Genesis (especially Abraham and Joseph), of Moses, and of David and Solomon. It refers to, but with less detail, Elijah, Jonah, and Job. Otherwise, the Qur'an includes only brief mentions of other characters or stories from the Hebrew Bible. All of this matters for a few reasons. First, the sort of Hebrew Bible material that is *not* mentioned in the Qur'an is significant. The Qur'an shows almost no interest in the prophets, mentioning none of the four major prophets (Isaiah, Jeremiah, Ezekiel, and Daniel). It shows very little interest in the Wisdom books. Notably, the only prophet from the biblical prophetic books whom the Qur'an does mention is Jonah (also the only minor prophet mentioned by name in the Gospels outside of the genealogy of Jesus), the one minor prophet whose book is (excluding the second chapter) a narrative. Moreover, the Qur'an's interest in the Wisdom book of Job is only in the prose narrative and not in the poetic wisdom material proper in the middle of the book. All of this seems to indicate a certain interest in narrative. The Qur'an (with some notable exceptions) largely passes over the legal, prophetic, wisdom, and poetic material of the Hebrew Bible.[26] It focuses on the stories.

More or less the same can be said for the Qur'an's engagement with the New Testament. In regard to Jesus the Qur'an is principally interested in miracle stories, including his birth. Very little of Jesus's teaching is found in the Qur'an. Missing are the parables, the Beatitudes, the sermons, and the long Johannine discourses. With the exception of certain turns of phrase (discussed above), which are likely the sort of thing that entered into the Qur'an from habits of speech in a largely Christian culture, the Qur'an shows little interest in, or knowledge of, the material of the rest of the New Testament, including the Acts of the Apostles, the letters of Paul, the catholic epistles, and the Book of Revelation. Again, the Qur'an focuses on the stories.[27] The Qur'an's interest in stories, I argue, points to a context in which Jews and Christians were orally narrating accounts of salvation history. There are some significant signs that the Qur'an emerged in particular in a context of Christian storytelling.[28]

The first case that points to this conclusion is the story of Adam and the fall of the devil.[29] In seven different Suras the Qur'an has God command the angels to bow before Adam. When the devil (Iblīs) refuses to do so, he is cursed and cast out of heaven. According to Karl-Heinz Pohlmann, the most primitive version of this account is that in Qur'an 38 (vv. 71–85).[30] In part it formed the source of the version in Qur'an 7 (vv. 11b–24; which in turn, according to Joseph Witztum, is older than the versions in Qur'an 20 [vv. 115–23] and Qur'an 2 [vv. 30–38]).[31] The relationship of the various occurrences of the fall of the devil account is disputed, and here I do not offer a new proposal for their relative chronology. Instead, I discuss the main features of the various versions of this account in order to illustrate different ways in which the Qur'an is engaging with the Christian legend.

In Sura 7 the Qur'an has God announce to its human audience: "We created you, then We shaped you, then We said to the angels: 'Bow yourselves to Adam'; so they bowed themselves, save Iblis—he was not of those that bowed themselves" (Q 7:11). In the following verse the Qur'an narrates how God confronts Iblīs: "Said He, 'What prevented thee to bow thyself, when I commanded thee?' Said he, 'I am better than he; Thou createdst me of fire, and him Thou createdst of clay'" (Q 7:12). Qur'an 2 adds a new element to the narrative. It has God announce to the angels his plan to create a man, naming him a *khalīfa* ("viceroy" or "representative"), and this before he has created him (v. 30). The angels initially resist God's plan: "And when thy Lord said to the angels, 'I am setting in the earth a viceroy.' They said, 'What, wilt Thou set therein one who will do corruption there, and shed blood, while We proclaim Thy praise and call Thee Holy?' He said, 'Assuredly I know that you know not'" (Q 2:30).

As in the other versions of this story, however, the angels in Qur'an 2 bow down to Adam in the end, with the exception of Iblīs (Q 2:34).

One final, and important, element of this account is found in four versions of it (Q 7:14–18, 15:36–43, 17:62–65, 38:79–86; cf. also 34:20–21), namely a sort of pact made between God and the devil after the devil's expulsion from heaven, but before his temptation of Adam and Eve in the garden of paradise. In Q 7:14–18 we read:

> 14 Said he, "Respite me till the day they shall be raised."
>
> 15 Said He, "Thou art among the ones that are respited."
>
> 16 Said he, "Now, for Thy perverting me, I shall surely sit in ambush for them on Thy straight path;
>
> 17 then I shall come on them from before them and from behind them, from their right hands and their left hands; Thou wilt not find most of them thankful."
>
> 18 Said He, "Go thou forth from it, despised and banished. Those of them that follow thee—I shall assuredly fill Gehenna with all of you."

This last element is important because with it one comes to see the Qur'an's larger interest in the account of Adam and the fall of the devil. The Qur'an is generally concerned with the enmity of Satan to humanity, that is, with its own audience. Fourteen of the nineteen occurrences in the Qur'an of the word "enemy" (Arabic *'adūw*) are references to Satan as the enemy of humans (2:36, 98, 168, 208; 6:142; 7:22, 24; 12:5; 20:117, 123; 28:15; 35:6; 36:60; 43:62).[32] The God of the Qur'an repeatedly warns believers to protect themselves against Satan, and indeed to consider him an enemy: "Surely Satan is an enemy to you; so take him as an enemy. He calls his party only that they may be among the inhabitants of the Blaze" (Q 35:6).

In this light one begins to see the coherence of the larger narrative regarding Adam and the fall of the devil. This narrative explains the enmity of the devil for humanity, for according to the narrative it was humanity who caused the devil's fall from heaven and who are responsible for the divine curse that he bears. More can be said here. The devil seems to be one of the angels who initially resisted the creation of humans as a *khalīfa.* Now, this term is alternatively translated "successor" or "viceroy/representative." It seems to me that the context suggests that the latter is the better understanding in the case of Q 2:30 (also in its use for David in Q 38:26), although elsewhere the word in the plural may be used in the sense of "successors" (Q 6:165; 7:69, 74; 10:14, 73; 27:62; 35:39). The point of Q 2:30 is that Adam is given a high station, one that merits veneration; for this reason it is appropriate for the angels to bow down (*sajada*) to him as they would bow down to God. However, the angels, knowing (although it is not explained how they know) that humanity's actions will be evil, initially resist God's plan.[33] How could it be that they are to show obeisance to a human? Indeed one of them, Iblīs, resists to the end and refuses to bow down to Adam, challenging that plan. When God asks the reason for his refusal he declares, "I am better than he; Thou createdst me of fire, and him Thou createdst of clay" (Q 7:12). He is then punished, made small for his desire to be great: "Get thee down out of it; it is not for thee to wax proud [*tatakabbar;* literally, 'act big'] here, so go thou forth; surely thou art among the humbled [*min al-ṣāghirīn;* literally, 'one of the small']." This leads to the "pact" between God and the devil mentioned above, which in turn leads to the constant enmity of the devil for humans, until the Day of Resurrection (Q 17:62, 38:79).

This narrative offers an important example of the way that the Qur'an develops material from earlier biblical tradition (broadly understood) for the sake of its own teaching on God and humanity. It is, essentially, leveraging an earlier story to explain why the devil is such a bother to humans, a dynamic that is at the heart of the qur'anic message about the need to take refuge in God.[34] The idea of the angelic resistance to the creation of Adam is found in a Jewish source, Sanhedrin (38b) of the Babylonian Talmud. There, God asks two groups of angels whether they agree with his plan to make a man in his image.[35] In turn, these groups ask about humanity's ultimate deeds from God (a detail not found in the Qur'an) and upon learning of them quote Ps 8:4–5:

> what is man that thou art mindful of him,
> and the son of man that thou dost care for him?
>
> Yet thou hast made him little less than God,
> and dost crown him with glory and honor.

At this they are destroyed by God. A third group is then brought forth and, knowing what has happened with the first two, declares submissively: "What did it avail the former [angels] that they spoke to Thee [as they did]? The whole world is Thine, and whatsoever that Thou wishest to do therein, do it."[36]

The qur'anic account (Sura 2) corresponds quite closely with the logic of the Talmud here. In both cases the angels know (or learn of) humanity's evil deeds; in both cases they question the honor given to Adam; and in both cases some of them, although not all, submit themselves to God. There is an important detail of the Qur'an, however, that is not part of the talmudic account, namely the particular demand to prostrate before Adam. It is here where the Christian subtext is key.

A number of late antique Christian accounts, most famously the Syriac text known as the *Cave of Treasures,* tell a story in which the angels recognize the glorious image of God (Gen 1:26) in Adam.[37] In the *Cave of Treasures* the angels hear the voice of God praising him ("I give you authority over everything I have created") and all prostrate before him, except for the devil and the "lesser order" of angels who followed him: "When the leader of the lesser order saw the greatness given to Adam, he became jealous of him and did not want to prostrate before him with the angels. He said to his hosts, 'Do not worship him and do not praise him with the angels. It is proper that you should worship me, since I am fire and spirit, not that I worship something that is made of dirt.'"[38] This version is evidently linked closely to that of the Qur'an. It includes both a report of angels "prostrating" (Syriac *sgad;* Arabic *sajada*) before Adam and a report in which the devil explains his refusal to do so on the grounds of his creation from fire and Adam's creation from dirt.

This might be compared to the version of this account in the *Life of Adam and Eve,* a work originally written in Greek between the first and third centuries CE (likely a Christian text that incorporates Jewish traditions).[39] It includes in certain later versions in Christian languages (Latin, Georgian, and Armenian) a report about a meeting in which Adam asks Satan to explain his enmity toward Eve and himself (manifested in the temptation in the garden). The devil then tells him the story of how God earlier announced that Adam was created in his image, how the archangel Michael bowed down before Adam, and how Michael commanded all of the other angels to do the same:

> 12.1 Satan also wept loudly and said to Adam, "All my arrogance and sorrow came to pass because of you; for, because of you I went forth from my dwelling; and because of you I was alienated from the throne of the cherubs who, having spread out a shelter, used to enclose me; because of you my feet have trodden the earth."
>
> 12.2 Adam replied and said to him,
>
> 12.3 "What are our sins against you, that you did all this to us?"
>
> 13.1 Satan replied and said, "You did nothing to me, but I came to this measure because of you, on the day on which you were created, for I went forth on that day.
>
> 13.2 When God breathed his spirit into you, you received the likeness of his image. Thereupon, Michael came and made you bow down before God. God said to Michael, 'Behold I have made Adam in the likeness of my image.'
>
> 14.1 Then Michael summoned all the angels, and God said to them, 'Come, bow down to god whom I made.'
>
> 14.2 Michael bowed first. He called me and said, 'You too, bow down to Adam.'
>
> 14.3 I said, 'Go away, Michael! I shall not bow down to him who is posterior to me, for I am former. Why is it proper for me to bow down to him?'

> 15.1 The other angels, too, who were with me, heard this, and my words seemed pleasing to them and they did not prostrate themselves to you, Adam.
>
> 16.1 Thereupon, God became angry with me and commanded to expel us from our dwelling and to cast me and my angels, who were in agreement with me, to the earth; and you were at the same time in the Garden.
>
> 16.2 When I realized that because of you I had gone forth from the dwelling of light and was in sorrows and pains,
>
> 16.3 then I prepared a trap for you, so that I might alienate you from your happiness just as I, too, had been alienated because of you."[40]

Now, there are some reasons why this account may seem less relevant to the Qur'an than the account in the *Cave of Treasures.* Unlike the *Life of Adam and Eve,* the *Cave of Treasures* is a Syriac text and thus theoretically could have been read in those regions of the Levant and Arabia where Syriac/Aramaic coexisted with Arabic. Moreover, the *Cave of Treasures* has a precise correspondence with the Qur'an in regard to the reason that the devil gives for refusing to bow to Adam, namely his creation from fire (as opposed to Adam's creation from clay or dirt). In the *Life of Adam and Eve,* Satan gives a different explanation, namely that he was created before Adam. For this reason Gary Anderson has argued persuasively that the *Life of Adam and Eve* is participating in a common discourse regarding divine election in the Hebrew Bible. The biblical authors often emphasize God's right to choose by telling stories in which the younger son is favored over the older son, contrary to expectations (Abel over Cain, Isaac over Ishmael, Jacob over Esau, Joseph over his brothers, all of whom except for Benjamin were older). Anderson points out that the authors of the *Life of Adam and Eve* develop this motif in a cosmological manner, by emphasizing the jealousy of Satan (and those who follow him) over God's election of Adam, who is younger than him. Indeed, it is interesting to note (as a final word about *khalīfa*) Anderson's argument regarding the meaning of *imago Dei* in the *Life of*

Adam and Eve (and in Milton's *Paradise Lost*): "Both Milton and the *Life of Adam and Eve* are interested in defining what it means to be created in 'the image of God.' Both come to a similar conclusion: *it means to be exalted over the angels.*"[41] One might argue that the Qur'an is participating in its own way in this exegetical tradition. It follows the tradition found in the *Life of Adam and Eve* by describing the exaltation of Adam above the angels (something not found in Genesis). However, for theological reasons it substitutes the notion of Adam as God's viceroy (*khalīfa*) for that of Adam as the image of God.

In the *Life of Adam and Eve* Satan refers to his temptation of Adam in the garden (16.3: "then I prepared a trap for you"). Something quite similar is found in the Qur'an. After the devil is expelled from heaven in the Qur'an, he declares his intention to God to lead humanity astray in what is evidently an act of vengeance. This declaration is found in Sura 7 ("Now, for Thy perverting me, I shall surely sit in ambush for them on Thy straight path," Q 7:16) and Sura 15 ("Said he, 'My Lord, for Thy perverting me I shall deck all fair to them in the earth, and I shall pervert them, all together," Q 15:38).[42] In each case the Qur'an, in a sort of midrash on Genesis 3 (at least Genesis 3 as understood by later Christians, with the serpent representing Satan), offers a reason for the animosity of Satan for humanity. This is particularly evident in Sura 7, as the devil's declaration is immediately followed by the story of his temptation of Adam and Eve in the garden (vv. 19–25).[43]

Before moving on to the case of Abraham and his father's idols, I would like to argue that there is something particularly Christian about the image of the angels bowing down before Adam. This image does appear in the *Life of Adam and Eve,* and some scholars hold that this text was originally written by Jews and only later added to, and transmitted by, Christians. Yet other Jewish sources have some hesitation regarding the tradition of the angels bowing before Adam. These are described by Anderson:

> One can see evidence of this subversive energy in the numerous rabbinic stories that polemicize against any venerating of Adam. In one tale, the angels mistake Adam for God and almost shout "Holy" before him (*Genesis Rabbah* 8:10).

> God averts this error by casting a deep sleep on Adam so that his mortal nature would be evident. Rabbi Hoshaya compares this story to a parable in which a king and his governor go forth in a chariot together. The subjects of the king wish to acclaim the king as *Dominus*. But the king, worried that his citizens might mistake the governor for him, quickly pushes the governor from the chariot. There was to be no confusion about just who was to be proclaimed lord. One should venerate God alone, never man.[44]

This point might be kept in mind when evaluating the attention given to the prostration of the angels before Adam in the *Cave of Treasures*. Indeed the drama with which the *Cave of Treasures* describes the prostration of the angels is revealing:

> God formed Adam with his holy hands, in His image and in His likeness. When the angels saw the image and the glorious appearance of Adam, they trembled at the beauty of his figure. . . . Moreover, the angels and celestial powers heard the voice of God saying to Adam, "See, I have made you king, priest and prophet, Lord, leader and director of all those made and created. To you alone have I given these and I give you authority over everything I have created." When the angels and the archangels, the thrones and dominions, the cherubims and seraphims, that is when all of the celestial powers heard this voice, all of the orders bent their knees and prostrated before him.[45]

In the *Cave of Treasures* the angels appropriately recognize the "image" and "glorious appearance" of Adam. This is before Adam's fall, and he still bears the untarnished image of God. Yet something more is going on here. The author tells us that the angels not only "prostrated," but also "bent their knees." One recognizes here an echo of the hymn in Philippians 2: "Therefore God has highly exalted him and bestowed on him the name which is above every name, that at the name of Jesus *every knee should bow,* in heaven and on earth and under the earth, and every tongue confess that Jesus Christ is Lord, to the glory of God the Father" (Phil 2:9–11, italics added). In other words, the image of Adam (before the fall) in the *Cave of Treasures* is distinctly Christological. Adam is the first man and Christ is the "second man," the new Adam ("The first man was from the earth, a man of dust; the second man is from heaven," 1 Cor 15:47). The image in the *Cave of Treasures* also reflects the language of Hebrews: "And again, when he brings the first-born into the world, he says, 'Let all God's angels worship him'" (Heb 1:6). The author of the *Cave of Treasures* evidently had in mind the angelic worship of Christ, alluded to in Philippians and Hebrews, in his depiction of the angelic worship of Adam. The divine address to Adam ("See, I have made you king, priest and prophet") redounds to the glory of Christ, who is given authority by the Father, who rules, and who offers his own life as a sacrifice of atonement.

Now, it is important to emphasize that the Qur'an does not participate in this sort of Christological reading of the Adam story. The Qur'an, after all, clearly rejects Christian doctrine on Christ's divinity (Q 4:171; 5:17, 72; 9:30). And while this is less salient in the text, the Qur'an also rejects Christian doctrine on Christ's atoning death; indeed one qur'anic verse (Q 4:157) may be read to deny that Christ died at all.[46] The point is that the presence of a story in the Qur'an that has angels bowing down before Adam is quite likely the reflection of a predominantly Christian cultural context. That the story appears at all in the Qur'an is interesting, since it shows that the Qur'an is participating in a tradition of exegesis on Genesis. That the story appears with the detail of the angelic prostration is especially interesting, since it suggests that the Qur'an is dialoguing especially with Christianity. That the story appears no less than seven times (and with the detail of the angelic prostration in each occasion) shows the prominence of this Christian legend in the Qur'an's cultural context. This story was important enough in that context for the Qur'an to leverage it for its own argument-making.

We will arrive at similar conclusions in regard to the Qur'an's interest in the tradition of Abraham and his father's idols. As with the story of the angelic prostration before Adam, this tradition too is not found in the Bible. Instead, it is born from certain rough edges in the biblical text that prompted exegetical or midrashic speculation. At the end of the Book of Joshua, in the course of Joshua's farewell address, he declares that Terah, the father of Abraham, "served other gods" (Josh 24:2). This is an interesting declaration, as nowhere in Genesis is Terah said to serve other gods. In fact, Genesis has almost nothing to say of Terah, except that he was Abraham's father (Gen 11:31–32). The turn of phrase in Joshua 24 led Jewish scholars to speculate on the contrast between Terah, servant of other gods, and Abraham, who came to represent the zealous worship of the Lord alone (even if this sort of zeal is not really explicit anywhere in Genesis). One fruit of this speculation is an episode in the second-century BCE text known as *Jubilees,* which is a sort of retelling of Genesis and parts of Exodus, preserved in an Ethiopic translation and in the original Hebrew (now known from the Dead Sea Scrolls). For our purposes it is important to note that although *Jubilees* was originally written by Jews, it was received and transmitted by Christians. Indeed in the Ethiopic church *Jubilees* (known in Geʿez as *Kufale*) is in lists (some, but not all, as is commonly assumed) of the biblical canon.[47] This is especially significant for our purposes in light of what we have noted already of Ethiopic vocabulary in the Qur'an. *Jubilees* is also cited regularly as an authoritative text by late antique Christian authors writing in Greek.[48]

Jubilees reports that even before he traveled to the promised land, Abraham rejected the worship of idols, and in order to remain unsullied by idolatry, he parted ways with his father ("he separated from his father so that he might not worship the idols with him"; Jub. 11:16). And yet before Abraham separates himself from his father, he confronts him and implores him to give up idol-worship: "What help or advantage do we have from these idols before which you worship and bow down? Because there is not any spirit in them, for they are mute, and they are the misleading of the heart. Do not worship them" (Jub. 12:2–4). This element of *Jubilees* is interesting in light of the way that the Qur'an has Abraham similarly confront and question his father. Eight different qur'anic passages refer to Abraham's confrontation with his father over the latter's idol worship (Q 6:74–83, 19:41–48, 21:51–67, 26:69–82, 29:16–25, 37:83–96, 43:26–27, 60:4). In a number of these, Abraham questions his father (and, in certain passages, his father's people) over the utility of this worship in a manner similar to that in *Jubilees* (here, Q 26:69–82):

69 And recite to them the tiding of Abraham

70 when he said to his father and his people, "What do you serve?"

71 They said, "We serve idols, and continue cleaving to them."

72 He said, "Do they hear you when you call,

73 or do they profit you, or harm?"

74 They said, "Nay, but we found our fathers so doing."

75 He said, "And have you considered what you have been serving,

76 you and your fathers, the elders?

77 They are an enemy to me, except the Lord of all Being

78 who created me, and Himself guides me,

79 and Himself gives me to eat and drink,

80 and, whenever I am sick, heals me,

81 who makes me to die, then gives me life,

82 and who I am eager shall forgive me my offence on the Day of Doom."

Here (and in Qur'an 21) Abraham questions his father and his father's people. In Qur'an 6 and 19 he questions only his father. As we saw regarding the qur'anic material on the angelic prostration before Adam, the Qur'an integrates its own theology into its presentation of an earlier legend. It is noteworthy that Abraham uses a qur'anic refrain by speaking of God as one who "makes me to die, then gives me life" (Q 26:81; cf. Q 2:28, 22:66, 30:40, 45:26), and that the Qur'an alludes to God's mercy on the Day of Judgment (*dīn;* Arberry translates "doom").[49] *Jubilees,* by contrast, shows no interest in the theme of eschatological judgment in its account of Abraham. Of particular interest is the way in which the Qur'an (unlike *Jubilees*) has Abraham's father (and his companions) explain their idol worship as an act of deference to the practice of their fathers (Q 26:74). This is an important theme in the Qur'an, which repeatedly refers to the imitation of the practice of one's fathers as the principal reason for the stubbornness of unbelievers, including those of its own day (see Q 2:170; 5:104; 7:28, 70; 10:78; 11:62, 87, 14:10; 21:53; 26:74; 34:43; 43:22–24). This, too, is not a salient concern in *Jubilees*. Nevertheless, the presence of this legend in the Qur'an is of great importance to our understanding of the Qur'an's historical context. Its presence in no fewer than eight Suras suggests both that it was well known in that context and that the author of the Qur'an found it useful for the advancement of the Qur'an's theological message (perhaps, principally regarding the problem of imitating one's fathers).

Nevertheless, there are signs that the Qur'an is not engaging directly with the version of this legend reported in *Jubilees*. For as the account in *Jubilees* continues, we learn that Abraham's father secretly agrees with the monotheism of his son but refuses publicly to reject idol worship (for fear of his compatriots). Abraham, however, burns down the temple, and the family flees from Ur (presumably to save themselves from the wrath of the idolaters). This element of the account in *Jubilees* appears to be an etiology meant to explain why Terah initially left Ur for Harran (see Gen 11:31).[50]

In another pre-qur'anic telling of this tale, things are different. The *Apocalypse of Abraham* makes Terah himself the idol maker and a stubborn defender of idol worship. Jon Levenson describes the *Apocalypse of Abraham* as "a Jewish book of uncertain date (but certainly written after the destruction of the Temple in 70 CE) that appears in no scriptural canon."[51] This is also the conclusion of Alexander Kulik regarding the *Apocalypse*, which exists only in Old Slavonic translations of an earlier Greek translation of (presumably) a Hebrew original.[52] Thus the origins of the *Apocalypse* are roughly similar to those of *Jubilees:* most likely a Hebrew Palestinian origin from the first or second century CE. With the *Apocalypse* as well it is important to note that although the text was originally written by Jews, it was translated, transmitted, and read by Christians (although unlike *Jubilees* it was not preserved as part of the canon by any ecclesial community).

The intriguing difference with the *Apocalypse* (vis-à-vis *Jubilees*) is that Terah never rejects idolatry or takes Abraham's side. Thus the *Apoca-*

lypse has Abraham confront his father and demand that he repent of the sin of idol-making and idol worship. The first half of the *Apocalypse* is a comical tale of Abraham, who is still a boy, and his observations of the inanity of idol worship. First, the head of an idol falls off as Abraham is holding it (Apoc. Ab. 1:6). Later, as Abraham is leading a donkey with five idols of his father, he meets some merchants with camels; the donkey is frightened by a camel and begins to run. When it does so, the idols fall off and three are smashed (Apoc. Ab. 2:4–6). Observing these things, Abraham reflects, "What is the profit of the labor which my father is doing? Is not he rather a god of gods, since by his sculpting, carving and skill they come into being? It would be more fitting for them to worship my father, since they are his work" (Apoc. Ab. 3:2–4). When Terah later, in gratitude for his son's service, declares that Abraham "gave honor to the gods" (Apoc. Ab. 4:2), he responds, "Hear Terah, [my] father! It is the gods who are blessed by you, since you are a god to them" (Apoc. Ab. 4:3).

This declaration strikes Terah as impious and impudent and he grows angry with Abraham, but things get still worse. Abraham sets an idol named Bar-Eshath, which Terah has made, near a fire meant for cooking, and it is enveloped by the flames. Abraham declares, mockingly, "Bar-Eshath, you certainly are able to kindle fire and cook food!" (Apoc. Ab. 5:10). Finally, Abraham confronts his father and proclaims to him in a sort of sermon:

> Listen, Terah, my father, I shall seek in your presence the God who created all the gods which we consider! For who is it, or which one is it who colored heaven and made the sun golden, who has given light to the moon and the stars with it, who has dried the earth in the midst of many waters, who set you yourself among the elements, and who now has chosen me in the distraction of my mind? Will he reveal himself by himself to us? [He is] the God! (Apoc. Ab. 7:11–12)

In a climactic moment Abraham then hears the voice of God telling him to flee from the idol shop of Terah (as Lot is told to flee from Sodom in Genesis 19): "In the wisdom of your heart you are searching for the God of gods and the Creator. I am he! Leave Terah your father, and leave the house, so that you too are not slain for the sins of your father's house!" (Apoc. Ab. 8:3–4).[53] Abraham goes out, and just as he departs, fire from heaven consumes the house of his father.

This dramatic confrontation between father and son, one an unbeliever and the other a believer, is central to the qur'anic Abraham material. It is found in the passage from Qur'an 26 quoted above, but a still closer connection is found with a passage in Qur'an 21 (cf. also 37:83–96) in which Abraham breaks the idols of his father's people (Q 21:51–67):

> 51 We gave Abraham aforetime his rectitude—for We knew him—
>
> 52 when he said to his father and his people, "What are these statues unto which you are cleaving?"
>
> 53 They said, "We found our fathers serving them."
>
> 54 He said, "Then assuredly you and your fathers have been in manifest error."
>
> 55 They said, "What, hast thou come to us with the truth, or art thou one of those that play?"
>
> 56 He said, "Nay, but your Lord is the Lord of the heavens and the earth who originated them, and I am one of those that bear witness thereunto.
>
> 57 And, by God, I shall assuredly outwit your idols, after you have gone away turning your backs."
>
> 58 So he broke them into fragments, all but a great one they had, for haply they would return to it.
>
> 59 They said, "Who has done this with our gods? Surely he is one of the evildoers."
>
> 60 They said, "We heard a young man making mention of them, and he was called Abraham."
>
> 61 They said, "Bring him before the people's eyes; haply they shall bear witness."

> 62 They said, "So, art thou the man who did this unto our gods, Abraham?"
>
> 63 He said, "No; it was this great one of them that did it. Question them; if they are able to speak!"
>
> 64 So they returned one to another, and they said, "Surely it is you who are the evildoers."
>
> 65 Then they were utterly put to confusion saying, "Very well indeed thou knowest these do not speak."
>
> 66 He said, "What, and do you serve, apart from God, that which profits you nothing; neither hurts you?
>
> 67 Fie upon you and that you serve apart from God! Do you not understand?"

The accounts of the *Apocalypse* and the Qur'an are meant to show the silliness of idol worship and to celebrate the monotheism of Abraham. However, there are important differences between the account in the *Apocalypse,* which features only Abraham's father, and this qur'anic account.[54] The most important difference is the anecdote of Abraham himself breaking the idols in Qur'an 21 (and Qur'an 37). This account is missing from the *Apocalypse,* but it is found in another pre-qur'anic work, the Jewish midrash known as Genesis Rabbah:

> Terah was a manufacturer of idols. He once went away somewhere and left Abraham to sell them in his place. A man came and wished to buy one. "How old are you?" Abraham asked him. "Fifty years," was the reply. "Woe to such a man!" he exclaimed, "you are fifty years old and would worship a day-old object!" At this he became ashamed and departed. On another occasion a woman came with a plateful of flour and requested him, "Take this and offer it to them." So he took a stick, broke them, and put the stick in the hand of the largest. When his father returned he demanded, "What have you done to them?" "I cannot conceal it from you," he rejoined. "A woman came

> with a plateful of fine meal and requested me to offer it to them. One claimed, 'I must eat first,' while another claimed, 'I must eat first.' Thereupon the largest arose, took the stick, and broke them." "Why do you make sport of me," he cried out, "have they any knowledge!" "Should not your ears listen to what your mouth is saying," he retorted.[55]

The importance of this account in Genesis Rabbah to appreciating the Qur'an's Abraham material becomes especially salient with what follows. In Genesis Rabbah the king of that place, who is Nimrod (a figure described in the Bible as a "mighty hunter" [Gen 10:9], but never a king), casts Abraham into a furnace as a punishment for his insolence, but Abraham is saved by the mercy of God.[56] This is precisely the order of things in the Qur'an. After the story of Abraham's breaking the idols comes the story of the furnace (both in Qur'an 21 [vv. 68–70] and in Qur'an 37 [vv. 97–100]). Both accounts are influenced, directly or indirectly, by the story of Shadrach, Meshach, and Abednego in Daniel 3.

It is also noteworthy that the Qur'an, like the *Apocalypse of Abraham* and the account of Genesis Rabbah, includes wittiness, even humor, in its material on Abraham. The *Apocalypse* seems to invite laughter at the scene of gods being trampled by a donkey, or Abraham's congratulating an idol for helping to cook some food. Genesis Rabbah and the Qur'an do the same by celebrating Abraham's cleverness when he declares that the only idol left standing must have broken the others, although the humor is admittedly less salient in the Qur'an.[57]

As mentioned above, the Qur'an is generally concerned with the problem of unbelievers stubbornly following the faith of their fathers and not converting to the message of its own prophet. One might argue that this above all accounts for the Qur'an's interest in this anecdote, which shows Abraham heroically standing up to a whole crowd of unbelievers, including his own father. Indeed in one passage (Q 19:46) the confrontation reaches the point where Abraham's father threatens to stone him. Yet this is only one example of a motif in the Qur'an of father-son conflict. The Qur'an portrays a dramatic conversation between Noah and a son who refuses to get in the ark and is ultimately consumed by the waves with the unbelievers (Q 11:42–43).[58] The Qur'an also makes

Pharaoh the adoptive father of Moses (Q 28:9; although in Exodus it is his daughter who adopts Moses) and thus sets up a confrontation between the two in which Moses preaches to his father of "the Lord of heavens and earth, and what between them is" (Q 26:24). In the account of Abraham and his unbelieving people the Qur'an clearly is concerned to undo a possible argument against conversion among hesitant members of its audience who insist on following the faith of their fathers. Yet there is also a prophetological aspect to the Qur'an's interest in this account. The Qur'an (which elsewhere declares that "this Prophet" is among those "closest to Abraham"; Q 3:68) means to present Muhammad as a new Abraham, to impute to him the courage and theological clarity (and perhaps the wittiness) of Abraham and thereby to make the case that he is a prophet.

Nevertheless, the case of Abraham's breaking the idols is an important example of the Qur'an's interest in a conversation with a Jewish tradition. What is to account for this interest? As Jon Levenson argues, there is good reason to suppose that the Qur'an's author agreed with Jews on iconoclasm, and so he found this Jewish account attractive.[59] Yet I think that there is still more to be said. I propose (although there is perhaps no clear proof of this in the Qur'an) that the Qur'an's author was aware that Christians were not (yet) iconoclastic. Indeed it is possible (and this has been suggested as an explanation for some of the qur'anic material on Jesus and Mary) that the Qur'an's author was aware of Christian iconography.[60] In other words, it is possible that this story is shaped not so much as a refutation of the (supposed) idolatry of the Meccan pagans, but rather as a condemnation of Christian icons, or sacred imagery more generally. Now, it is true that the earliest Islamic coins have images, but these images are largely replicas of earlier Sasanian and Byzantine images and are largely explained as the product of a concern to ensure the recognition of the new coins.[61] Otherwise, Islam seems from the early material record to have been aniconic, especially in religious contexts.[62] Notably, early Islamic mosques do not have frescoes or mosaics of holy prophets, angels, or saints. In other words, I am proposing that the Qur'an has used a Jewish account (which has its own midrashic purpose connected to Genesis) to develop an argument against Christian practice.

Our third example of a story from the Qur'an's biblical subtext, that of Joseph, also involves thinking through the Qur'an's theological relationship with Judaism and Christianity. One dramatic difference between the qur'anic story of Joseph and our first two examples is the attention given to the Joseph story in one Sura (Qur'an 12, named "Joseph" by tradition) in contrast to the various allusions to the Adam/Iblīs story (in seven places) or the Abraham and his father story (in eight places). The use of the term "story" for this passage in Sura 12 seems especially appropriate, as the Qur'an itself seems to name it such when it has God declare in Q 12:3, "We will relate to thee the fairest of stories [*aḥsan al-qaṣaṣ*]." The length of the Joseph story has led to an enormous amount of interest in its literary characteristics.[63] Among other things, scholars have debated whether it is necessary to read the qur'anic story in the light of the biblical story. Thus Marilyn Waldman writes:

> It is now possible to restate and answer the questions raised in the beginning: Is it helpful to think of the Qur'anic Joseph as a version of the Biblical one? Not if it precludes us from approaching both as equally "basic" tellings whose "real" form logically can never exist apart from a given telling.
>
> Is it necessary to be aware of the Biblical story, or forms of it that might have been current in Muḥammad's milieu, in order to understand the Qur'anic one? Not unless we are prepared to compare the two scriptures in order to discover the integrity of each. An affinity between the two exists only to an extent; formal similarities do not necessarily mean they tell the same story in a thematic, moral, or theological sense.[64]

Waldman alludes here to other "forms" of the Joseph story (the only allusion in the article to post-biblical, pre-qur'anic versions of the Joseph story). She does not make anything more of this, and otherwise her analysis falls into the trap into which so many other analyses fall: direct comparison between Genesis and Sura 12. This trap is more evident in light of the sparse evidence for a pre-Islamic Arabic translation of the Bible. In other words, she is right to resist a simplistic comparison between the Bible and the Qur'an, but for the wrong reasons, and she is wrong to avoid comparison altogether. As Joseph Witztum has now shown (and we rely on his work extensively in what follows), a whole number of elements in the Qur'an become clearer when one appreciates the Joseph material of the late antique Near East, and particularly the material in Syriac tradition. Now, one can ignore this material (and most do just that), but those who do so will lose a wonderful resource that adds to, and does not take away from, the message of the Qur'an.

As Witztum has noted, early critical ("orientalist") scholarship on the qur'anic Joseph story tended to work from the premise that it was shaped by the influence of Jewish, not Christian, sources.[65] An interesting case in point is a 1923 German dissertation by Heinrich Näf, generally forgotten until Witztum brought it to light, on Joseph in the Syriac tradition but that includes some attention to the Qur'an as well.[66] While Näf shows interest in the Syriac tradition (including works of Narsai, Balai, and Jacob of Serugh) and the Qur'an, he nevertheless assumes that the Qur'an must be drawing on Jewish sources (even when there is no clear Jewish subtext) because Muhammad knew Jews (and not Christians) in Medina.[67] It seems to me that what Näf states is left unstated, yet still operative, in the works of a number of orientalists. The prevalent view that in cases such as the Joseph story the Qur'an must be reliant on Jewish sources seems to be a reflection of orientalist confidence in traditional reports, which have Muhammad deal often with Jews (even if Qur'an 12 is considered a Meccan Sura, one could argue that Jews were close by in Medina) but rarely with Christians. I also suspect (although it seems to be a quite elementary mistake) that scholars tend to forget that the Hebrew Bible is also (more or less) the Christian Old Testament. Indeed for our purposes it is important to note how significant the Old Testament was to the Syriac fathers, who frequently articulate their claims about Jesus (at times with Jews as real or imagined opponents) through Christological readings of it.[68]

In any case, Witztum's dissertation dramatically challenged the premise of predominant Jewish influence. In his thesis he brings to bear on the study of the qur'anic Joseph story a number of fourth- to sixth-century texts written by Christians in Syriac, including a prose narrative known as the *Syriac History of Joseph* (falsely attributed to Basil of Caesarea) and a number of metrical homilies, variously attributed to

Ephrem (d. 373), Balai (ca. early fifth century), Narsai (d. 503), and Jacob of Serugh (d. 521).[69] Still, it is important to emphasize that Witztum is nuanced in his assessment of this Christian literature and the Qur'an. He notes certain elements of the Joseph story that do not have precedents in this literature, and generally he is concerned to balance an appreciation for the Christian subtext (my word, not his) of the Qur'an and its Jewish subtext. He writes, "My argument is not that the Syriac tradition provides the entire background for the Quranic Joseph story, but that it played a major role in the formation of the Quranic version."[70] With that important caveat we might begin to explore Witztum's findings and their importance for the argument we are developing in this book.

A helpful way to start might be by offering an overview, following Witztum, of the various ways in which the qur'anic account of Joseph departs from that of Genesis.[71] These include:

1. The Qur'an, unlike Genesis, begins the story with the report of one dream (not two) of Joseph and does not mention the opening details regarding Jacob's preference for Joseph, the robe Joseph receives, and the brothers' resentment of Joseph.
2. The Qur'an (Q 12:8–9) has the brothers plot to kill Joseph while at home, whereas in Genesis (Gen 37:18–20) the brothers spontaneously decide to kill Joseph when they are out shepherding flocks at a site named Dothan.
3. The Qur'an speaks of a wolf (Q 12:13–14, 17) that kills Joseph, but Genesis has the brothers speak of a "wild animal" (Gen 37:20, 33).
4. The Qur'an, but not Genesis, has Joseph receive a divine message/revelation while he is stuck in the bottom of a pit (*jubb*) (Q 12:15, Gen 37:24).
5. Jacob, in the Qur'an (unlike Genesis), sees through the brothers' fabrication of a story by which Joseph was killed (Q 12:18).

6. Whereas in Genesis (Gen 39:20) Potiphar throws Joseph in prison for the alleged assault of his wife, in the Qur'an Potiphar recognizes Joseph's innocence (Q 12:28–29) and recognizes his wife's guilt (but nevertheless Joseph is thrown into prison, Q 12:35).
7. The Qur'an, unlike Genesis, has Potiphar's wife confess her crime and deceit (Q 12:52–53; unless these words are not attributed to her).
8. The Qur'an (Q 12:96), but not Genesis, has Jacob recover from blindness when Joseph's shirt is placed on his face.
9. The Qur'an reports an enigmatic statement by the brothers regarding Benjamin (who is unnamed), namely, "They said, 'If he is a thief, a brother of his was a thief before'" (Q 12:77; an apparent allusion to Joseph). This has no clear precedent in Genesis.
10. In Genesis (Gen 45:27–28) Jacob realizes that Joseph is alive when he sees the wagons that Joseph sent to him. In the Qur'an (Q 12:96) he declares openly that Joseph is alive (although he seems to have known this earlier, when he detects his scent in v. 94) only when Joseph's garment is placed on his face.
11. In the Qur'an (Q 12:97–98), but not in Genesis, the brothers ask Jacob's forgiveness for their crime against Joseph.

Thus on these eleven points (and Witztum identifies six more) the Qur'an departs notably from the Joseph narrative in Genesis. The notable differences between the Joseph account in the two scriptures (and not only on these narrative features, but also in regard to the more pious language of the Qur'an) have led scholars to comment on the reasons for the Qur'an's unique telling of the tale. Mustansir Mir writes of the literary brilliance (as he sees it) of the qur'anic version: "For its sheer readability, the Qur'anic story of Joseph, told in S. 12, is perhaps unsurpassed in the whole of the Qur'ān. The less than one hundred verses of the narrative telescope many years, present an amazing variety of scenes and characters in a tightly-knit plot, and offer a dramatic illustration of some of the fundamental themes of the Qur'an."[72] Later he comments:

> In a sense, *Sūrat Yūsuf* is a story in which there are no losers. All the "villains" are reformed in the end. In spite of that, one continues to feel that the distinction between the good and the bad characters is not completely erased. Although the brothers repent and Potiphar's wife admits her mistake (as do the noblewomen), the atmosphere remains charged with the conflict that took place between the good and the not-so-good characters, and the tensions created in the plot remain vividly in the reader's mind.[73]

Although Mir generally refrains from explicit comparisons with Joseph in Genesis, he nevertheless highlights those elements of the qur'anic account that, in his opinion, are remarkable and praiseworthy. The qur'anic Joseph story, in his analysis, is exceptional, for its "amazing variety of scenes and characters," its "tightly-knit plot," and the "tensions" that "remain vividly in the reader's mind." I do not care here to assess Mir's claims of the quality of this story, although I do think they are open to reconsideration.[74] Indeed I recognize the importance of the larger point of Mir in his *Muslim World* article, namely to emphasize the Qur'an's perspective and voice, and above all theological concerns in its telling of the Joseph story.

Less nuanced is the treatment of Muhammad Abdel Haleem in his chapter on Joseph in the book *Understanding the Qur'an.* Abdel Haleem makes explicit comparisons of the Genesis Joseph story and the qur'anic Joseph story. Like Mir, his description of the qur'anic storytelling technique is filled with praise: "It is truly remarkable that with all the gaps and great economy of style in the Qur'an, the story is very clear in Arabic and does not require anything from outside the Qur'an to be appreciated and its message fully understood." He adds, "In the Qur'anic version, the story is structured very tightly." Regarding the Genesis Joseph story Abdel Haleem writes that it "forms part of the national history of the Jews." He concludes:

> The function of a revealed text in Islam is not to give a national history; Muslims are not used to this, and the Qur'an does not contain a history of Muhammad's tribe. . . . Joseph's religious side is also far more emphasized in the Qur'an than any other aspect of his personality. . . . Although he is also guided by God in Genesis, other aspects of his character and of the whole story gain clear prominence. He appears also as a pleasant, handsome, gifted and able Hebrew economist who played an important role in the history of his nation.[75]

These observations are arguably valid in part, but as a whole they miss a larger point regarding the Joseph story, namely that the Qur'an is not the first text to tell the story in explicitly religious terms. Indeed, and as we argue below, the Qur'an is continuing a tradition of post-biblical, Christian interpretation of the Genesis Joseph story and is *not* engaging directly with Genesis at all.

This is precisely the point of Witztum (at least, as I understand it), namely that the Qur'an is not principally in conversation with the text of Genesis in its articulation of the story. In other words, the ways in which the plot of the qur'anic Joseph story departs from that of Genesis do not redound to the qur'anic author's dissatisfaction with the way the story is told in the Bible. Instead, they reflect the conversation of the Qur'an with later, post-biblical Jewish and (principally) Christian retellings of the Genesis Joseph story. This is a point that is almost always lost in popular discourse on the Qur'an and the Bible and, to a surprising degree, often lost in academic discourse on the Qur'an and the Bible as well.

I now look at the eleven points of difference (among the seventeen that Witztum notes) introduced above between the Genesis and qur'anic Joseph stories and, following Witztum, illustrate how they reflect *not* the Qur'an's willful departure from Genesis, but rather its conversation with post-biblical Jewish and Christian traditions. All of this is meant as evidence for the larger argument of this chapter, namely that the nature of biblical material in the Qur'an reveals the prominence of Jews and especially Christians in the Qur'an's context. It is meaningful that the Qur'an develops the Joseph story in ways that reflect the thought and traditions of late antique Near Eastern Christians, as preserved in Syriac literature. Again, it is important to emphasize that what follows is largely a synopsis of Witztum's observations and not new discoveries that I have made.

Point 1. The Qur'an, unlike Genesis, mentions one dream (not two) of Joseph at the opening of the story, involving the stars, sun, and moon. This dream is not reported as part of the narrative; rather, the Qur'an quotes Joseph seeking out the meaning of his dream from his father Jacob ("When Joseph said to his father, 'Father, I saw eleven stars, and the sun and the moon; I saw them bowing down before me'"; Q 12:4). Joseph then receives advice from his father ("[Jacob] said, 'O my son, relate not thy vision to thy brothers, lest they devise against thee some guile. Surely Satan is to man a manifest enemy'"; Q 12:5). In this the Qur'an is very close to the fifth-century homily of Pseudo-Narsai: "Jacob said: 'Be quiet child. Do not reveal [your dreams] / lest there be envy among your brothers and they kill you.'"[76] It is also interesting to note that Ephrem, in his *Commentary on Genesis,* does not mention Jacob's preference for Joseph or the gift of a coat (both of which also go unmentioned in the Qur'an).

Point 2. The Qur'an also incorporates a tradition found in the homily of Pseudo-Narsai when it has the brothers plot against Joseph while still at home. Although Genesis (as mentioned above) makes the plot a spontaneous reaction to seeing Joseph at Dothan, Pseudo-Narsai writes:

> Then the brothers of righteous Joseph heard these [dreams];
> they were smitten with envy and they planned to do away
> with him.
> When righteous Jacob saw that they were biting him
> [= Joseph]
> he sent them to pasture the flock at Shechem.[77]

Point 3. While Genesis has the brothers speak of a "wild animal" (Gen 37:20, 33) killing Joseph, the Qur'an makes it a wolf (*dhi'b;* Q 12:13–14, 17). As Witztum notes, this discrepancy helps underline the Qur'an's particular indebtedness to Christian tradition. Jewish rabbinic traditions usually identify the "wild animal" as Judah (symbolically a lion in Gen

49:9) or Potiphar's wife.[78] Christian traditions, however (including Pseudo-Narsai), refer to Joseph's brothers as wolves (*dēbē*) and Joseph as a lamb.[79] This is likely a reflection of the prominence of sheep-herding as a metaphor in the Gospels.

Point 4. The Qur'an's description of a revelation to Joseph in a pit (*jubb;* Q 12:15) follows likewise from a report in Pseudo-Narsai of revelation to Joseph (in the pit; Syriac *gubbā*). The Syriac text describes how God goes down with Joseph into the pit and comforts him.[80]

Point 5. Genesis has Jacob lament Joseph's apparent death ("And he recognized it, and said, 'It is my son's robe; a wild beast has devoured him; Joseph is without doubt torn to pieces'"; Gen 37:33), making an apparent contrast with the Qur'an ("And they brought his shirt with false blood on it. He said, 'No; but your spirits tempted you to do somewhat. But come, sweet patience! And God's succour is ever there to seek against that you describe'"; Q 12:18). As Witztum shows, a number of pre-qur'anic Christian texts have Jacob not mourn but think through things and conclude that the brothers' account of Joseph's death must be false. A cycle of homilies attributed to both Ephrem (d. 373) and Balai (d. fifth century) has Jacob wonder why Joseph's robe was neither ripped (if he were killed by animals) nor stolen (if he were murdered).[81]

Point 6. Potiphar's knowledge of Joseph's innocence (found in the Qur'an, Q 12:28–29, but not in Genesis) is a feature of a number of post-biblical Jewish (including Genesis Rabbah 87:9) and Christian traditions. However, it is only in Christian traditions (e.g., Pseudo-Narsai) that we find Potiphar, as in the Qur'an, arguing for Joseph's innocence by referring to the garment.[82]

Point 7. The confession of guilt by Potiphar's wife (Q 12:52–53) is a dramatic departure from the Genesis account, in which her last appearance is to accuse Joseph. In the Qur'an she appears again, after Joseph's imprisonment. Context is again offered to this scene in the Qur'an by Pseudo-Narsai, who relates that Potiphar was frightened when he heard of Joseph's rise to power. After successfully supplicating Joseph, Potiphar returns home and speaks to his wife of Joseph's clemency. At this she confesses her crime, first to her husband, and then in the presence of Joseph.[83] Not only does this Syriac subtext provide a narrative context to Q 12:52–53, it seems to confirm that the words in these verses are spoken by Potiphar's wife (and not Joseph or Potiphar), something debated in Islamic exegesis.[84]

Point 8. The Qur'an has Joseph tell his brothers to cast his shirt on his father's face when they return to him, that he might regain his sight (Q 12:93), and it subsequently reports that Jacob indeed "saw once again" when they did so (Q 12:96). As Witztum explains, Genesis merely reports that Jacob's ("Israel's") eyes were "dim [literally, 'heavy'] with age" (Gen 48:10), but there is nothing about blindness or recovering from blindness.[85] Witztum notes that this anecdote is also not found in pre-qur'anic Jewish sources but *is* found in Christian sources. A number of Syriac authors use the biblical turn of phrase "to lighten eyes," which idiomatically means "to gladden." Thus, for example, the psalmist asks of God to "lighten my eyes" (Syriac *w-anhar ʿaynay;* Ps 13:3; cf. Ps 19:8, Prov 15:30, Tob 10:5) not in the sense of "heal my blindness" but rather in the sense of "hear my prayer" or "bring me joy." Syriac authors seem to use this phrase as well in a metaphorical sense to express the grief of Jacob.[86] It may be significant that in Narsai's homily he is looking at Joseph's blood-stained garment as he speaks of his blindness, as the Qur'an connects the healing of Jacob's blindness with that garment. Thus it seems likely that the qur'anic author knew of Christian traditions, and even Christian turns of phrase, regarding Jacob's grief and made a metaphorical statement about his eyes into a literal report that Jacob was blind and was healed by Joseph's garment (or, in the Qur'an, "shirt," *qamīṣ*).[87] This would not be the only case where the Qur'an takes a metaphor or parabolic element from earlier biblical tradition and makes it into a plot element.[88]

Point 9. In Q 12:77 the brothers say regarding Benjamin, apparently to Joseph (whom they do not yet recognize), "If he is a thief, a brother of his was a thief before." There is nothing of this in Genesis; in the parallel scene the brothers defend Benjamin and seek to save him from the punishment of enslavement ("We said to my lord, 'The lad cannot leave his father, for if he should leave his father, his father would die'"; Gen 44:22). The explanation for this contrast, as Witztum shows, is evidently in the way in which the business of Benjamin carrying a stolen cup (although unbeknownst to him) is parallel to his (and Joseph's) mother Rachel carrying stolen idols. As Rachel is pursued by her father Laban and questioned about the idols earlier in Genesis (Gen 31:19–35), Benjamin is pursued by his brother Joseph and questioned about the cup (Genesis 44). Pseudo-Narsai develops this parallel by having the other brothers (who are not children of Rachel) say to Joseph (in a way that is close to Q 12:77), "He resembles his mother who stole the idols of her father Laban / and his brother Joseph resembled him and was worse than him."[89] Although Pseudo-Narsai does not directly call Joseph a thief, it is not hard to see how the comparison here could lead the qur'anic author to take the next step and do so. This is an interesting case where elements of the biblical tradition that are not prominent in the Qur'an (in this case the relationship between Benjamin/Joseph, beloved sons of Rachel, and the other brothers), but are prominent in the biblical tradition, are still reflected in a qur'anic turn of phrase.

Point 10. Witztum very astutely notices a contrast between the Peshitta (and Septuagint and Vulgate) reading of Gen 45:22–23 and that of the Masoretic Text of the Hebrew Bible. The Hebrew Bible has, "To each and all of them he gave festal garments; but to Benjamin he gave three hundred shekels of silver and five festal garments [v. 22]. To his father he sent as follows: ten asses loaded with . . ."; whereas the Peshitta has, "And to his father he sent such things as well as [*hākkanā w-*] ten donkeys . . ." (v. 23). The Syriac conjunction *w-* suggests that Joseph *also* sent garments to Jacob, since Gen 25:22 mentions garments that Joseph gave the brothers. Witztum notes that this leads Syriac authors to report that Joseph gave garments to Jacob.[90] This might explain in part why the Qur'an has Joseph send his shirt to Jacob (Q 12:93). Such an explanation might initially seem like a stretch, since the Syriac sources intend new, fancy Egyptian garments and the Qur'an seems to have in mind the same shirt that Jacob once gave to Joseph. Still, it is interesting to note that in the poem of Balai, Jacob becomes convinced that Joseph is alive only when Benjamin gives him garments from Joseph.[91] This is an interesting anticipation of the way the Qur'an has Jacob "perceive" ("smell" might be better for *ajidu rīḥa*) Jacob's scent when the brothers' caravan approaches carrying Joseph's garment (v. 94).

Point 11. Whereas the qur'anic report of the brothers asking forgiveness of Jacob (Q 12:97–98) has no parallel in Genesis, Witztum points out that it does have a parallel in Balai, who has the brothers—after Joseph has forgiven them—ask Jacob to forgive them as well. Remarkably in both texts Jacob also asks God to forgive them. Balai has Jacob say:

> But I also call my God
> not to judge you according to what you did.
> Let him not avenge through you
> the afflictions that my old age endured.[92]

Qur'an 12:98 reports: "[Jacob] said, 'Assuredly I will ask my Lord to forgive you; He is the All-forgiving, the All-compassionate.'" Witztum suggests convincingly that Balai (and thereby the Qur'an) has Jacob forgive the brothers because of Gen 50:15–17 where, after Jacob's death, the brothers send a message to beg for Joseph's forgiveness, noting how Jacob had told them to do so.

It is important to note that these eleven examples do not exhaust the differences between the qur'anic and Genesis Joseph stories. As mentioned above, Witztum identifies seventeen instances of difference and concludes that some of them are not to be accounted for (at least, in our current state of knowledge) by the pre-qur'anic Syriac Christian tradition. These include, for example, the way in which the Qur'an implies that "Potiphar" (named *al-ʿazīz*) adopts Joseph (Q 12:21).[93] More likely this is a case of applying a qur'anic motif, namely an unbelieving father and a believing son (note how the Qur'an seems to have Moses as the adopted son of Pharaoh; see Q 28:9).[94] He notes two further examples of differences that are not obviously explained by Syriac Christian tradition. First, in Genesis (Gen 42:28, 35) the brothers are dismayed to find money in their sacks upon their return to Canaan (because they fear an accusation of theft), whereas in the Qur'an they are grateful (Q 12:65). Second, Genesis (Gen 44:9–10) has the brothers suggest death for whoever has stolen Joseph's cup (but Joseph's steward judges that the thief become a slave), whereas the Qur'an (Q 12:75) has the brothers suggest that the thief become a slave.[95]

The final example of Christian narratives and the Qur'an is the case of the qur'anic Companions of the Cave who appear in Sura 18. The appearance of these companions, and the connection of their story with the Syriac Christian legend of the Seven Sleepers of Ephesus, has been noted by numerous scholars. The rather exact narrative (although not linguistic) correspondence between the qur'anic story and the Christian legend has been detailed in various studies, notably in a book chapter by Sidney Griffith.[96] Not all scholars, however, pause to think through the significance of this correspondence. With a few exceptions, including that of Joseph just mentioned, the qur'anic material on the Seven Sleepers is longer than any other qur'anic passage on Jewish or Christian narratives. That the Qur'an would show this level of interest in a Christian legend not found in the Bible seems to reflect, on the one hand, the usefulness of a story that is essentially (as we will see) an argument for the resurrection of the body, a doctrine of great importance to the Qur'an, and on the other hand, the prominence of this story in the Qur'an's context. That is an interesting point since (even if the story might have been originally written in Greek) the Seven Sleepers of Ephesus circulated almost exclusively in Syriac in the late antique Near East. In fact, in its narrative sequence and details the Qur'an follows closely the version of this story as recounted in a homily by Jacob of Serugh. This tells us a lot about the proximity of the Qur'an to lived Christian culture.

The qur'anic story of the Companions of the Cave also nicely illustrates a larger point about the Qur'an and Christian legends: the Qur'an depends on its audience's knowledge of a legend while it shapes that legend for its own theological purposes. It is important to note, for example, that the Qur'an includes what seem to be anti-Christian proclamations at both the beginning and the end of the story:

> . . . and to warn those who say, "God has taken to Himself a son." (Q 18:4)
>
> Say: "God knows very well how long they tarried. To Him belongs the Unseen in the heavens and in the earth. How well He sees! How well He hears! They have no protector, apart from Him, and He associates in His government no one.'" (Q 18:26)

These "bookend" notes seem to reveal a particular interest of the Qur'an in leveraging this story for the purpose of making an argument against Christians (the very group from which it received this story).[97]

As for the story itself, a few things can be said. First, the story of the Seven Sleepers of Ephesus was originally written by a Christian in the fifth century who intended to argue against certain of his coreligionists who doubted the resurrection of the body (but not the eternality of the soul). Griffith summarizes the scholarly assessment of the story's origins:

> The currently prominent opinion is that a record of their miraculous survival after more than three hundred years of entombment was first composed in Greek by Bishop Stephen of Ephesus between the years 448 and 450, albeit that the earliest extant texts are in Syriac and date from the sixth century. . . . Nevertheless, the alternative opinion of a Syriac original, strongly seconded by Theodor Nöldeke in 1886, and bolstered by the remark of St. Gregory of Tours (d. 594) that he owed his account of the "Seven Sleepers" to a Latin translation from a Syriac original, still survives. The thought among those who support this opinion is that the legend arose in the Syriac-speaking churches in connection with the "Origenist" controversies of the sixth century, in which differing opinions about the doctrine of the resurrection of the body were an issue.[98]

The story is related to an account recorded in a Jewish text from the second century CE known as 4 Baruch or the *Paraleipomena of Jeremiah* (which is likely the subtext of Q 2:259).[99] Both stories involve people falling asleep and then being woken up after an improbably long period of time. The Seven Sleepers of Ephesus involves young Christian men who faithfully refuse to offer incense at the altars of Zeus, Apollo, and Artemis as ordered by the pagan (Christ-hating) emperor Decius (r. 249–251). The youths are initially imprisoned but then escape, flee the city, and hide in a cave. There, God casts a miraculous sleep upon them and leaves a "watcher" (Syriac *ʿīrā*) to guard their bodies. The emperor, however, learns where they are and has the cave sealed to finish off the young men. Their sad story is transmitted in the Christian community, and one of them goes to the cave; he records on a tablet the names of the young men along with the date and reason for their flight from Ephesus. In his homily on the sleepers, Jacob of Serugh (who is responsible for the earliest extant version of the story) writes:

> They made tablets of lead and placed them beside them;
> They wrote the names of the sons of light on them,
> And the reason why the youngsters went to hide in the cave,
> And in what time period they had fled from Decius the king.[100]

Many years later, however, God wills to awaken the "sons of light"; in the reign of the (Christ-loving) emperor Theodosius II (r. 408–450) a man dismantles the wall that sealed off the cave for use as a sheepfold. As the cave is opened, the "young" men awaken; soon they send one of their members to buy food. This young believer is amazed to see that Ephesus has been transformed into a Christian city with a public display of crosses. When he attempts to buy food, however, the merchant he meets notices the (now) ancient coin of the young man. He assumes that the young man has found a buried treasure. This rumor travels quickly until a crowd gathers and takes the boy to a church, where the coin is recognized as belonging to the time of Decius. The boy tells his story, which spreads widely until the emperor Theodosius himself comes to Ephesus, not to persecute the young men as Decius once had, but to see the miracle for himself. He reads the lead tablet and offers to build a temple (Syriac *hayklā*) for them in Ephesus, but they choose to be buried back in their cave. Before they return to "sleep," however, the young men explain to Theodosius that they have been brought back only for his sake. They tell him that all of this is so "you could see and affirm that there is truly a resurrection."[101]

The correspondence between the qur'anic Companions of the Cave account and the Syriac legend of the Seven Sleepers of Ephesus is impressive. The Qur'an speaks of youths (*fitya,* Q 18:10, 13) who take refuge in a cave (Jacob also describes the protagonists as "youths," Syriac *ṭlāyē*), evidently for the sake of their religious convictions. In

Q 18:15 they declare: "These our people have taken to them other gods, apart from Him. Ah, if only they would bring some clear authority regarding them! But who does greater evil than he who forges against God a lie?" The Qur'an speaks of their miraculous protection and preservation in the cave, and also curiously mentions a dog "stretching its paws on the threshold" (Q 18:18). The dog, as Sidney Griffith has argued, seems to correspond to the "watcher" of the Christian legend. The presence of a dog in the Companions of the Cave account is particularly interesting. The only other mention of a dog in the Qur'an seems to be pejorative.[102] So what is a dog doing in the cave of the God-fearing young men?

To answer this question one needs to return to the Christian legend. Jacob tells the story of the Seven Sleepers by developing the Gospel metaphor (best known from the "Good Shepherd" discourse of John 10) of faithful believers as "sheep" protected by Jesus the shepherd. The believers (in Jacob's story) call on Jesus as the Good Shepherd and speak of Decius as a ravenous "wolf": "We beseech you, Good Shepherd, who has chosen His servants, / Guard your flock from this wolf who thirsts for blood."[103] It is in response to this prayer that God sends a "watcher" to guard them. Griffith insightfully notes that the Qur'an seems to complete or fulfill this Christian metaphor by making this (perhaps angelic) "watcher" a dog. After all, what other animal would a shepherd use to protect his sheep from a wolf? Griffith comments, "It may not be too far a leap to suppose that it was this 'watcher' of the Syriac tradition which became the watch-dog of the Arabic Qur'an."[104] Now, Griffith argues that this was a "leap" for the Qur'an, since in Syriac Christian tradition the term "watcher" generally refers to an angel (and indeed, as he notes, in one version of Jacob's homily on the Seven Sleepers precisely this explanation for "watcher" appears).[105] In fact, however, there is a pre-Islamic Christian text that suggests this "leap" had already been taken by Christians themselves. The account of a sixth-century pilgrim named Theodosius (not to be confused with the Christ-loving emperor) to the holy land (which he visited around 530) includes a reference to the legend of the Seven Sleepers. Tellingly, Theodosius describes Ephesus as the city of "the seven sleeping brothers, and the dog Viricanus at their feet."[106] Thus he not only confirms that Christians had begun to identify the "watcher" of the legend with a sheepdog, he also provides the dog's name.

There are a number of other significant correspondences between the legend of the Seven Sleepers and the qur'anic account of the Companions of the Cave. Like the Christian legend, the qur'anic account has one of the young men enter the city to buy food with a coin (Q 18:19).[107] The Qur'an's account does not speak of the emperor Decius (whose image would have been on the coin as the merchant inspected it), and so one would need some knowledge of the Christian legend in order to recognize the significance of the coin in the unfolding of the plot in the Qur'an. This is one sign that the Qur'an is engaging with an audience that is already familiar with this Christian tale.

It is also significant that the Qur'an has the people of the place declare, "We will raise over them a place of worship" (*masjid;* Q 18:21). This corresponds with the declaration of the emperor in the Christian legend that he would build a temple (Syriac *hayklā*) over them. Moreover, Griffith adds a very important observation in this regard. In the version of the Christian legend as preserved in the *Ecclesiastical History* of Zacharias of Mitylene, the author writes that at the site of the cave (not in Ephesus) a "house of prayer" (*bēt ṣlūtā*) was built over the bodies of the sleepers.[108] This seems to correspond still more closely with the qur'anic account (which speaks of a "place of prostration," *masjid*).

Finally, it is also important (for our purposes) to consider the final section of the Companions account, where the narrative shifts from a recounting of the story to a sort of intervention into debates regarding the story. First, in Q 18:22, the Qur'an notes different opinions regarding the number of companions:

> They will say, "Three; and their dog was the fourth of them." They will say, "Five; and their dog was the sixth of them," guessing at the Unseen. They will say, "Seven; and their dog was the eighth of them." Say: "My Lord knows very well their number, and none knows them, except a few." So do not dispute with them, except in outward disputation, and ask not any of them for a pronouncement on them.

Second, in Q 18:25–26, the Qur'an seems to intervene into another debate, namely the length of time the companions were "asleep":

> 25 And they tarried in the Cave three hundred years, and to that they added nine more.
>
> 26 Say: "God knows very well how long they tarried. To Him belongs the Unseen in the heavens and in the earth. How well He sees! How well He hears! They have no protector, apart from Him, and He associates in His government no one."

In the first case, the Qur'an does not provide a definitive answer (regarding the number of companions) but rather counsels Muhammad (apparently, since the imperative verbs are in the second-person singular) not to get involved with this debate. In the second case, the Qur'an both provides an answer (they slept for 309 years, Q 18:25) and then uses this as a moment to celebrate God's ability to know such things (Q 18:26).

Again, Griffith is extremely insightful here. He notes that there was indeed a dispute in Syriac tradition over the number of sleepers: "According to the *mêmrâ* of Jacob of Serugh and the *Ecclesiastical History* of John of Ephesus, the number is consistently eight . . . while the *Ecclesiastical History* of Zacharias of Mitylene speaks of 'their leader Akleides and his six companions.' In other early Christian language traditions the youths are usually called the 'Seven Sleepers of Ephesus.'"[109] Likewise, Griffith notes how the Christian sources debate the length of the youths' sleep in the cave. Now, one would think that the Christian sources should say something around two hundred years (calculating the date range between Decius and Theodosius II), but not everyone seems to have had a clear sense of the chronology (this may explain why the Qur'an speaks of 309 years). Griffith explains:

> In the pre-Islamic Syriac texts there is in fact disagreement about the number of years the youths stayed asleep in the cave. For the most part the differences seem to come from the methods of computing the number of years which elapsed between the reigns of the emperors Decius (249–51) and Theo-

> dosius II (408–50). Recension I of Jacob of Serugh's *mêmrâ* says of Decius, "According to the numbering and the reckoning of the Greeks, he was the king three hundred and seventy-two years ago," but recension II says, "According to the numbers and the reckoning of the Greeks, Decius passed on three hundred and fifty years ago." The *Ecclesiastical History* of John of Ephesus says that the coinage of Decius in the youths' possession was current three hundred and seventy years ago; in the *Ecclesiastical History* of Zacharias of Mitylene, the bishop of Ephesus tells the youth Dionysius that Decius reigned "two hundred years ago, more or less." With this reckoning, the bishop would seem to be "more or less" correct; the number of years which elapsed between the end of the reign of Decius (d. 251) and the last year of the reign of Theodosius (d. 450), when the youths were discovered, is roughly 199.[110]

What the Qur'an is up to in this "coda" to the Companions of the Cave account is of critical importance to appreciating its historical context, as it shows both a remarkable familiarity with and a remarkable interest in a Christian debate. Put otherwise, one could imagine a scenario according to which the Qur'an's author had only a vague acquaintance with the Christian legend of the Seven Sleepers of Ephesus. In this scenario the Qur'an's author, who clearly is fervently interested in constructing arguments in support of the Qur'an's teaching on the resurrection of the body, might have found this story useful for the sake of that teaching. In this scenario the legend might have made it to the Qur'an's author through storytellers who may have been Christian. However, the coda of the Companions of the Cave suggests that the actual scenario was different. The qur'anic author does not simply tell or retell the story of the Seven Sleepers. He expresses concern and offers advice for ongoing debates over that story. Evidently, in the Qur'an's very context there were disputes—the same disputes that are recognizable from the documentary record of the Syriac Christian sleepers legend—over both the number of sleepers and the length of their sleep. This is a highly suggestive clue that the historical context of the Qur'an—at least at the time and place of the composition of Qur'an 18 (which, by tradition, is "Meccan")—was marked by a substantial presence of Christian communities, communities that were reading (or at least recounting) legends known to us from Syriac literature.

As a concluding note to this chapter it is important to emphasize that what we have seen of the evidence for the presence of Christians in the Qur'an's historical context *in no way* implies that there were not also Jews in that context. Although I have highlighted some notable turns of phrase and legends that suggest a special relationship between the Qur'an and Christianity, this does not preclude the existence of a relationship between the Qur'an and Judaism. There is simply no reason why the Qur'an might not be engaging with both significant monotheistic communities of the late antique Near East. Indeed, the example of the phrase discussed above (Q 2:93, 4:46), "We hear, and rebel" (*samiʿnā wa-ʿaṣaynā;* cf. Hebrew *we-shāmaʿnū wa-ʿāsīnū;* Deut 5:27, cf. Exod 24:7), which seems to be a thoughtful play on Hebrew, shows that the Qur'an does engage directly with Jewish texts. A second example of a remarkable play on a Hebrew word may appear with *rāʿinā* in Q 2:104.[111] Meanwhile, we also saw that the legend of Abraham and his father's idols seems to come principally from Jewish and not Christian tradition. Another example of this is the "court of the ladies" in the qur'anic Joseph story (Q 12:30–35), a story involving Potiphar's wife and her friends that is not found in earlier Christian tradition but seems to have a Jewish subtext.[112]

Nevertheless, in the following two chapters I argue, first on historical grounds and then on theological grounds, that the Qur'an is particularly concerned with Christianity (which, after all, was by far the larger of the two communities). For now, however, it perhaps suffices to conclude that the Qur'an engages robustly with biblical tradition. As Tannous explains: "Not only are these figures, places, texts, concepts, and ideas referred to and used in the Qur'ān, but the text itself seems to assume that its audience will know who and what exactly these people, places, things, and categories are. Put slightly differently: the allusive style of the Qur'ān seems to presuppose a world in which biblical ideas and characters are reasonably well known."[113] We turn now to examine historical evidence that shows how important Christianity was to that world.

T•H•R•E•E

Christianity in the Qur'an's Historical Context

In his lucid discussion of the biblical world of the Qur'an, Jack Tannous addresses a number of indications that Christianity had spread widely among Arabic speakers in the centuries just preceding Islam.[1] In this chapter I cite and discuss some of those indications, add a few more, and note also the notable absence of pagan inscriptions in both North and South Arabia in the century before the rise of Islam in the early seventh century. It is true that the absence of evidence is not evidence of absence, and that an argument from silence is not the most compelling sort of argument. Nevertheless, this final point, when seen together with the other points raised in this book, suggests that Islam emerged from a context in which Arabic speakers had largely set aside polytheism and adopted monotheism, and Christianity above all. This historical evidence will largely confirm the literary evidence of the previous chapter. We saw there that the Qur'an uses Christian turns of phrase and engages closely with Christian stories. In this chapter we put this in perspective and argue that the Qur'an's interest in Christian stories corresponds with the significant presence of Christians in Arabia.[2]

Arabic and Other Languages in the Qur'an's Historical Context

One interesting approach to this exploration is to begin not with religion but with language. As already discussed, the Qur'an shows exceptional interest in its own language. Although I am hardly the first to point this out, this is nevertheless a topic that is too often missed in discussions of the origins of Islam. The Qur'an's repeated declarations that it is Arabic suggests that other languages were around and that earlier scriptures were found in those other languages and not in Arabic.[3] Why else would the Qur'an be so concerned to underline its Arabic language? In Sura 12 the divine voice of the Qur'an declares, "We have sent it down as an Arabic Koran; haply you will understand" (*innā anzalnāhu qurānan ʿarabiyyan la-ʿallakum taʿqilūna;* Q 12:2; cf. 43:3);[4] the Qur'an elsewhere speaks of itself as "a Book whose signs have been distinguished as an Arabic Koran for a people having knowledge" (*kitābun fuṣṣilat āyātuhu qurʾānan ʿarabiyyan li-qawmin yaʿlamūna;* Q 41:3).[5] Such verses imply that the Prophet's proclamations (his "Koran" or "recitation") *could* have been in another language, and that his book *could* have been a non-Arabic "Qur'an" (*qurʾān*).

In other words, there is something new about an Arabic scripture, which explains why the Qur'an so often speaks of its own language (something that is quite unusual in religious literature, including late antique Near Eastern religious literature). The Qur'an (Q 14:4) claims that God sends messages in the language of the people for whom they are intended. Thus the new scripture is God's special or particular message for Arabic speakers.

Another verse seems to confirm this perspective. In Sura 41 (*Fuṣṣilat*) the Qur'an declares: "If We had made it a barbarous [*aʿjamī*] Koran, they would have said, 'Why are its signs not distinguished [*fuṣṣilat*]? What, barbarous and Arabic?' Say: 'To the believers it is a guidance, and a healing; but those who believe not, in their ears is a heaviness, and to them it is a blindness; those—they are called from a far place'" (Q 41:44).[6] Here the Qur'an itself entertains (hypothetically) the possibility of a "barbarous" Qur'an. The translation of Arberry is appropriate inasmuch as "barbarous" implies an unintelligible language (the original sense of Greek *barbaros*). The idea behind this verse seems to be that the unbelievers have criticized the Qur'an for being Arabic; the Qur'an, rhetorically, notes that if it had been instead "barbarous" (that is, non-Arabic), they *still* would have criticized it, since after all the unbelievers are deaf and blind to the truth.

Equally interesting for our purposes is a passage in Qur'an 26. There the Qur'an first declares, "Truly it is the revelation of the Lord of all Being brought down by the Faithful Spirit upon thy heart that thou mayest be one of the warners, in a clear, Arabic tongue" (Q 26:192–95). A few verses later we read, "If We had sent it down on a barbarian [*'alā ba'ḍi l-a'jamīna*] and he had recited it to them, they would not have believed in it" (Q 26:198–99). This second passage is still more interesting because by raising this hypothetical scenario the Qur'an implies that "barbarians," people who spoke a non-Arabic language, were around.

Although the Qur'an does not describe itself as the first or only Arabic scripture explicitly, one can infer this much. When the Qur'an declares that it is in Arabic "so that" (Arberry uses the antiquated "haply") its audience will understand (Q 12:2), it suggests that this is something different from the other "recitations" which the people do *not* understand. One has the sense that now (finally!) the Arabs are to receive a revelation in their own tongue.

One final verse that is critical to this discussion of *'arabī* and *a'jamī* is Q 16:103: "And We know very well that they say, 'Only a mortal is teaching him.' The speech of him at whom they hint is barbarous; and this is speech Arabic, manifest." Here again, one can infer that there were "barbarians" around Muhammad. Indeed the Qur'an seems to have one specific "barbarian" in mind when it says "the speech of him at whom they hint" (*lisānu alladhī yulḥidūna ilayhi*). While the Qur'an does not let us know who this mysterious figure is, it does at least let us know that he spoke another language.[7]

Here the insights of Al-Jallad about Arabic and other languages at the dawn of Islam are particularly important. In his book on the Damascus Psalm fragment Al-Jallad meticulously argues that the language of the qur'anic text (or more precisely, the Qur'anic Consonantal Text, or QCT) was essentially that of the dialect of the Hijaz.[8] The scenario that he envisions is that this "Old Hijazi" initially became a prestige language (and accordingly is reflected in texts such as the Greek-Arabic Psalm fragment of Damascus) but coexisted along with a poetic register of the language associated with Central Arabic (and more particularly the tribe of Maʿadd).[9] Classical Arabic was formed when Hijazi was adapted to this poetic register: "normative Classical Arabic is Old Ḥigāzī in Maʕaddite garb," Al-Jallad writes.[10] He goes on to argue—and this is a still more important point for our purposes—that when the Qur'an speaks of its own language as *ʿarabī,* it means "the local vernacular language as opposed to traditional monotheistic liturgical idioms," namely Aramaic, Hebrew, Greek, and Ethiopic.[11] In articulating this idea Al-Jallad is responding to a few earlier studies by Jan Retsö and Peter Webb that argued for the idea that *ʿarabī* marked a special register of Arabic that was distinct to soothsayers (*kuhhān*) and poets.[12] Al-Jallad astutely argues that any similarity between the register of the Qur'an and that of soothsayers or poets has to do with the nature of the texts they produced: "It is more likely that the similarities between the Qur'an and other ritualistic forms of speech stem from its content, that is, divine communications, and its stylistics, that is, its rhymed and rhythmic language."[13]

Al-Jallad holds that the key takeaway from this is that the Qur'an was produced in the vernacular (Arabic) language of the people and so is different from the "monotheistic liturgies in this period" (one thinks of the recitation of the Torah or the Psalms among Jews and Christians). To this end he quotes Q 14:4 (alluded to above), "And We have sent no Messenger save with the tongue of his people, that he might make all clear to them." This could imply that the revelation is in a language actually spoken (and not some formalized, liturgical register of the language). However, it seems to me, especially in light of the play between *ʿarabī* and *aʿjamī* that we see elsewhere in the text, that the Qur'an means that God has proclaimed the Qur'an in Arabic and not in one of the languages of the *ahl al-kitāb* (Hebrew, Aramaic, Syriac, Greek, or Ethiopic). Qur'an 14:4 might be read together with Q 42:7: "And so We have revealed to thee an Arabic Koran, that thou mayest warn the Mother of Cities and those who dwell about it, and that thou mayest warn of the Day of Gathering, wherein is no doubt—a party in Paradise, and a party in the Blaze."[14]

If the "Mother of Cities" is Mecca, as the tradition claims (and really, even if it is not), this verse tells us that the Qur'an is in Arabic because Arabic was spoken in its environment. Again, one infers a situation in which, previously, monotheism was preached in a non-Arabic language, and now (finally) it is preached in Arabic.[15] Nicolai Sinai largely follows Al-Jallad's perspective on *'arabī*. He helpfully notes that the Qur'an explicitly indicates in Q 30:22 (where it speaks of *ikhtilāfu alsinatikum*) an awareness of the diversity of languages.[16]

The distinction between *'arabī* and *a'jamī* in the Qur'an seems to correspond roughly to the distinction between *ummī*/*ummiyyūn* (introduced briefly in Chapter 2) and *ahl al-kitāb* ("The People of the Book"). The Qur'an uses the phrase *ahl al-kitāb* to refer to Jews and Christians. They are the communities that have received revelation previously, and in non-Arabic languages. The divine voice of the Qur'an commands the Prophet to make an appeal to them,[17] and to dispute with them even while affirming that they are monotheists: "Dispute not with the People of the Book save in the fairer manner, except for those of them that do wrong; and say, 'We believe in what has been sent down to us, and what has been sent down to you; our God and your God is One, and to Him we have surrendered'" (Q 29:46). In this verse the Qur'an clearly wants to position itself vis-à-vis the earlier scriptures. Jews and Christians, it implies, have received authentic revelation (and the new believers are meant to affirm what "has been sent down" to them), but the Qur'an too is an authentic revelation.

Thus the *ahl al-kitāb* are Jews and Christians and Muhammad does not claim to be one of them. The Qur'an speaks of Muhammad as the *ummī* prophet (Q 7:157) and the people to whom he is sent as the *ummiyyūn:* "It is He who has raised up from among the common people [*ummiyyīn*] a Messenger from among them, to recite His signs to them and to purify them, and to teach them the Book and the Wisdom, though before that they were in manifest error" (Q 62:2). Arberry's translation here of *ummiyyīn* as "common people" rests on a sociological explanation for Islam's rise as a movement among the masses (rising up against the aristocrats). A better translation of *ummiyyūn* is simply "the gentiles" if one can expand this term to mean more than non-Jews (and also non-Christians), or perhaps, as Sinai has it, "the unscriptured" (which does nicely capture the point that the *ummiyyūn* do not have a scripture in their language).[18]

Because other scriptures were around, the Qur'an had to make space for itself, which it does in part by celebrating its own brilliance, and in part by forming arguments against Christianity and Judaism. Indeed the Qur'an's salient concern with disputation, visible for example in its extraordinary use of counterdiscourse, is best understood in the light of this sectarian (and multilingual) milieu.[19]

Although I focus on language and not ethnicity here, it is perhaps necessary to add that the words "Arab" and "Arabia" are ancient terms, appearing already in Assyrian inscriptions and in the Bible (1 Kgs 10:15; 2 Chr 9:14).[20] The Arabic inscription of Namara, written in Nabataean script and dated to 328 CE, speaks of a man named Mar al-Qays son of ʿAmro, "king of all the Arabs."[21] Al-Jallad has also written on two pre-Islamic Ancient North Arabian inscriptions that use the root *ʿ-r-b* as a self-designation (he argues that here the root does not mean simply "nomads" as there is no definite article).[22] Thus there does seem to have been a general idea of Arabic speakers as a people before Islam (in addition to a use of *ʿ-r-b* that coincided with its use for Bedouins in particular, e.g., in the qur'anic *aʿrāb*), even if we must be cautious not to impose an idea of nineteenth- or twentieth-century Arab nationalism on late antiquity.[23]

In speaking of the qur'anic author's decision to compose his scripture in Arabic, Robert Hoyland deftly writes, "It was an idea whose time had come."[24] In fact, before Islam Arabic-speaking Jews and Christians continued to read, or more likely listen to, scriptures in other languages. However, they had begun to write down Arabic in inscriptions and had even developed a specific script, adapted from Nabataean Aramaic script, for that purpose. It is possible, perhaps likely, that they had begun to write Arabic as well on perishable materials, none of which have remained. In any case, a Christian inscription from 567 CE from southern Syria (a town named Harran) notably has both Greek and Arabic (the Arabic in Arabic script) (see more below). The key point is that the Arabic script was developed only a few centuries before the rise of Islam and was used in the sixth century (at least) by Christians for religious purposes. It then took just one more step to make Arabic a scriptural language. That is a big step, however, and Hoyland comments, "Even if not the very first to use Arabic for a public text, Muhammad was certainly breaking new ground and this is presumably why he made such a show about the fact that the Qur'an was written in Arabic."[25]

Hoyland cautions that it would be simplistic to think of the Qur'an as simply indebted to Aramaic or Syriac. Words that might appear to be inherited from Syriac in the Qur'an (e.g., the word for soothsayer, *kāhin*, or priest, *qissīs*) often can be found in other Semitic languages, including Ancient North Arabian dialects of Arabic. However, this does not mean that Aramaic was not found in the Qur'an's historical context. Hoyland describes two early Aramaic funeral texts from the northern Arabian Peninsula, one each from Tayma and Hegra, which seem to confirm that Aramaic *was* regularly used in late antique Arabia.[26] What all of this means is that the linguistic situation in the Qur'an's context was "complex."[27]

Hoyland suggests, both on the basis of the pre-Islamic inscriptions and on the basis of the Qur'an (two questions that we explore below), that Christianity had spread widely among Arabic speakers before Islam. He advances this in part by studying Q 2:259, which includes a legend of a man who falls asleep for a hundred years that was known before Islam from 4 Baruch, a first- or second-century text that circulated among Christian communities in the Middle East. He adds that this matches an increasing amount of material evidence: "I would suggest that Arabophone Christianity was a lot more developed than has previously been thought. A careful analysis of a variety of texts, including papyri and inscriptions, reveals that places like Najran, Hira, Petra, Nessana, and Jabiya were home to substantial communities of Arabic-speaking Christians."[28] To this one might note the alliance of the Jacobite Ghassānid/Jafnid Arabs (centered in Jabiya, Syria) with the Byzantines,[29] and the thriving Christian community (in part Church of the East) in Hira (Iraq), the center of the Lakhmid/Nasrid kingdom.[30] Ilkka Lindstedt concludes, "By the beginning of the mission of the prophet Muḥammad in the early seventh century, most northern Arabian tribes appear to have converted to Christianity."[31] The evidence of the Qur'an suggests that Christianity was also thriving in the Hijaz.

Pre-Islamic Arabic Inscriptions

Before turning (back) to the Qur'an, I here discuss how the evidence of pre-Islamic Arabic (and Arabian) inscriptions helps shed light on the Qur'an's context. Work in this field has developed rapidly in recent years. What I offer is mostly a synthesis of this research and a discussion of how it helps us better to understand the relationship between Christianity and the Qur'an.

Before discussing a number of relevant pre-Islamic inscriptions, I offer a brief overview of the pre-Islamic Arabian linguistic situation. In the south of the Arabian Peninsula pre-Islamic inscriptions are known in both a monumental and a miniscule script (most of the latter sort of inscriptions are on small sticks or palm bark). The language of most of these inscriptions is *not* Arabic but rather languages—principally Sabaic, Minaic, Qatabanic, and Ḥaḍramitic—that fall within the Ancient South Arabian (ASA) family of Semitic languages to which Arabic does *not* belong.[32] However, as they are Semitic languages they include many cognate words with Arabic. As we will see, moreover, Arabic language inscriptions in the early Arabic (or Paleo-Arabic) script have also been found in the south (especially around Najran).

To the north (but also in the center) of the Arabian Peninsula a variety of Ancient North Arabian (ANA) languages coexisted with Aramaic (and Greek). These ANA languages (unlike ASA languages) are best considered a part of the Arabic language family (if not simply dialects of Arabic), in different varieties or stages of development. They are written in a number of different scripts, usually labeled Safaitic, Hismaic, Taymanitic, Dadanitic, Thamudic, and eventually Nabataean and early (Paleo-) Arabic. Both ASA and ANA languages/dialects, and their inscriptions, provide valuable information about the religious and historical context in Arabia at the time of Islam's emergence.

Beginning in the year 384 CE, monotheistic inscriptions in South Arabia begin to replace polytheistic inscriptions. The one God is generally addressed as *rḥmnn,* meaning "the Merciful" (the last *n* represents the definite article), closely related to the qur'anic Arabic term for God: *al-raḥmān.* Some of these inscriptions are so general that it is not clear whether they are written by a Jew, a Christian, or another, basically unknown, sort of monotheist (although this latter category may be only a hypothetical construct). However, other inscriptions are distinctly Jewish, as indicated by personal names or references to synagogues or to Jews (*yhd*), or to Israel.[33]

In 525, however, the armies of the Christian Kingdom of Axum in Ethiopia invaded South Arabia and imposed or disseminated Christianity there. Al-Jallad comments regarding the south of the Arabian Peninsula: "By the fourth century CE, references to the pagan gods disappear almost entirely from the inscriptions, ushering in what scholars have termed the 'monotheistic period.'"[34] Intriguingly, both the earlier Jewish inscriptions and the Christian inscriptions of the "Ethiopian" period refer to God as "the Merciful" (*rḥmnn*). An inscription dated to 552 CE, which mentions the South Arabian Christian king Abraha (who, according to Islamic tradition, attacked Mecca with an elephant in the year of Muhammad's birth), refers to "Rḥmnn and his messiah." Both Carlos Segovia and Illka Lindstedt find something strange here. Segovia argues that this formulation reflects a low Christology among South Arabian Christians, while Lindstedt speaks of "non-conventional Christological formulae."[35] Both wonder whether the Qur'an's discourse about Jesus could reflect some sort of idiosyncratic South Arabian Christological ideas. In fact, it is possible that this formula, that is, the reference to Jesus as God's "messiah" instead of God's son, is meant to send a message to Jews in South Arabia about the messiah. The most sober conclusion, however, is that it does not provide enough information to make a reliable assessment of the nature of sixth-century South Arabian Christology, let alone any possible relationship with the Qur'an.

Looking to the north we find a fundamentally different linguistic situation. Although there are certain outliers that might represent independent languages, ANA inscriptions are now recognized as belonging to a spectrum of the Arabic language (even if many, although not all, of them use *h*- and not *al*- as the definite article).[36] A similar trend toward monotheism is evident in these northern inscriptions. The ANA inscriptions in Safaitic, Hismaic, Taymanitic, or Dadanitic generally do not include references to Christianity or to Byzantine history, and so it is likely that none of them dates later than the fifth century CE. However, in their place we find inscriptions from the sixth century that are written in a transitional form of the Arabic script. Many (if not all) of these Paleo-Arabic inscriptions were written by Christians.[37] The move to monotheism appears a bit later than it does in South Arabia, but it occurs definitively before Islam. "By the sixth century," writes Al-Jallad, "the pagan gods had completely disappeared from the inscriptions of North Arabia."[38] These inscriptions refer to one God, usually as *al-ilāh,* a form close to the qur'anic name for God: *allāh.* It is quite likely that *al-ilāh* is a calque on Greek *ho theos,* although one should keep in mind as well how close it is to Syriac *alāhā.*

In thinking through the linguistic situation in North (and Central) Arabia at the time, it is also important to note that the Nabataean kingdom, which stretched down into the northern part of the Arabian Peninsula (including the cities of Dūmat al-Jandal and Hegra), used Aramaic for its official inscriptions, but (on the basis of names, technical terms, and Arabic traits in the Aramaic inscriptions) it seems quite likely that the spoken language of the kingdom was a form of Arabic.[39] This multilingual situation is quite interesting for our purposes. I do not mean to speculate too much about sociological phenomena, but this situation, where Aramaic is the official (imperial, if that term might be used for the kingdom) language and Arabic is the language of the people, might be connected to what we have observed above regarding the Qur'an. It may provide some insight into the Qur'an's declaration that it is (finally) offering the people a scripture in their own language, or better, in the language "of the people."[40] In any case we will see that Aramaic words seem to have entered into the pre-Islamic Arabic dialects well beyond the confines of the Nabataean kingdom.

As mentioned, for the most part inscriptions in Ancient North Arabian scripts are pagan, but one apparent and significant inscription dating to the fourth century CE might include a reference to Jesus. In their article "The Pre-Islamic Divine Name ʿsy and the Background of the Qurʾānic Jesus," Ahmad Al-Jallad and Ali Al-Manaser discuss an inscription in the Safaitic script found in northeastern Jordan (in the basalt desert known as the *ḥarrah*). Al-Jallad and Al-Manaser were particularly interested in this inscription because it seems to be the first witness to the use of the root *ʿ-s-y* for Jesus in pre-Islamic Arabia, and thus to help solve the mystery of why the Qur'an uses ʿĪsā for Jesus when one would expect from other Semitic languages (and the original Hebrew proper noun *yēshûaʿ*) something like *yasūʿ*, which indeed is the Christian Arabic form of Jesus's name. There is perhaps no reason to enter here into a detailed summary of their argument in this regard, but the inscription does seem to be Christian: its final clause, "O ʿsy help him against those who deny you" (*h ʿsy nṣr-h m-kfr-k*), may indeed be an invocation to Jesus, named *ʿsy* (against those who do not believe in him).[41] It is notable that both the Arabic roots *n-ṣ-r* ("help") and *k-f-r* ("deny") are common in the Qur'an and are used specifically in passages involving Jesus, for example in Q 61:14: "O believers, be you God's helpers [*anṣār*], as Jesus [*ʿĪsā*], Mary's son, said to the Apostles, 'Who will be my helpers [*anṣār*] unto God?' The Apostles said, 'We will be helpers [*anṣār*] of God.' And a party of the Children of Israel believed, and a party disbelieved [*kafarat*]. So We confirmed those who believed against their enemy, and they became masters." If the interpretation of this inscription as a Christian invocation and its dating to the fourth century are correct, then it would be the first Arabic witness to Christianity. Al-Jallad and Al-Manaser note that both the place and time would generally match with the stories of "holy men and ascetics venturing out into the deserts to convert its nomadic inhabitants," including St. Hilarion (d. 371), who was active around the Dead Sea among the "Saracens."[42] If they are right, then this inscription would be evidence of the spread of Christianity among Arabs well before the rise of Islam, albeit far from the Hijaz. It does show, in any case, that the sort of religious vocabulary that the Qur'an uses for Jesus was in use in Arabic a few centuries earlier.

As for pre-Islamic Arabic inscriptions written in the Arabic script—which (as mentioned above) developed out of the Nabataean form of the Aramaic script—they are all monotheistic. The known Paleo-Arabic inscriptions are relatively few in number. Among them are three inscriptions from Syria: an inscription dating to 512 CE found in Zebed, one dating to 529 CE found in Jabal Says, and another dating to 569 CE in the village of Harran. The inscription of Harran—which today is on the lintel of a modern house in the village—is written in Greek and Arabic; it originally was on a tomb for a Christian martyr (identified as "the holy John" in the Greek version). Recently, Christian Robin and colleagues have studied a number of Arabic-script, Arabic-language inscriptions from southern Arabia, near Najran (perhaps left by northern Arabs who had settled in the south); meanwhile, Leila Nehmé has studied an Arabic-script, Arabic-language Christian inscription from the region of Dūmat al-Jandal in northwestern Saudi Arabia.[43] We discuss these Christian Arabic inscriptions further below.[44]

Before turning to those Christian inscriptions, I discuss some other inscriptions that, although not explicitly Christian, testify to the presence of Aramaic vocabulary in the pre-Islamic Arabic inscriptions. First is an inscription dated 267 CE and known as the epitaph of Raqōsh bint ʿAbd Manōtō, which has been discussed by Al-Jallad and before him by Joshua Blau.[45] Following Al-Jallad, I have made boldface the Aramaic words found in the inscription and quoted his translation:

1. ***dnh*** *qbrw ṣnʿ-h kʿbw br*
2. *ḥrtt l-rqš* ***brt***
3. *ʿbdmnwtw ʾm-h w hy*
4. *hlkt py ʾl-ḥ grw*
5. *šnt* ***mʾh w štyn***
6. ***w tryn b-yrḥ tmwz w lʿn***
7. ***mry ʿlmʾ*** *mn yšnʿ ʾl-qbrw*
8. *d[ʾ] w mn yptḥ -h ḥ šy (w)*
9. *wld-h w lʿn mn yqbr w {y}ʿly mn-h*

> Translation: (1) This is the tomb which Kaʿbō son of Ḥāreṯah built (2) for Rqwš daughter (3) of ʿbd mnwtw his mother, and she (4) died in ʾal-Ḥegrō (= Ḥegrā) (5) in the year one hundred and sixty (6) two in the month of Tammūz so may (7) Mry-ʿlmʾ (lit. lord of eternity) curse whosoever alters this tomb (8) or opens it except (9) his children and may he curse whosoever buries or removes from it [a body].

Al-Jallad argues convincingly that this inscription is not the work of an author who did not know Aramaic well (and so had recourse to Arabic when necessary), but rather the work of a bilingual author. For our purposes it is interesting to note how the author refers to God as *mry ʿlmʾ*, which Al-Jallad renders as "lord of eternity." It shows that this author was likely a monotheist,[46] even if the deceased is named daughter of ʿAbd Manōtō ("Servant of [the pagan goddess] Manāt");[47] moreover, this formula is roughly equivalent to the qur'anic Arabic *rabb al-ʿālamīn* ("Lord of the worlds" or "Lord of humanity"), found for example in Q 1:2. This inscription is from Hegra in northwestern Arabia (as indicated in line five), approximately three hundred kilometers north of Medina and at the edge of the Nabataean realm. From approximately the same time is the En Avdat inscription farther north, from the Negev desert, which includes two lines of Arabic in an otherwise Aramaic text.[48]

Similar is an inscription discussed and translated in a 2018 study of Laïla Nehmé, written principally in Aramaic but with a few words in Arabic, from a route that connects Hegra (Madāʾin Ṣāliḥ) with Petra. This inscription (which she labels UJadhNab 538) is dated to 303 CE (thus a few decades after the Raqōsh epitaph discussed above) and seems to have been left to us by a Jew named Shullay son of Awshū, as it refers to the Feast of Unleavened Bread (Passover) with the Arabic expression *ḥajj al-faṭīr.* As Lindstedt has noted in his discussion of the inscription, it thus confirms the presence of bilingual (Aramaic-Arabic) Jews in northwest Arabia in the early fourth century.[49] To my knowledge, however, no unambiguously Jewish inscriptions have been found in the region with later dates, something that could cast doubt on the significance of a Jewish presence in Muhammad's Hijaz.

These examples of Aramaic-Arabic bilingualism very helpfully show us that these two languages coexisted in the Nabataean sphere of influence for centuries before the rise of Islam. One can thus infer that the author of the Qur'an likely did not himself "borrow" Aramaic terminology (such as *qissīs* for "priest," *ṭāghūt* for "error," *qurbān* for "sacrifice," or *rūḥ al-qudus* for the Holy Spirit) or proper nouns (Isḥāq, Ismāʿīl, or Maryam) for his scripture but rather that Aramaic terms were commonly used among Arabic speakers in his context.

To the north, toward Syria, there is reason to think of a trilingual context, with an important presence of Greek. This is indicated by the inscription of 512 CE in Zebed, which includes first a Greek/Syriac bilingual text and then a brief Arabic "addendum" (as Hoyland puts it): "May God be mindful of Sirgū son of ʾAmt-Manāfū and Ha{l.n}ī son of Maraʾ l-Qays and Sirgū son of Saʿdu and Š/Syrw and Š/S{.}ygw."[50] The

Zebed inscription is part of a "martyrion," a shrine dedicated to the martyr St. Sergius, and thus is Christian. While the Zebed inscription is near Aleppo (in northern Syria), another sixth-century Christian Arabic inscription, the Harran text, is dated to 569 and is found in a village approximately seventy kilometers south of Damascus. As mentioned briefly above it is only in Greek and Arabic, but in this case the Arabic is roughly equivalent in content to the Greek.[51] Like the inscription of Zebed, the Harran inscription was (originally) on a martyrion (in this case to a certain St. John). The Arabic inscription reads: "1. I Šaraḥīl son of Ẓālim built this martyrion 2. [in] the year 463, after the rebellion [?] 3. of Khaybar 4. by one year."[52]

The inscription of Jabal Says, located on a desert mountain approximately one hundred kilometers southeast of Damascus and dated to 528/529 CE, is the work of a "frontier guard." This inscription is only in Arabic and states simply, "Ruqaym son of Ma'arrif the Awsite; Al-Ḥārith the king sent me to; Usays, as a frontier guard, [in] the year; 423 [= 528/529 CE]." The reference to al-Ḥārith indicates the Jafnid (or Ghassanid) king al-Ḥārith ibn Jabala (r. 528–569). Although there are no Christian markers in this inscription, the reference to the Christian king al-Ḥārith, who is generally seen as an enthusiastic sponsor of Christianity, makes it very likely that "Ruqaym" was a Jafnid and a Christian.[53] Finally, a mosaic found in a church in Nebo (present-day Jordan) seems to include the Arabic formula *bi-l-salām*, "in peace" (perhaps "rest in peace"), across from a name (in Greek letters), Saola.[54] Together, these inscriptions point to a robust, linguistically Arabic, Christian culture in northern Arabia and Syria in the sixth century.[55]

Other pre-Islamic Christian inscriptions bring us closer to Mecca and Medina. In 2018 a study appeared of eleven Greek Christian inscriptions from al-ʿArniyyāt and Umm Jadhāyidh in northwestern Saudi Arabia (approximately five hundred kilometers from Medina). These inscriptions include Christian names (e.g., Petros/Peter) and, in one instance, a cross.[56]

In addition to these inscriptions, several recent discoveries of pre-Islamic Christian Arabic inscriptions (in Arabic script) might now be added, bringing us closer to the Hijaz. These include a text from Dūmat al-Jandal, or al-Jawf, studied by Nehmé.[57] Dūmat al-Jandal is well to the north of Medina (approximately 650 kilometers), although still in modern-day Saudi Arabia. This Arabic-script, Arabic-language inscription, which is dated to 548/549 CE (and thus roughly in the same time period as the Christian inscriptions discussed above), was found along with a large number of inscriptions in the Nabataean script. It reads: "May be remembered. May God remember Ḥgʿ{b/n}w son of Salama/Salāma/Salima {in} the m[onth] (gap) year 443 [AD 548/549]." At the end of the inscription, after the series of letters that represent the year, is a sizeable cross. It is notable that the word for God here is *al-ilāh,* close to qur'anic *allāh* and identical with the term for God in the Zebed inscription (and in the Ḥimā inscription discussed below).

This text also includes two Aramaic words, namely *yarḥ* for "month" (not fully legible, however) and *bar* for "son." Thus (unless these words are logograms), this inscription seems to reflect some sort of ongoing bilingualism in the Nabataean region in the sixth century. Still, Nehmé argues that the appearance of these words in the formulaic part of the text suggests the author was "likely an Arabic-speaking individual."[58]

Further important inscriptions for our knowledge of the pre-Islamic Arabian linguistic and religious context were discovered and studied by Christian Robin and others in Ḥimā, which lies not in the north but to the south of Mecca and Medina, near the southern Saudi Arabian city of Najran.[59] Of particular interest are a group of eleven inscriptions, ten of which include monumental crosses and which are all written in a "Nabataean-Arabic" script close to that found in the Syrian inscriptions such as Zebed, although they are located in the south.[60] One of these (Ḥimā-Sud PalAr 1) is dated to 364 in the scheme of the Roman Arabian Province, equivalent to 470 CE (and thus perhaps offers a rough date for this group of inscriptions, although several different hands are present). All of these inscriptions are short and consist principally of names, but it is interesting to note a number of biblical names among them: Isaac (Ḥimā-Sud PalAr 2), Elijah (Ḥimā-Sud PalAr 5), and Moses (Ḥimā-Sud PalAr 8). Ḥimā-Sud PalAr 10 includes the name of God in the typical pre-Islamic Arabic form (seen in Zebed, Dūmat al-Jandal, and elsewhere) of *al-ilāh.* A number of other names are repeated, which suggests that all of these texts come from the same time and from the same group of people (eight have the name Thawbān son of Mālik). It is also important to note the presence of Aramaic words, as we have seen in other Arabic Christian inscriptions, even this far to the south.[61] These include the words for month (*yrḥ*), son (*br*), and year (*sht*). The definite article is *al-*, as in Classical Arabic.

Al-Jallad argues that these short inscriptions, even if they were discovered in the south, were made by travelers from the north, as two of them use dating from the era of the Roman Arabian Province.[62] However, Robin is cautious on this matter and ultimately concludes that these inscriptions point to a community that had settled in South Arabia.[63] One reason to agree with Robin is his argument about the commemorative nature of these inscriptions; although they are not on tombs, they seem to be written in honor of the deceased. Thus they seem to be the work of a settled community that was remembering its dead. Robin also underlines the prominence of the crosses in these inscriptions, which says something about the importance of the Christian faith to this community.[64] This case is interesting for our purposes because it seems to show that Christians from northern Arabia were traveling to the south and settling there, making it at least conceivable that Christianity had a presence in between as well.

Still, thus far the Christian Arabic inscriptions (a number of which include Aramaic vocabulary) we have discussed are from North Arabia and South Arabia. One might reasonably ask whether the religious culture that produced these inscriptions was limited to the outskirts of the Hijaz. Perhaps Arabic-speaking Christians were in the south and north of Arabia but not in the region of Mecca and Medina itself. Perhaps the view of Aziz Al-Azmeh (presented in Chapter 1), essentially shared by Stephen Shoemaker, that western Arabia was a "pagan reservation" can still be maintained.[65]

However, an inscription from a site just outside of Mecca known as Riʿ al-Zallālah, recently examined, studied, and reread by Ahmad Al-Jallad and Hythem Sidky, suggests otherwise.[66] Although the Riʿ al-Zallālah inscription does not have a cross or explicitly Christian language, it does include monotheist (and specifically biblical) vocabulary. This inscription (which had been photographed in the 1950s and later studied by A. Grohmann)[67] is located in a pass (Riʿ al-Zallālah) that leads from Ṭā'if in the south into an open desert plain known as al-Sayl al-

Kabīr. From there one can head to the southwest to Mecca, approximately seventy-five kilometers away. Thus Riʿ al-Zallālah is on one of the principal routes of travel between Ṭāʾif and Mecca, and it is reasonable to assume that this inscription was made by someone moving between these two cities. The inscription reads simply (according to the new reading of Al-Jallad and Sidky):

May our Lord bless you
I am Qurrah
son of Sd[68]

The vocabulary in the first line, the Arabic of which is *brk-[k]m rb-n'*, is important. The use of *rb* ("Lord"), which is rendered definite by the pronominal suffix, might correspond with Hebrew *adonai* (or the Tetragrammaton) as used by Jews for "the Lord," or Greek *kurios,* much as *al-ilāh* (found in other inscriptions) might correspond to the use by Christians and Jews of *ho theos* for God. In any case, neither of these two roots is typical of the early pagan inscriptions. Al-Jallad and Sidky write: "The combination of *brk* and *rb* is quite spectacular from the perspective of the pagan Arabian inscriptions. In the tens of thousands of these documented so far—across North Arabian, South Arabian and Nabataean scripts—*rb* is never used as an epithet of the old gods and the verb *brk* 'to bless' is virtually absent from invocations in the pre-monotheistic period."[69] In light of this observation it seems extremely likely that this inscription comes from a monotheist, presumably a Jew or a Christian. Al-Jallad and Sidky write, "Both appear to be part of the stock of monotheistic vocabulary borrowed into Sabaic from Hebrew and Aramaic in the fourth century CE."[70] Whereas Grohmann dated the inscription to the first or second century AH (making it Islamic), this new reading (and the similarity of the script to the inscriptions of Ḥimā) strongly suggests that it is a pre-Islamic Jewish or Christian inscription. It is consistent neither with the early pagan inscriptions nor with later Islamic inscriptions. Al-Jallad and Sidky date it between 470 and 513 CE.[71] It is true that the Riʿ al-Zallālah inscription bears no telltale sign of Christianity, like the crosses in Ḥimā, but there is no reason to exclude that the author here (as in the majority of the inscriptions of this type now known to us) was a Christian. Al-Jallad and Sidky note that the known inscriptions of this type or class, which they call (following Robin) Paleo-Arabic, are all monotheistic, and those that can be identified further are all Christian. They conclude compellingly:

> These texts together imply the widespread penetration of monotheism across Arabia in the late pre-Islamic period, even in areas previously believed to have been late bastions of paganism, such as Dūmat al-Ǧandal and Ṭā'if itself, which Ibn al-Kalbī regarded as the centre of Allāt's cult in the sixth century. The discovery of the present text in the area between Ṭā'if and Mecca confirms this trend and demonstrates the expansion of monotheism to the very environment of nascent Islam.[72]

More perspective on the trend toward monotheism in Arabia is offered by an inscription in the south, the Jabal Dhabūb inscription. Like that at Riʿ al-Zallālah, the inscription found on Jabal Dhabūb includes the use of *rb* ("Lord") for God. When it was initially found, this inscription created quite some excitement, since the authors of the first Arabic study of it announced that it begins with a sort of *basmala* (the tripartite invocation with which all but one of the Qur'an's Suras begin).[73]

The Jabal Dhabūb inscription is not "Paleo-Arabic," and so it is different in nature from the others we have discussed. However, it dates from a similar period and is evidently the work of a monotheist. This inscription is exceptionally written in the miniscule Ancient South Arabian script (otherwise used for writing on small sticks and palm bark; it is also known as the *zabūr* script) and in a language that is related to late Sabaic; however, the inscription includes a number of lexemes found also in Arabic. The inscription also includes *rb smwt,* which in Arabic would be *rabb al-samāwāt* or "Lord of the heavens" (see Q 19:65). According to Al-Jallad this formula is typical of monotheism in South Arabia.[74] In North Arabia the title *mr' smayn* was used instead, with Aramaic *mr'* (also "lord") instead of Arabic *rb.*

Al-Hajj and Faqʿas, the authors of the first study and initial reading of the inscription, render its first words as *bsmlh rḥmn rḥmn.* Notably, they take the *n* at the end of the second *rḥmn,* but not the first *rḥmn,* to be the Sabaic definite article suffix (and thus equivalent to "the *raḥīm*"). In this way they were able to render these two words as *raḥmān* and *al-raḥīm.* Thus they concluded that the phrase is equivalent to Arabic *b-ismi llāhi l-raḥmāni l-raḥīm,* that is, roughly parallel to the invocation at the beginning of all of the Qur'an's Suras except Sura 9 (it is v. 1 in Sura 1). This invocation has been considered by some as a sort of theological response to the Christian invocation (based on Matt 28:19) "in the name of the Father and of the Son and of the Holy Spirit," a question to which we will return.[75]

In any case, the initial reading seemed to suggest a spectacular find. The qur'anic invocation would seem to have a precedent (although correlation is not causation) in a South Arabian inscription. Al-Jallad, however, reads this inscription differently. We follow his argument here, which in its own way leads to a conclusion that is no less spectacular. Al-Jallad notes that there is no compelling reason to conclude that the *n* is playing one role in the first *rḥmn* and a different role in the second *rḥmn.* He also questions why either of the two *n*'s should be seen as the Sabaic definite article when the word at the end of that same line, *smwt* (meaning "heavens"), which in principle should be definite as it is part of the compound *rb smwt* (as mentioned above), does not have the *-n* definite article. This line of questioning leads him to argue that the second *rḥmn* is, rather, an imperative verb with a first-person plural object suffix. Thus he reads the inscription:

> *bsm lh rḥmn,* "In the name of Allāh, the Raḥmān"
> *rḥm-n rb s^{1}mwt,* "have mercy upon us, O lord of the heavens"
> *rzq-n m-fḍl-k,* "satisfy us by means of your favor"
> *w-'ṯr-n mḫ-h s^{2}kmt 'ym-n,* "and grant us the essence of it at the end of our days / the gift of our days"

Al-Jallad accordingly sees the Jabal Dhabūb inscription as an invocation followed by three imperative appeals to God. It is interesting to note the reference to God as Allah (a possible reading of *lh*) in this pre-Islamic inscription (this sets it apart from the Paleo-Arabic inscriptions that use *al-ilāh*).[76] Al-Jallad, in fact, argues that this inscription reflects an effort to join together the use of *lh* to refer to God (typical in northern Arabia) and the use of *rḥm* to refer to God (typical in southern Arabia). He writes, "'The Raḥmān' was much more than an epithet—it was the proper name of Ḥimyar's deity, and was not used in North Arabia."[77]

Al-Jallad also provides a potential context for this "joining together" of two divine names. In the mid-sixth century the Christian South Arabian king Abraha led military campaigns into Central Arabia.[78] We know from his military activities that he was an ambitious ruler and from his inscriptions that he used Christian invocations.[79] Perhaps he sought to bring his subjects together under his religion and accordingly encouraged them to use both *al-raḥmān* and *allāh* for God. Thus Al-Jallad suggests that one might think of the first line above as "In the name of Allah, *who is* al-Raḥmān." This would make the inscription close in spirit to Q 17:110: "Say: 'Call upon God [*Allāh*], or call upon the Merciful [*al-Raḥmān*]; whichsoever you call upon, to Him belong the Names Most Beautiful.'"[80]

It is also important to recognize elements of the Jabal Dhabūb inscription that seem to reflect not some sort of unaffiliated monotheism, but specifically biblical monotheism. As Al-Jallad explains, both of the last two lines in the inscription reflect language from Psalm 90:

> Jabal Dhabūb inscription, line 3: Satisfy us by means of your favor
>
> Ps 90:14: Satisfy us in the morning with thy steadfast love
>
> Jabal Dhabūb inscription, line 4: and grant us the essence of it at the end of our days / the gift of our days
>
> Ps 90:12: So teach us to number our days / that we may get a heart of wisdom

Now, it is important to note that the words behind English "satisfy" in line 3 and Ps 90:14 are not from the same root. The root in the inscription is *r-z-q* (to "nourish" or "provide for," a common root in the Qur'an), and the root of Hebrew Psalm 90 (as in the Syriac Peshitta) is *s-b-ʿ* (literally, to "make full" or "satisfied"), but the meaning of these two roots is close. That this inscription would have language flavored by the Psalms is perhaps not surprising, as the Psalms represented the main text for liturgical use (and private prayer) in the Eastern Church (as they did in the Western Church) and in the synagogue. If the inscription is indeed connected to the religious agenda of Abraha, then it might in fact be the work of a Christian, even if it has no cross or mention of Christ.

According to Al-Jallad's reading of the inscription, it does not include *the basmala,* as we know it in the Qur'an, but it does include *a basmala.* The inscription has a bipartite *basmala* ("In the name of God/ Allāh who is al-Raḥmān") and the Qur'an has a tripartite *basmala* ("In the name of God, al-Raḥmān, the merciful"). But why would the Qur'an use not a bipartite formula but a tripartite formula? Al-Jallad has an answer, which is connected to an argument articulated by Angelika Neuwirth: "The addition of the third element may have been motivated by, and perhaps even regarded as a response to, Christian invocations of the trinity, which would have been widely known as they are displayed on public royal inscriptions in Arabia."[81] Thus even the Qur'an's theological language may reflect a Christian culture, a point to which I return in the following chapter.

From South Arabia we might move back to the Hijaz to mention one final monotheistic inscription, this time from the city of Ṭā'if (approximately seventy-five kilometers from Mecca), also studied by Al-Jallad and Sidky.[82] Although Ṭā'if is described by the tradition to be a bastion of paganism, the author of this inscription, "located on a prominent boulder approximately 100 meters uphill from an abandoned mosque allegedly built by the caliph ʿAlī b. Abī Ṭālib," was evidently a pre-Islamic monotheist.[83] He identifies himself as "Ḥanẓalah [son of] ʿAbd ʿAmrw." The inscription is written in Paleo-Arabic script (and thus likely dates to the sixth or very early seventh century) and reads (according to the translation of Al-Jallad and Sidky), "In your name, our Lord, I am Ḥanẓalah [son of] ʿAbd ʿAmrw. I urge [you] to be pious towards God." The absence of the *basmala,* and the wording generally (particularly of the final clause, "I urge you," *wṣy b-br llh*), is typical of pre-Islamic monotheistic inscriptions.[84]

Al-Jallad and Sidky propose that this Ḥanẓalah is a companion of Muhammad named Ḥanẓalah b. Abī ʿĀmir (d. 3 AH/625 CE). Islamic tradition says some interesting things (for our purposes) about him, namely that Ḥanẓalah b. Abī ʿĀmir was not from Ṭāʾif but from Yathrib (Medina). His father, tellingly, was nicknamed "the monk" (*al-rāhib*) and is said to have "become a monk," *tarahhaba,* and wore monastic garb (*wa-labisa l-musūḥ*).[85] Islamic tradition even records a contentious dialogue between Abu ʿĀmir, who indeed was also known as ʿAbd ʿAmr, and Muhammad himself. When Muhammad announced to ʿAbd ʿAmr that he had come with the religion of Abraham, *al-ḥanīfiyyah,* the latter assured Muhammad that he (ʿAbd ʿAmr) was already a *ḥanīf.* Not only this, ʿAbd ʿAmr accused Muhammad of corrupting *al-ḥanīfiyyah* (*innaka adkhalta yā muḥammad fī al-ḥanīfiyya mā laysa minhā*), called him a liar, and cursed him.[86] He never converted to Islam but fled Yathrib for Mecca and then (when Muhammad conquered Mecca) to Ṭaʾif; then, when Muslims took control of Ṭāʾif as well, he fled to Christian Syria, where he died.[87] On the other hand Ḥanẓalah, his son, converted to Islam in Yathrib and even participated in the battle of Uḥud (in which he was martyred). The inscription in Ṭāʾif presumably would have been written by Ḥanẓalah before his conversion to Islam, that is, when he would have still followed the Christian religion of his father. If the authors are right in associating this inscription with Ḥanẓalah b. ʿAbd ʿAmr of Islamic tradition, then it is a remarkable record of a pre-Islamic Arab Christian of the Hijaz.[88] Yet even if they are not right, the implications of this inscription are still significant.

Al-Jallad and Sidky observe here that the monotheistic character of this inscription, found literally down the road from Mecca, confirms that the Arabian pre-Islamic turn to monotheism did not skip the Hijaz:

> The Paleo-Arabic texts discussed in this article confirm that the Ḥijāz experienced the same religious transformation as the rest of the Peninsula. They record devotion to only one deity, Allāh. Not only that, but the introduction of new religious formulae and vocabulary demonstrate a break with the past. God is referred to with Hebrew-Aramaic vocabulary, *brk, rb,* he is to be obeyed and the object of piety, *wṣy b-br ʾllh,* and his forgiveness is to be sought . . . , all features shared

> in common with the Qur'an but alien to the pagan cults attested in early texts.[89]

Before moving on to the final section of this chapter, I mention one other element of material evidence. Jack Tannous notes that in Dūmat al-Jandal, the very site where the mid-sixth-century Arabic Christian inscription studied by Leila Nehmé (discussed above) was found, excavators also found a silver hand bell with a clapper in a Byzantine layer underneath a mosque associated with ʿUmar b. al-Khaṭṭāb.[90] The bell, according to Romolo Loreto, the author of the study on the excavation at Dūmat al-Jandal, is typical of that used in Eastern liturgical life. He also notes, "In Islamic tradition, bells are forbidden" and that "there is no textual evidence of a Christian community at Dūmat al-Jandal after the *ridda* [rebellion] wars that took place after the death of Prophet Muḥammad."[91] In light of this he concludes that the bell "could suggest that the previous role of the ʿUmar mosque was a church, at least in the early seventh century AD just before the Islamic conquest."[92] Thus we have evidence not only for the presence of Christian individuals who left inscriptions behind them in different parts of Arabia, but also, in Dūmat al-Jandal at least, for the church of a settled Christian community. All of these points, together with the absence of pagan inscriptions from the sixth (and seventh) century, suggest that by the rise of Islam, Christianity was widespread in Arabia.

Qur'anic Evidence for Christianity

Yet was Christianity also a significant presence in Mecca and Medina? How can we get closer to understanding the religious situation in the immediate context of the Qur'an (according to the traditional scenario)? In the absence of any substantial archaeological work in these two cities, and in light of the contested sources that place a Christian here or there in Mecca or Medina, we might turn to the one documentary witness of their religious context in the early seventh century: the Qur'an itself.[93] So what can the Qur'an tell us of the presence of Christians in the communities where its author was active? In what follows I argue from the premise that the Qur'an, even if it went through a process of redaction that would have shaped and reshaped its wording, nevertheless reflects the traditional Hijazi context of Mecca and Medina.

In this I follow the insights of Stephen Shoemaker in his provocatively titled work *Creating the Qur'an* in regard to oral transmission, but I disagree with his contention that significant qur'anic texts were first composed in the post-prophetic context of "Syro-Palestine." Shoemaker argues that the Qur'an reflects Muhammad's original proclamations in the Hijaz, but that these proclamations were substantially developed through a process of oral transmission and "recomposition" as the community moved to the north (where more Jews and Christians were found) after the conquests. The argument of the present chapter is that there is enough evidence to take a simpler approach to the Qur'an's Jewish and Christian material: Muhammad's original proclamations (which indeed almost certainly went through a process of "recomposition") already included engagement with Judaism and Christianity because there were Jews and Christians in the Hijaz.[94] This approach is simpler in part because it matches the early carbon-14 dating of Hijazi Qur'ans and the other arguments that have been put forward (such as the absence of anachronisms) for an early origin of the qur'anic text.[95]

The orientalist approach to the Christian material in the Qur'an is to hold that Muhammad met Christians somewhere in Syria, or when a few Christian souls wandered into Mecca.[96] As a rule the orientalists trust the Islamic traditions of Muhammad's travels as a youthful merchant, the "first hijra" of Muslims to Ethiopia and so on. One report from the classic biography of the Prophet relates how Muhammad would travel with his uncle Abū Ṭālib to Syria and how on one occasion he met a monk named Baḥīrā near Buṣrā.[97] Perhaps, then, Muhammad knew Christianity only from the memory of travel in distant lands. We will see, however, that the Qur'an suggests otherwise—that there were Christian communities, with priests, monks, churches, and monasteries, in the *immediate* context of the Qur'an.

First, one might note those qur'anic passages that suggest the Qur'an's author, and his followers, interacted directly with Christians. This is seen in a passage of Sura 2 in which the Qur'an seems to be responding to the theological attitudes encountered (on the streets of

Medina?) among Jews and Christians. Qur'an 2:111 includes a quotation of Jews and Christians, "And they say, 'None shall enter Paradise except that they be Jews or Christians.' Such are their fancies. Say: 'Produce your proof, if you speak truly'" (Q 2:111). This verse might be read as the product of real social interactions between Christians (and Jews) and Muslims. The line of counterdiscourse ("None shall enter Paradise except that they be Jews or Christians") probably should not be seen as a verbatim quotation (indeed, it is hard to imagine both Jews and Christians speaking these Arabic words in unison).[98] Still, it might reflect historical theological debates between Christians (and Jews) and members of the new religious movement. Specifically, this verse might be a challenge to a theological exclusivism that would put the new believers on the outside looking in, which after all was rather typical of the soteriology of more or less everyone in late antiquity. It matters too that Q 2:111 has the God of the Qur'an tell his prophet how to speak with Jews and Christians ("Produce your proof, if you speak truly"). This suggests that there really were Jewish and Christian communities around with whom he could speak, "produce his proof," and argue (cf. also Q 3:64 and 4:171 for examples of God's giving Muhammad words to address Christians).

Although in Q 2:111 the Jews and the Christians are lumped together, two verses later the Qur'an points to divisions between them: "The Jews say, 'The Christians stand not on anything'; the Christians say, 'The Jews stand not on anything'; yet they recite the Book. So too the ignorant say the like of them. God shall decide between them on the Day of Resurrection touching their differences" (Q 2:113). While this verse might reflect the long history of apologetics and polemics in late antiquity between Jews and Christians, it might also be intended to undermine missionary arguments of Jews and Christians in the Qur'an's context by showing the divisions between them.

That there is some merit to this latter idea is suggested by Q 2:120, which implies that Jews and Christians were actively seeking to convert Muslims: "Never will the Jews be satisfied with thee, neither the Christians, not till thou followest their religion. Say: 'God's guidance is the true guidance.' If thou followest their caprices, after the knowledge that has come to thee, thou shalt have against God neither protector nor helper." On the basis of this verse, one would conclude not only that Christians are a real presence in the community (along with Jews), but also that they were putting pressure on the new believers to convert to Christianity. Thus it seems that the Christians in the Qur'an's context were evangelistic (which would match the notion that during this time Christian missions had spread into Arabia and had a role in the formation of the Arabic script). The Qur'an indeed seems concerned enough with their evangelism that it adds a threat of divine judgment to dissuade any possible converts: "If thou followest their caprices, after the knowledge that has come to thee, thou shalt have against God neither protector nor helper." This is precisely the sort of statement a preacher might make who is concerned for the fidelity of his flock.

What's noticeable about this sequence of verses is that the Qur'an is not engaging with Christian (or Jewish) theology. In other passages the Qur'an criticizes Christian Christology, but not here. The problem here is not with what Christians (or Jews) believe; the problem is what they are doing. They are, apparently, causing trouble by appealing to Muslims to convert, and the Qur'an is pushing back.

In what follows in Sura 2 we see that the Qur'an develops a rational, scriptural argument in its attempts to push back, and it does so by bringing up the figure of Abraham. Qur'an 2:135 appeals to Abraham (who was before Moses and Jesus): "And they say, 'Be Jews or Christians and you shall be guided.' Say thou: 'Nay, rather the creed of Abraham, a man of pure faith; he was no idolater.'" We return to this point in the following chapter, but for now the key insight is that the recourse to Abraham (which also occurs in Sura 3) seems to be a thoughtful, deliberate response to efforts by Christians and Jews to convert Muslims.[99] A similar point is advanced a few verses later, but now with reference to Abraham's descendants. Again the Qur'an denies that they were Jews or Christians: "Or do you say, 'Abraham, Ishmael, Isaac and Jacob, and the Tribes—they were Jews, or they were Christians'? Say: 'Have you then greater knowledge, or God? And who does greater evil than he who conceals a testimony received from God? And God is not heedless of the things you do'" (Q 2:140).[100]

That there were real engagements with Jews and (perhaps especially) Christians is suggested by a few other verses in different Suras that have God counsel the Muslims as to how to engage in debate. In

Q 29:46 the divine voice declares, "Dispute not with the People of the Book save in the fairer manner, except for those of them that do wrong; and say, 'We believe in what has been sent down to us, and what has been sent down to you; our God and your God is One, and to Him we have surrendered.'" Here the Qur'an, besides advising general goodness in one's debates, also gives Muslims the very words that they should use while debating with Christians or Jews ("say, 'We believe in what . . .'"). While nothing in this verse suggests that Christians in particular were the concern of the Qur'an's author, there is such a suggestion in a second verse: "Say: 'People of the Book! Come now to a word common between us and you, that we serve none but God, and that we associate not aught with Him, and do not some of us take others as Lords, apart from God.' And if they turn their backs, say: 'Bear witness that we are Muslims'" (Q 3:64). This second verse appears after a long section in Sura 3 that deals first with the stories of Mary, John, and Jesus (Q 3:35–57) and then specifically forms an argument for Islamic teaching on Jesus and against Christian teaching on Jesus (Q 3:59). Notably, in Q 3:61 the Qur'an even seems to propose a sort of contest between Muslims and Christians (presumably, over who is right regarding Jesus): "And whoso disputes with thee concerning him, after the knowledge that has come to thee, say: 'Come now, let us call our sons and your sons, our wives and your wives, ourselves and your selves, then let us humbly pray and so lay God's curse upon the ones who lie.'"

This passage is traditionally explained with a story about a delegation of Christians from the southern Arabian city of Najran, although there is no reference here (or elsewhere in the qur'anic text) to this city or to any such delegation, which refused to accept this challenge.[101] What the nature of the contest (sometimes referred to as a *mubāhala*) was to be is never explained by the Qur'an, but it is often thought to be a sort of mutual cursing. For our purposes the point is that a contest is mentioned only because Christians were around who could, theoretically, engage in it (even if it were raised principally for rhetorical purposes).

In any case, this preceding section in Sura 3 suggests that in the "common word" verse (Q 3:64) the Qur'an is principally interested in Christians. This seems to be confirmed by the wording of the verse. It is not in fact an invitation to open dialogue, for the "common word" is made up of principles that the Qur'an holds up to make a scandal of Christianity, including the (supposed) deification of a man (Jesus): "that we serve none but God, and that we associate not aught with Him, and do not some of us take others as Lords" (Q 3:64).[102] The end of this verse is also interesting; the Qur'an declares, "And if they turn their backs, say: 'Bear witness that we are Muslims.'" What Arberry renders as "if they turn their backs" is in Arabic *in tawallaw,* which could mean simply "to desist," but it does mean idiomatically "to turn the back, to turn away (from [someone])."[103] In its context of Q 3:64 what seems to be evoked is Christians refusing the proposition of Muslims (it also appears in v. 63 in the context of the proposed *mubāhala*). Again, this sort of practical advice regarding what to do in the context of a debate seems to bespeak real interactions between Muslims and Christians. The Muslims who challenge Christians face to face should turn their backs on them when the Christians prove to be stubborn.[104]

Notably, this passage in Sura 3 is followed by a passage that is closely related to the section in Sura 2 mentioned above. In Q 3:65–68 (as in Q 2:135) the Qur'an invokes Abraham to construct an argument against Jews and Christians:

> 65 People of the Book! Why do you dispute concerning Abraham? The Torah was not sent down, neither the Gospel, but after him. What, have you no reason?
>
> 66 Ha, you are the ones who dispute on what you know; why then dispute you touching a matter of which you know not anything? God knows, and you know not.
>
> 67 No; Abraham in truth was not a Jew, neither a Christian; but he was a Muslim and one pure of faith; certainly he was never of the idolaters.
>
> 68 Surely the people standing closest to Abraham are those who followed him, and this Prophet, and those who believe; and God is the Protector of the believers.

It is only putative to assign this Sura 3 passage to a later period than the Sura 2 passage discussed above, even if this would be the standard order of both medieval Muslim scholars and the early orientalists (it is also possible to see these two as parallel passages that have their origin in separate recensions of one original composition). Still, for argument's sake, or as a thought experiment, one could consider whether this passage in Sura 3 is a more developed version of the passage from Sura 2. The Qur'an's author possibly found the argument with recourse to Abraham (introduced in the early "Medinan" Sura 2) serviceable. Here (in Sura 3), then, he notes additionally that the Torah and Gospel are later than Abraham (Q 3:65; proposing, therefore, that Jews and Christians have no special knowledge about him). He has developed the argument to include scripture. He also adds explicitly that Abraham was not a Jew or a Christian (Q 3:67), affirming what is only suggested in Q 2:135. Finally a completely new argument appears, namely that "this Prophet" is among those who are closest to Abraham (Q 3:68). Qur'an 2:135 argues that Muhammad's message is the "Creed of Abraham" (*millat Ibrāhīm*),[105] a "man of pure faith" (*ḥanīf*).[106] The argument there, in other words, is about the teaching of Abraham and the teaching of Muhammad. In Q 3:68 the argument becomes about Muhammad himself, who is claimed to be like Abraham. His personal status, in other words, is now a central question.

All of this seems to bespeak a context in which Muslims were really arguing with Christians. This does not appear to be a hypothetical debate with opponents who dwelled far away or who have long since disappeared, but rather a context in which arguments have been developed and new points have been made. One can only imagine that Jews and Christians in the Qur'an's context made a particular claim on Abraham (as mentioned, this was a regular element of Jewish-Christian polemics in late antiquity), to which the Qur'an is responding. One imagines that the Jews and Christians questioned Muhammad's authority to give them lessons on Abraham; after all, their communities had been around much longer. The Qur'an responds (Q 3:68) that Muhammad is just like Abraham. He is as "close" to Abraham as those who followed him.

Although I admit the speculative nature of these last remarks, I would draw attention to the very next verse, which speaks specifically of a group (*ṭāʾifa*) of the People of the Book who are particular troublemakers: "There is a party of the People of the Book [who] yearn to make you go astray; yet none they make to stray, except themselves, but they are not aware" (Q 3:69). The reference here to one particular group again suggests that these polemical arguments are not hypothetical, that there are certain troublemaking Jews or Christians who have annoyed the Qur'an's author. This is not the only place where the Qur'an singles out a particular group among the People of the Book.

Later in Sura 3 we find a remarkable passage that involves both a violent criticism of the People of the Book and an immediate cautionary note that they are not actually all bad. It is the nature of that cautionary note, which seems to be the product of actual observation of religious practice, that is interesting for our purposes (Q 3:110–14):

> 110 You are the best nation ever brought forth to men, bidding to honour, and forbidding dishonour, and believing in God. Had the People of the Book believed, it were better for them; some of them are believers, but the most of them are ungodly.
>
> 111 They will not harm you, except a little hurt; and if they fight with you, they will turn on you their backs; then they will not be helped.
>
> 112 Abasement shall be pitched on them, wherever they are come upon, except they be in a bond of God, and a bond of the people; they will be laden with the burden of God's anger, and poverty shall be pitched on them; that, because they disbelieved in God's signs, and slew the Prophets without right; that, for that they acted rebelliously and were transgressors.
>
> 113 Yet they are not all alike; some of the People of the Book are a nation upstanding, that recite God's signs in the watches of the night, bowing themselves,[107]
>
> 114 believing in God and in the Last Day, bidding to honour and forbidding dishonour, vying one with the other in good works; those are of the righteous.

In verse 110 the Qur'an distinguishes between those of the People of the Book who believe and those who are "ungodly" (or "sinful," *fāsiqūn*). In verse 112 the Qur'an, apparently speaking of the ungodly among the People of the Book, declares "abasement shall be pitched on them" and "they will be laden with the burden of God's anger" (*ghaḍab*). Thus the Qur'an remarkably distinguishes between "believers" and "ungodly" among the People of the Book.

There is good reason to conclude here that the Qur'an is not distinguishing among Jews and Christians but rather between them. The polemical remarks of verse 112, regarding a people with whom God is angry, suggests that the ungodly here *are* the Jews, as the Qur'an regularly refers to the Jews as a people with whom God is angry. Fourteen of twenty references to God's anger in the Qur'an involve the Israelites, and the description of them as a people who "slew the Prophets" seems to confirm that the Qur'an is concerned here with Jews.[108] In Q 2:61 the Qur'an describes how the Israelites complained to Moses about receiving only one sort of food (manna). It then relates: "And abasement and poverty were pitched upon them, and they were laden with the burden of God's anger [*ghaḍab*]; that, because they had disbelieved the signs of God and slain the Prophets unrightfully; that, because they disobeyed, and were transgressors." This verse is very close to Q 3:112; indeed it (at least this part of Q 2:61) makes up a doublet with Q 3:112. It also seems to confirm that Q 3:112 is specifically anti-Jewish in character and that the *fāsiqūn* or "ungodly" of Q 3:110 are the Jews.

A second passage related to Q 3:110–12 is found in Sura 2. There the Qur'an condemns the Jews for refusing to listen to God's prophets, (again) for killing the prophets (Q 2:87), and for declaring that their hearts are covered, or literally "uncircumcised" (Q 2:88).[109] The Qur'an then declares: "Evil is the thing they have sold themselves for, disbelieving in that which God sent down, grudging that God should send down of His bounty on whomsoever He will of His servants, and they were laden with anger upon anger [*ghaḍab ʿalā ghaḍab*]; and for unbelievers awaits a humbling chastisement" (Q 2:90). All of this sheds light on what the Qur'an means when it subsequently declares, in Q 3:113, "Yet they are not all alike," and goes on to speak of a praiseworthy group among the People of the Book. In light of the evidence from Sura 2 (and, as we will see, of what follows in Sura 3) it seems this other group from the People of the Book are Christians, something asserted by Régis Blachère and Arthur Droge.[110]

On this verse Abdullah Yusuf Ali writes: "In Islam we respect sincere faith and true righteousness in whatever form they appear. This verse, according to Commentators, refers to those People of the Book who eventually embraced Islam."[111] His comment is a bit ambiguous. The second sentence seems to negate the first; it is not clear whether he sees this verse as honoring pious non-Muslims or only those pious non-Muslims who embrace Islam (that is, Muslims!). In any case, he seems to miss that this verse appears to allude in particular to Christians, and to distinguish them from Jews (who are condemned in Q 3:110–12).

This might seem like a rather surprising reading of this passage. It is not entertained at all by the *Study Qur'an,* which (following various commentators) offers (like Yusuf Ali) that this verse might be praising certain Jews or Christians who converted to Islam, or that in this case Muslims themselves are the upright community among the People of the Book.[112] And yet if it seems unlikely or unseemly that the Qur'an would so clearly favor Christians over Jews, one might compare Q 3:110–13 with Q 5:82–83, a passage that explicitly does just this:

> 82 Thou wilt surely find the most hostile of men to the believers are the Jews and the idolaters; and thou wilt surely find the nearest of them in love to the believers are those who say "We are Christians"; that, because some of them are priests and monks, and they wax not proud;
>
> 83 and when they hear what has been sent down to the Messenger, thou seest their eyes overflow with tears because of the truth they recognize. They say, "Our Lord, we believe; so do Thou write us down among the witnesses."[113]

In verse 83 the Qur'an has the Christians say "we believe," *āmannā,* whereas in Q 3:110 we read of a group among the People of the Book who are believers (*mu'minūn*). In verse 82 the Qur'an speaks of the Jews (along with the idolaters [*alladhīna ashrakū*]) as "the most hostile" to the believers and the Christians as "nearest of them in love" to the believers. It also seems to reflect direct interaction with Christians. It is interesting that verse 82 speaks of what the Christians "say." In two other verses in this Sura (Q 5:17, 72), the Qur'an speaks of the things that the Christians "say" (in both cases the Qur'an declares, "They are unbelievers who say, 'God is the Messiah, Mary's son'"). And in one other verse (Q 5:18), the Qur'an speaks of what both the Jews and the Christians "say" ("Say the Jews and Christians, 'We are the sons of God, and His beloved ones'"). Again, these "group declarations" are not to be thought of as verbatim quotations, but they do seem to bespeak a context in which Muslims were interacting with Christians. We have already noted how in Q 29:46 the Qur'an gives instructions to Muslims to do just that ("Dispute not with the People of the Book save in the fairer manner").

Also interesting is the way in which the Qur'an has God in verse 83 speak to Muhammad (presumably) about the times when he has (apparently) seen Christians weep from what they have heard of his proclamations. Thus one has the sense that Christians were living in Muhammad's community and listening to what he was saying, and that the Qur'an had a relatively high opinion of them as a community (principally because of their positive, possibly emotional, reaction to Muhammad's proclamations).

A passage in Qur'an 17 (vv. 107–9) seems to paint a similar picture—one of a group who have received earlier "knowledge" and then who fall down prostrating when they hear the new revelation recited:

> 107 Say: "Believe in it, or believe not; those who were given the knowledge before it when it is recited to them, fall down upon their faces prostrating,
>
> 108 and say, 'Glory be to our Lord! Our Lord's promise is performed.'"
>
> 109 And they fall down upon their faces weeping, and it increases them in humility.

In light of the similarity of this passage to Q 5:82–83 one can assume that here too the Qur'an has Christians in mind. The Christians in Muhammad's town, apparently, either really cried (or fell down) when they heard him proclaim his message, or at least are being presented as doing such (perhaps as a way further to castigate the Israelites for their stubbornness, or in order to send a message to Christians about how they should respond to Muhammad's message).[114]

All of this seems to confirm my reading of Q 3:110–13 as a condemnation of the Jews and a commendation of the Christians. If the Christians are indeed the "upright community" (*umma qā'ima*) of Q 3:113, then it becomes particularly interesting to note how the Qur'an describes (with approval) that members of this community "recite God's signs in the watches of the night, bowing themselves [*yasjudūn*]." By our reading this would then be a reference to the monastic practice of night vigil and to Eastern Christian monastic prostration (in Greek, *proskynesis;* in Syriac, *segdtā*). This is not a new idea, but rather was already proposed by Wilhelm Rudolph in 1922.[115] In any case, if Rudolph was right more than a hundred years ago that this is a reference to the ritual practices of Eastern monks, then it might be read together with Q 48:29, which seems to refer to the followers of Muhammad bowing in prostration:

> Muhammad is the Messenger of God, and those who are with him are hard against the unbelievers, merciful one to another. Thou seest them bowing, prostrating, seeking bounty from God and good pleasure. Their mark is on their faces, the trace of prostration. That is their likeness in the Torah, and their likeness in the Gospel: as a seed that puts forth its shoot, and strengthens it, and it grows stout and rises straight upon its stalk, pleasing the sowers, that through them He may enrage the unbelievers. God has promised those of them who believe and do deeds of righteousness forgiveness and a mighty wage.

The Qur'an here alludes to a "mark" (*sīmā,* perhaps coming from Greek *sēma*) on the faces of the believers as a "trace [*athar*] of prostration." This is generally taken as a reference to a callus (known in certain Arabic-speaking countries today as a *zabība,* "raisin") that can develop on a person's forehead from repeated prostration. After painting this picture the Qur'an immediately declares that "their likeness [*mathal*]" is in the Torah and the Gospel. It then seems to describe this *mathal* by speaking of a seed that grows into a plant, perhaps a play on the parable of Mark 4:26–32, or Matt 13:1–23.[116] Thus the Qur'an closely associates the prostration practice of Muhammad's followers with a New Testament image from the Gospels. I would speculate (although perhaps it cannot be proved) that this verse reflects the indebtedness of the earliest qur'anic community's prayer practice to the practice of Eastern Christian monks.

Monks and Books in the Qur'ān

With this we might begin to explore the Qur'an's interest in monks and monasticism. As has been noted by numerous scholars before me, both monks (*ruhbān*) and monasticism (*rahbāniyya*) appear in the qur'anic text. To this one might note that the word *ṣawāmiʿ*, likely meaning "monastic cells" or "hermitages" (rendered by Arberry as "cloisters"), also appears in Q 22:40, a verse that also mentions *biyaʿ* ("churches"), *ṣalawāt* ("oratories"), and *masājid* (Arberry renders this as "mosques," but historically speaking perhaps Paret has a better idea with "Kultstatten," i.e., "places of worship").[117] It should be emphasized that this verse speaks of these buildings (the first two of which are certainly Christian) as sanctuaries that *need to be defended:*

> . . . who were expelled from their habitations without right, except that they say "Our Lord is God." Had God not driven back the people, some by the means of others, there had been destroyed cloisters [*ṣawāmiʿ*] and churches, oratories and mosques, wherein God's Name is much mentioned. Assuredly God will help him who helps Him—surely God is All-strong, All-mighty.

Thus the Qur'an does not simply mention the sanctuaries of Christians; it shows a religious concern for them. This concern for Christian ecclesial buildings logically follows from the passages we have studied above, which reflect an admiration and esteem for Christian prayer practices and for Christians. Arberry renders *ṣawāmiʿ* as "cloisters," although it possibly refers to monastic cells or hermitages. Here and there one finds scholars speculating that individual hermits lived in the Arabian desert (perhaps this idea reflects the stories involving the monk Baḥīrā, whom Muhammad is said to have met during a journey to Syria, as mentioned above). Wilhelm Rudolph speculates that the sight of a hermit's cell, with its light flickering at night as the solitary monk performed his devotions, might somehow be behind the famous "light verse" of the Qur'an, which declares, "the likeness of His Light is as a niche wherein is a lamp (the lamp in a glass, the glass as it were a glittering star) kindled from a Blessed Tree, an olive that is neither of the East nor of the West whose oil well-nigh would shine, even if no fire touched it" (Q 24:35).[118] Rudolph's idea may not be wild speculation, for the following verses in Sura 24 seem to refer explicitly to prayer houses, perhaps to monasteries:

> 36 in temples God has allowed to be raised up, and His Name to be commemorated therein; therein glorifying Him, in the mornings and the evenings,
>
> 37 are men whom neither commerce nor trafficking diverts from the remembrance of God and to perform the prayer, and to pay the alms, fearing a day when hearts and eyes shall be turned about,
>
> 38 that God may recompense them for their fairest works and give them increase of His bounty; and God provides whomsoever He will, without reckoning.

In verse 36 Arberry renders the simple Arabic word *buyūt* (literally "houses") as "temples"; this may be a bit fanciful, but it does reflect the likelihood that the Qur'an is referring here to monasteries (Richard Bell writes that these lines "can hardly indicate anything but Christian places of worship").[119] Indeed the identification of these *buyūt* as monasteries seems to be confirmed by their description as houses where God's name is "commemorated" (*yudhkaru fīhā ismuhu*), which matches the description of churches and monastic cells in Q 22:40 (*yudhkaru fīhā ismu llāh*).[120] Thus it seems clear that the Qur'an has a rather remarkable awareness of Christian monasteries, and indeed an *astoundingly* positive view of them. It speaks of the men in these monasteries (Q 24:37) as those who "commerce nor trafficking diverts from the remembrance of God and to perform the prayer, and to pay the alms, fearing a day when hearts and eyes shall be turned about." It even includes an invocation calling on God to bless them: "God may recompense them for their fairest works and give them increase of His bounty" (Q 24:38). Here we might keep in mind that the very reason the Qur'an gives in Q 5:82 for why Christians are those who are closest in friendship to the believers is "because some of them are priests and monks, and they wax not proud."

Now, these positive assessments of monks and monasteries should be read together with other passages that criticize monks. Qur'an 9:34 (cf. Q 5:63) accuses some monks (and rabbis) of seeking profit and blocking people from God: "O believers, many of the rabbis and monks indeed consume the goods of the people in vanity and bar from God's way. Those who treasure up gold and silver, and do not expend them in the way of God—give them the good tidings of a painful chastisement." Here the Qur'an seems to accuse monks (*ruhbān*) of sinful behavior that is precisely the opposite of the good behavior (apparently) attributed to them in Q 24:36–38.[121] A second polemical verse in regard to monks is found a few verses earlier: "They have taken their rabbis and their monks as lords apart from God, and the Messiah, Mary's son—and they were commanded to serve but One God; there is no god but He; glory be to Him, above that they associate" (Q 9:31). The two verses are of course connected, as the authority of monks (and rabbis; Q 9:31) might allow them to collect money and bar people from the way of God. These verses critical of monks are often read together with Q 57:27, which, while praising certain positive qualities of Christians, also seems to accuse Christians of "innovating" monasticism:

> Then We sent, following in their footsteps, Our Messengers; and We sent, following, Jesus son of Mary, and gave unto him the Gospel. And We set in the hearts of those who followed him tenderness and mercy. And monasticism they invented—We did not prescribe it for them—only seeking the good pleasure of God; but they observed it not as it should be observed. So We gave those of them who believed their wage; and many of them are ungodly.

I will not attempt here to reconcile the positive description of monks in Qur'an 24 and the negative description of monks (or monasticism) in Qur'an 9 and 57. It is possible that the different descriptions reflect a change in attitude over time. There may be a hint of this in Q 9:34, where the Qur'an declares that the rabbis and monks do not spend their money "in the way of God." This might suggest that the Qur'an's author is angry that Christian monks have not donated money for the sake of the military campaigns of the Muslims. It is also possible that there are two sorts of sources from which the Qur'an is drawing on here, one of which had a positive assessment of monasticism, and the second of which had a negative assessment of monasticism. In matters like this there is simply not enough data to make a compelling argument.

Yet for our purposes the principal point is not whether the Qur'an likes or does not like monks (even if that is a question that is worth consideration in another study). Our point is simply that the Qur'an is engaging with monks, monasteries, and monasticism in a way that suggests that they were part of the landscape in the Qur'an's context.

Some mention in this regard should also be made of the way in which the Qur'an speaks of scripture (apparently) being written down. A number of verses should be considered in this regard:

> Had We sent down on thee a Book on parchment [*qirṭās*] and so they touched it with their hands, yet the unbelievers would have said, "This is naught but manifest sorcery." (Q 6:7)

> They measured not God with His true measure when they said, "God has not sent down aught on any mortal." Say: "Who sent down the Book that Moses brought as a light and a guidance to men? You put it into parchments [*qarāṭīs*], revealing them, and hiding much; and you were taught that you knew not, you and your fathers." Say: "God." Then leave them alone, playing their game of plunging. (Q 6:91)

These two verses, which both appear in the same Sura, seem to refer to a community other than the new believers, who put down scripture in *qirtās/qarāṭīs,* a word rendered by Arberry as parchment/parchments, but in light of the use of this root in Syriac might mean simply "page" or "pages."[122]

The second verse (Q 6:91) is particularly revealing, as it addresses a community that is putting down on *qarāṭīs* the "Book that Moses brought." One would assume that the Qur'an means Jews here, especially since it includes an accusation of scriptural falsification ("and hiding much"), a charge that the Qur'an specifically levels against the Jews on a number of occasions.[123] These two verses might be read together with Q 20:133, "They say, 'Why does he not bring us a sign from his Lord?' Has there not come to them the clear sign of what is in the former scrolls?"[124] The word here rendered by Arberry as "scrolls" is simply *ṣuḥuf*, which likely means any sort of folio or page (not necessarily a scroll) and contextually is more or less synonymous with *qarāṭīs*.[125] One might note in this context as well Q 52:2, which (in the context of an oath) speaks of *kitab masṭūr*, rendered by Arberry as "a Book inscribed." The term *masṭur* (related to the phrase *asāṭīr al-awwalīn* or "stories of the early peoples," which appears nine times in the Qur'an) may be related to the Syriac/Aramaic root *sh-ṭ-r* (although there is possibly a relation with Greek *historia*).[126] The Qur'an continues in the next verse (Q 52:3), "in a parchment unrolled" (*raqq manshūr*), using the word *raqq*, which may indeed refer specifically to parchment (although *manshūr* might mean simply "spread out," not unrolled, which implies unrolling scrolls).[127] In any case, the plural reference to "former scrolls" (or better, "former writings/books") in Q 20:133,[128] might be an allusion to *both* the writings of the Jews and the writings of the Christians, another sign of the historical presence of both Jews and Christians in Muhammad's context.

A few further verses add additional evidence to the argument that the Qur'an is engaging not with Christianity in the abstract but with Christians in its own community. In Q 9:30 (just before the verse that accuses the People of the Book of taking rabbis and priests as lords, an impious action) the Qur'an accuses the Jews and Christians of an impious saying: "The Jews say, 'Ezra is the Son of God'; the Christians say, 'The Messiah is the Son of God.' That is the utterance of their mouths, conforming with the unbelievers before them. God assail them! How they are perverted!" The interesting point for our purposes is the insistence of the Qur'an that these impious statements are the "utterance of their mouths" (*dhālika qawluhum bi-afwāhihim*). Here the Qur'an seems to testify of direct conversations with Jews and Christians. Again, a few verses later (after accusing them of deifying their religious leaders, Q 9:31), the Qur'an refers to the "mouths" of Jews and Christians: "desiring to extinguish with their mouths God's light; and God refuses but to perfect His light, though the unbelievers be averse" (Q 9:32). Now, the Qur'an refers to "mouths" on a number of occasions (Q 3:118, 167; 5:41; 9:8, 30, 32; 14:9; 18:5; 24:15; 33:4; 36:65; 61:8), often to describe some sort of hypocrisy, where the saying of one's mouth does not match one's interior disposition. Again, we should be careful not to imagine that this sort of language implies that the Qur'an is recording verbatim the statements of its opponents.[129] Still, even if we take this language to be part of a sort of mise-en-scène, it still seems likely that it reflects an historical context where Christians (and Jews) were speaking to the first Muslims.

More light on that context is shed by Q 16:103, which refers to an unnamed speaker of a non-Arabic language: "And We know very well that they say, 'Only a mortal is teaching him.' The speech of him at whom they hint is barbarous; and this is speech Arabic, manifest." The term rendered here as "barbarous" by Arberry is *aʿjamī*, a term that has been discussed above. There is good reason to think, in light of what we have seen of Aramaic-Arabic bilingualism in inscriptions close to the Hijaz, that the language (*lisān*) alluded to here is Aramaic. If this is right then we have a remarkable reference in Q 16:103 to an Aramaic speaker who apparently had interactions with the qur'anic Prophet. It is highly likely that this Aramaic speaker was either a Jew or a Christian, as Aramaic in the late antique Near East was overwhelmingly spoken by Jews and Christians. Although it is hardly compelling evidence, the reference to the Holy Spirit, or "spirit of holiness" (*rūḥ al-qudus*) and "good tidings" (*bushrā*) in the previous verse (Q 16:102), might suggest that the speaker of Q 16:103 was a Christian. This verse is perhaps to be read together with Q 25:5, which includes an accusation that Muhammad listened to "old tales" (*asāṭīr al-awwalīn*) twice a day: "They say, 'Fairy-tales of the ancients that he has had written down, so that they are recited to him at the dawn and in the evening.'"

There is perhaps no way to identify who this speaker of Q 16:103 might be, although the tradition has various guesses.[130] Although I would not make much of the attempts to localize particular qur'anic verses, it is perhaps worth mentioning that by tradition Sura 16 is a Meccan Sura and to remember that according to the biography of Muhammad there is more or less no reason to expect Jews or Christians in Mecca, beyond a few slaves or travelers.[131]

Yet we have seen that a careful reading of the Qur'an suggests that Christianity and Christians were in fact a significant presence in Muhammad's Mecca (and Medina). Christians were among the groups with whom he interacted regularly. These Christians, apparently, were not rogues who had wandered far away from their community in the heartlands of the Byzantine Empire or Ethiopia. Instead, their community was in the Hijaz. Muhammad knew of priests, churches, monks, monastic cells, liturgies, and monasteries, matching what we saw in the previous chapter of the Qur'an's remarkable engagement with Christian legends.

A Final Thought: The Importance of Christian Missions

In order to make sense of this surprising discovery, namely the Christianity of the Hijaz, it is important to appreciate the missionary nature of late antique Near Eastern Christianity. The early church, motivated by a shared conviction that Jesus had appointed the apostles not simply to save themselves, but to save the world, encouraged and celebrated the sharing of the Gospel with new peoples and new lands. Indeed a number of scholars, including Jack Tannous, have pointed out that the Christian nature of the pre-Islamic Arabic inscriptions (discussed earlier in this chapter) strongly suggests that the development of the Arabic alphabet was at least in part the work of Christian missionaries. Tannous quotes the *Encyclopedia of Islam* article on Arabic by Chaim Rabin, who writes: "The Christian character of the dated inscriptions suggests that the Arabic script was invented by Christian missionaries, as were so many eastern alphabets."[132] Tannous also quotes Robert Hoyland (who is a bit more cautious): "The fact that all pre-Islamic Arabic inscriptions in the Arabic script are from a Christian context suggests that there is some connection between Christianity and the emergence of the Arabic script."[133] As Tannous notes, it is possible that Christians did not invent the Arabic script but rather "used a preexisting script with a limited diffusion for their religious ends."[134] Either way, the point to appreciate for our purposes is the incredible energy of Christian missions in the late antique Near East. To this one might add the observation that the normal unfolding of things in Christian missions (in the East, at least) was not the imposition of new language but rather the adaptation of the Gospel to the local languages. Tannous writes:

> Viewed from a wider angle, therefore, the spread of Christianity across the late ancient and medieval worlds had important linguistic consequences: the Greek, Hebrew, and Aramaic texts of the Christian Old and New Testaments were translated wholly or partially (and sometimes more than once) into a number of different languages; these included Armenian, Christian Palestinian Aramaic, Coptic, Geʿez, Georgian, Gothic, Latin, Nubian, Slavonic, Sogdian, Syriac, and Caucasian Albanian. Christian material was even translated into Chinese. Indeed, a notable characteristic of Christianity throughout its nearly two-thousand-year history has been one of translation.[135]

This wave of missionary energy swept down into Arabia. Now, Tannous leverages this point to suggest the likelihood of the translation of some or all of the Bible into Arabic before Islam.[136] As the reader will know by now, I find it unlikely that such a translation existed. However, Tannous's emphasis on the larger phenomenon of Christian missions in the Near East (and beyond) is important for appreciating not only the likelihood of a significant Christian presence in the Hijaz, but also the importance of this presence to the genesis of the Qur'an (and Islam). Christian missionaries did not go into new lands simply to settle and mind their own business. They went to evangelize. The principal method of evangelization was to develop arguments, on the basis of scriptural (or nonscriptural) stories, and on the basis of reason or logic.[137] This argument-making is central to almost all of the Syriac homilies of Jacob of Serugh. The very purpose of his homilies is to inculcate right teaching about God and Christ. Intriguingly, Jacob invokes divine help in this task. Here, for example, is the opening of Jacob's homily *On Faith*, as translated by Philip Forness:

> Bend your exalted word down to me, O Son of God,
> So that your great story might be spoken with an exalted voice.
> I am your creation, O Lord. Establish my tongue so that I might sing to you
> Sounds of glory with the love of the soul without contention.
> You formed me, and I became a speaking vessel for the glory of your name:
> May the word that I received as a gift from you not fail in me!
> Yours are all the readings,[138] all the interpretations,
> All the discourses, all the homilies, and the canticles.
> From your own, give beauty for the narrative of your faith,
> So that by your gift the homily might be enriching for those who listen.[139]

In his study on Jacob, Forness explains the nature of this homily:

> The exposition of doctrine follows immediately after the introduction. Jacob treats, in turn, the incarnation, the crucifixion, the Trinity, the church, salvation, and Christology. Each doctrine poses challenges to understanding Christ as fully God and fully human. The incarnation, for example, leads him to ask: "The wisdom of the world only looks on nature: / 'How is it that God dwelled in a girl?'" Jacob's responses to these guiding questions move the homily's narrative forward. Jacob then exhorts his audience to be faithful to the doctrines he has just discussed.[140]

Now, Jacob is writing a homily and so is addressing Christian believers and seeking to confirm their faith. His is therefore a different sort of address from what one might expect from a missionary addressing unbelievers. Still, it is interesting to note that even in the one line that Forness quotes from the homily (in the paragraph immediately above) there is attention to the skepticism of non-Christians. Jacob notes how these unbelievers scoff at the doctrine of the incarnation. One is tempted to notice a certain parallel between their challenge (as quoted by Jacob) "How is it that God dwelled in a girl?" and the sorts of questions that the Qur'an poses: "The Creator of the heavens and the earth—how should He have a son, seeing that He has no consort?" (Q 6:101). I do not mean to suggest any direct connection here, but merely to point out that the Qur'an seems to reflect the same culture of argument-making, including the use of rhetorical questions, in which Jacob too participated.

In this homily Jacob is preparing his audience to understand their faith so that they might make arguments with unbelievers in order to evangelize them. Jacob even gives them specific counsel to this effect, encouraging them not to trust in their own intelligence but in the message of love in the Gospel:

> When the narrative of the Son is spoken by the wise,
> It hides itself so that they do not place it in their disputes.
> In the discourse of the scribes—however much they rouse up their questions—
> He cannot be discussed through their ingenious explanations.
> But, look!, he is revealed to the simple and rises as a light,
> And he allows himself to be discussed with love.
> He hates wisely worded retorts,
> For with a simple teaching he subdued the whole world.
> He chose the simple and the poor to preach about him,
> And he sent them to speak of him in various places.
> So that everyone would perceive that because the one who is speaking is God,
> The world received him from preachers who were not wise.[141]

This section of Jacob's homily is meant to give courage to his listeners to proceed to the task of evangelization, whatever their concerns may be about their own capacity for debate. Yet it also says something about the fundamental nature of the Christian message—that God has surprised the world with the radical nature of salvation through the incarnation, suffering, death, and resurrection of his son. He has confounded thereby the wise. One thinks of Paul's argument near the opening of 1 Corinthians:

> 18For the word of the cross is folly to those who are perishing,
> but to us who are being saved it is the power of God. 19For it
> is written,
>
> > "I will destroy the wisdom of the wise,
> > and the cleverness of the clever I will thwart."
>
> 20Where is the wise man? Where is the scribe? Where is the
> debater of this age? Has not God made foolish the wisdom of
> the world? 21For since, in the wisdom of God, the world did
> not know God through wisdom, it pleased God through the
> folly of what we preach to save those who believe. (1 Cor
> 1:18–21)

Can the Qur'an then be understood as a response to Christian missions and to the sorts of arguments that Christians made about God's work of salvation in Christ? Above we discussed how Chaim Rabin sees the Arabic script as the product of Christian missionaries. Earlier scholars too saw a place for Christian missionaries in the story that led ultimately to the Qur'an and the rise of Islam. Tor Andræ, writing in 1932, famously imagines (rather fancifully) that Muhammad might have met a Christian missionary at a market in Ukaz:

> We know that none of the Oriental churches carried on so active a missionary programme as did the Nestorians, who established important Christian churches in Central Asia, India, and China. It is not overbold to assume that Nestorian monks from the Arabian churches in Mesopotamia, or from Nejran in Yemen after the Persians had conquered this

> country in 597, in the course of their preaching tours among their pagan countrymen, visited Hejaz, with whose capital city the Christian Arabs maintained a lively contact. As a matter of fact tradition tells of a Christian preacher named Quss ibn Sa'ida, who is said to have been Bishop of Nejran, but who belonged to a tribe living at Hira in Mesopotamia, whom Mohammed is supposed to have heard preaching in the market at Ukaz.[142]

Now, Andræ, and more forcefully Joseph Azzi (whose work is discussed in Chapter 1), seems to think of Christians as "informers" of Muhammad. But what if the Qur'an was not informed by Christianity, but rather was a response to Christianity? This sort of speculation has largely gone out of style. But what if scholars who have been looking at the Qur'an for signs of Christian influence here or there have missed the possibility that the Qur'an is fundamentally, substantially, shaped by a concern to respond to Christian ideas? These are the questions that we explore in the next chapter.

F • O • U • R

The Qur'an in Conversation with Christianity

In 1997 Mahmoud Ayoub published an article in the journal *Islam and Christian-Muslim Relations* titled "Nearest in Amity: Christians in the Qur'an and Contemporary Exegetical Tradition." In it Ayoub is not particularly interested in the Qur'an's response to Christian teaching (about Jesus or otherwise), but rather in the Qur'an's view of Christians themselves. Notably, he identifies a number of passages that, he argues, reflect a positive assessment of Christians, including passages that do not explicitly refer to *naṣārā*, the qur'anic term for Christians. Among these is a passage in Sura 28, which opens with the declaration "Those to whom We gave the Book before this believe in it" (Q 28:52) and, a few verses later, notes, "When they hear idle talk, they turn away from it and say, 'We have our deeds, and you your deeds. Peace be upon you. We desire not the ignorant'" (Q 28:55). Ayoub comments: "Although the verses here cited do not specifically mention the Christians they no doubt refer to them. This is because they clearly echo other verses which extol their piety and humility. . . . It should also be noted that these verses closely resemble verses describing the piety and humility of 'God's faithful servants' among the Muslims."[1] Now, Ayoub's interest in noting these positive assessments of Christians in the Qur'an is to make an argument that the Islamic scripture itself has a sort of program for Muslim-Christian friendship.[2] In this chapter, however, I discuss such cases not for the sake of interreligious dialogue but for the sake of the larger argument of this book, namely that the Qur'an is regularly engaged in a conversation with Christianity. Christianity is the Qur'an's ever-present, although sometimes invisible, conversation partner. The Qur'an, I argue, has Christianity in mind when it articulates its own teaching, *even when it does not explicitly refer to Christians or Christian teaching.* Passages like Q 28:52–55 (along with others that we have discussed in previous chapters) suggest that Christians and Christianity were a significant presence in the Qur'an's original context. What remains to be shown is that the Qur'an is attentive to this presence even in the articulation of its own theology.

Before returning to the Qur'an it might be worth simply restating an axiom regarding speech and composition generally. The ways in which speakers express themselves are shaped by the context in which they are speaking. Politicians and prophets alike change their discourse according to their setting and in particular according to the people who make up their audience. In his *Rhetoric,* after discussing effective oral composition, Aristotle declares, "We can now see how to compose our speeches so as to adapt both them and ourselves to our audiences."[3] Now, Aristotle is concerned with *effective* adaptation of one's speech, but some sort of adaptation of speech for an audience is inevitable. Compositions, and perhaps especially compositions (like the Qur'an) meant to persuade, are necessarily adapted to their audience. In this chapter I argue that the Qur'an regularly speaks in ways that reflect the significant presence of Christianity in its context.

To put this point otherwise, one might say that Christianity is nowhere and everywhere in the Qur'an. There is no Arabic word for "Christianity" (either *naṣrāniyya* or *masīḥiyya*) in the Qur'an, and the term for "Christians" (*naṣārā*) appears only fifteen times in the text. The task of the present chapter, however, is to argue that a concern for Christianity appears consistently throughout the Qur'an. To make this case we might begin at the beginning, with the Qur'an's opening Sura, *al-Fātiḥa.*

The *Fātiḥa*

The first Sura in the Qur'an, the *Fātiḥa,* has no explicit reference to Christianity, and yet it seems to respond to Christianity in both its first and last verses. The first verse of the *Fātiḥa* consists of the *basmala,* the invocation that opens 113 of the Qur'an's 114 Suras (although it is counted as a verse only in *al-Fātiḥa*). The *basmala* is notably a tripartite invocation of God: "In the name of God, the Merciful, the Compassionate" (*bi-smi llahi l-raḥmāni l-raḥīm*). That the Qur'an's Suras would open with a tripartite invocation of God is suggestive of Trinitarian Christian language, as has been argued by Angelika Neuwirth.[4] Late antique Christian prayer and Christian liturgy (notably baptismal formulas) regularly involve the tripartite, Trinitarian invocation of God known from Matt 28:19: "In the name of the Father and of the Son and of the Holy Spirit."[5] The use of the Trinitarian formula in Matthew is part of a command to baptize, and indeed it was clearly part of baptismal rites from the earliest period. Irenaeus (d. 202) wrote in *The Demonstration of the Apostolic Preaching*: "First of all it bids us to bear in mind that we have received baptism for the remission of sins, in the name of God the Father, and in the name of Jesus Christ, the Son of God, who was incarnate and died and rose again, and in the Holy Spirit of God. And that this baptism is the seal of eternal life."[6] Nicolai Sinai writes more generally about the Trinitarian formula: "We can safely assume this Christian parallel [that is, the Trinitarian invocation and the *basmala*] to have been known in the Qur'anic milieu."[7]

We might also note again the study of Ahmad Al-Jallad on an Ancient South Arabian inscription found in Yemen (Jabal Dhabūb) and first studied by M. A. Al-Hajj and A. A. Faq'as in 2018 (see Chapter 3). Al-Jallad provocatively titled his article "A Pre-Islamic Basmalah: Reflections on Its First Epigraphic Attestation and Its Original Significance." He argues that the text (written in the "miniscule" variant of Ancient South Arabian) dates to the late fifth century CE. While other interpretations hold the opening of the inscription (*bsmlh rḥmn rḥmn*) to be a "proto-basmalah," Al-Jallad reads it to be an invocation of God as *raḥmān* and then an imperative (opening line 2) "Have mercy upon us" (*rḥm-n*), thus altogether: "In the name of Allāh, the Raḥmān, have mercy upon us."[8] He argues that in part the point of this invocation is to invoke God both as Allah (typical of Ancient North Arabian) and as Raḥmān (typical of Ancient South Arabian).[9] Al-Jallad contends that the work the invocation is doing is similar to Q 17:110: "Say: 'Call upon God, or call upon the Merciful; whichsoever you call upon, to Him belong the Names Most Beautiful.'

And be thou not loud in thy prayer, nor hushed therein, but seek thou for a way between that." In other words, according to Al-Jallad's interpretation this inscription anticipates a move that the Qur'an would later make, namely to unite monotheists in the Arabian Peninsula by accommodating the two principal manners in which God was invoked there.

The key point here, however, is how Al-Jallad also argues that the qur'anic innovation is to add another attribute to God, *al-raḥīm,* and thereby to use a *three-part* invocation. Al-Jallad speculates that this was a sort of response to Christian invocations of the Trinity. The Qur'an, without embracing Trinitarian doctrine, provides an alternative tripartite invocation that is meant to challenge and replace the Christian invocation. That this might indeed be the case is suggested by the redundant nature of this added term (something that has long troubled commentators and translators alike). Already *al-raḥmān* signals "mercy," and so the precise semantic contribution of *al-raḥīm* is unclear (although, of course, many speculative guesses have been offered).[10] It could be indeed that the addition of *al-raḥīm* is not meant to add any additional meaning, but rather expressly to create a tripartite invocation that might compete with, and ideally replace, the Christian Trinitarian invocation.[11]

If the beginning of *al-Fātiḥa* seems to have a connection to Christianity, so too does the end. The Sura concludes with the following prayer (Q 1:6–7):

> 6 Guide us in the straight path,
>
> 7 the path of those whom Thou hast blessed, not of those against whom Thou art wrathful, nor of those who are astray.

Classical Muslim exegetes frequently argue that the references in verse 7 are not general, that the Qur'an means specific communities. The people with whom God is "wrathful" are the Jews and those "astray" are the Christians. This is reported by Ibn al-Jawzī (who quotes a prophetic hadith to this effect) and many other commentators.[12] The opinion is so widespread that it is taken up in (one version of) the exegetical translation (endorsed by Saudi Arabia) of the Moroccan Muhammad Taqi-ud-Din al-Hilali (d. 1987) and the Afghani Muhammad Muhsin Khan

(d. 2021). They render verse 7 as follows: "The Way of those on whom You have bestowed Your Grace, not (the way) of those who earned your Anger (such as the Jews), nor of those who went astray (such as the Christians)."[13] In a note they explain (translating the hadith alluded to by Ibn al-Jawzī) that Muhammad himself offers this interpretation in a hadith on the authority of 'Adī b. Ḥātim.[14]

Khaleel Mohammed takes issue with this interpretation of Q 1:7, and in particular with the effect of the Saudi-sponsored Hilali-Khan translation, in an online article titled "Produce Your Proof: Muslim Exegesis, the Hadith, and the Jews." He grants that most exegetes, including Ṭabarī and Ibn Kathīr (d. 774 AH/1373 CE), identify the people with whom God is wrathful as the Jews and the people who are astray as the Christians. He notes Ibn Kathīr's explanation that people who know the truth (he seems to mean in regard to Muhammad) but do not follow it (the case of the Jews) are subject to divine anger, while people who simply do not know the truth (the case of the Christians) are astray. Mohammed responds, however, after referring to the aforementioned scholar Mahmoud Ayoub, that there is no reason to insist on specific referents for these expressions when the Qur'an itself is intentionally (as he sees it) general: "The text makes no specific reference to any religious community, but rather refers to two types of people."[15] Mohammed is worried that the Hilali-Khan translation—well-known among English-speaking Muslims—might encourage anti-Semitism.[16]

Mohammed is of course right that readers are not bound to follow Hilali-Khan here. Indeed, even if the Qur'an's author originally intended (as I argue) to refer to Jews and Christians with this verse, readers of scripture today are free to find new meanings. That is, Muslims today have every right to advance an inclusivist or pluralist reading of the Qur'an and in the process refute the traditional idea regarding verse 7 of *al-Fātiḥa*. Nevertheless, the relevant material elsewhere in the Qur'an suggests that the traditional idea, and thus the translation of Hilali-Khan, is correct (even if most exegetes advance that idea on the basis of hadith).

As for the question of divine wrath, fourteen of twenty references to God's anger (*ghaḍab*) in the Qur'an involve the Israelites or the Jews contemporary to Muhammad. For example, in Sura 2 the Qur'an condemns the Jews for refusing to listen to God's prophets, for killing the prophets (Q 2:87), and for declaring that their hearts are covered, or literally, "uncircumcised" (*ghulf;* Q 2:88). Two verses later we read: "Evil is the thing they have sold themselves for, disbelieving in that which God sent down, grudging that God should send down of His bounty on whomsoever He will of His servants, and they were laden with anger upon anger; and for unbelievers awaits a humbling chastisement" (Q 2:90). Earlier in the same Sura the Qur'an describes how the Israelites complained to Moses about receiving only one sort of food (manna), and declares, "And abasement and poverty were pitched upon them, and they were laden with the burden of God's anger [*ghaḍab*]; that, because they had disbelieved the signs of God and slain the Prophets unrightfully; that, because they disobeyed, and were transgressors" (Q 2:61).

The accusation against the Jews of killing God's prophets and consequently earning God's wrath returns in Q 3:112. The Qur'an has God warn the Israelites of his wrath if they disobey his commands (Q 20:81). They do just that by worshipping a calf as an idol, for which they merit God's anger (Q 7:150, 152; 20:86; see also Q 5:60, 58:14, 60:13). In Sura 20 God warns the Israelites not to violate food laws in the following manner: "Eat of the good things wherewith We have provided you; but exceed not therein, or My anger shall alight on you; and on whomsoever My anger alights, that man is hurled to ruin" (Q 20:81). Thus the Qur'an repeatedly refers to the Jews as a people with whom God is wrathful. As I alluded to earlier (Chapter 2), this rather violent rhetoric against the Israelites seems to be intended in part to present Muhammad as a prophet in the line of Jesus. The Qur'an emphasizes the Jewish rejection of Jesus (Q 3:52, 61:6). Indeed it has the Jews celebrate (wrongly) their killing and crucifixion of Jesus (Q 4:157). Meanwhile, the Qur'an also emphasizes that the Jews (along with pagans) are "greatest in enmity" (Q 5:82) to the (Muslim) believers. All of this material has long been a sensitive topic for observers of the Qur'an, as it has been connected to the supposed conflict between Muhammad and the Jews of Medina. It seems to me that it can plausibly be disconnected from any historical scenario and understood as a literary creation meant to make Muhammad a righteous prophet who (like Jesus) faced the opposition of a people with whom God is wrathful. As I have argued elsewhere, many of the anti-Jewish accusations in the Qur'an, such as the "killing of prophets," are prominent motifs in early Christian anti-Jewish writings.[17] Thus even in the manner in which it criticizes Israelites the Qur'an seems to be in conversation with Christianity.

But what about the Christians as a people who have gone astray? The active participle *ḍāll* in Q 1:7, rendered by Arberry as "astray," appears fourteen times in the Qur'an and never explicitly refers to Christians. Instead, it refers often to those who are heedless of God's will generally. Qur'an 2:198 looks back at the time when the believers were "formerly" astray (*wa-in kuntum min qablihi la-mina l-ḍāllīn*). Qur'an 3:90 speaks of those who have left belief for unbelief and describes them as "astray" (*ḍāllūn*). In Q 6:77 Abraham declares, "If my Lord does not guide me I shall surely be of the people gone astray." Many more such examples could be cited (Q 23:106; 26:20, 86; 37:69, passim), and even more if we consider all of the 191 occurrences of the root *ḍ-l-l* in the Qur'an. Notably, the Qur'an speaks of God's ability to "lead astray" (*yuḍillu;* e.g., Q 2:26; 4:119, 143 passim).

Meanwhile, Q 3:69 speaks of a "party [*ṭā'ifa*] of the People of the Book" who "yearn to make you go astray" (*waddat . . . yuḍillūnakum*), implying that these Jews or Christians are themselves astray. When this is seen together with a concern with those who were believers but have now gone "astray" in Q 3:90 (which appears twenty-one verses later), it seems possible that the Qur'an is concerned with members of Muhammad's community who have converted to Christianity. Indeed, the Qur'an seems *very* concerned with this prospect: "Surely those who disbelieve after they have believed and then increase in unbelief—*their repentance shall not be accepted; those are the ones who stray*" (Q 3:90, italics added).

Qur'an 4:44 speaks of those of the People of the Book who "purchase error" (*yashtarūna l-ḍalālata*). Other verses associate "being astray" explicitly with *shirk* (Q 4:116), something of which Jews and Christians are accused (Q 9:31) but which arguably is a particular concern with Christians. Qur'an 5:77 seems directly to warn the People of the Book—and in my opinion Christians in particular (in light of the emphasis in Qur'an 5 on Christians)—of *ḍalāla:* "Say: 'People of the Book, go not beyond the bounds in your religion, other than the truth, and follow not the caprices of a people who went astray [*ḍallū*] before, and led astray [*aḍallū*] many, and now again have gone astray [*ḍallū*] from the right way.'" There may be no compelling argument that *ḍāllīn* in Q 1:7 refers specifically to Christians, since in certain cases (including the group who "leads astray" in Q 5:77) the root clearly has a more general meaning. However, there is at least a circumstantial case to be made for the connection between Christians and "being astray" in the Qur'an. After all, the Qur'an's fundamental argument against Christians is that they were rightly guided until they forgot part of what God revealed to them (*nasū ḥaẓẓan mimmā dhukkirū bihi;* Q 5:14), which presumably is why the Qur'an cites the words of Jesus to them as a sort of reminder: "'Children of Israel, serve God, my Lord and your Lord. Verily whoso associates with God anything, God shall prohibit him entrance to Paradise, and his refuge shall be the Fire; and wrongdoers shall have no helpers'" (Q 5:72). The Qur'an uses Jesus to remind the Christians of what they have forgotten regarding God's will.[18] By quoting Jesus the Qur'an means to remind Christians of the teaching that (in the Qur'an's perspective) they forgot. What is more, if the Jews are indeed meant with the reference to divine anger in Q 1:7, then there is an additional reason to connect the reference to those who are astray with the Christians, since the Qur'an on a number of occasions refers to the Jews and the Christians together (Q 2:111, 113, 135, 140; 3:65, 67; 5:13–15, 18, 51). It is plausibly doing so here.

In addition, one must keep in mind the various historical, textual, and material witnesses advanced by the present book to the abundant presence of Christians in the Qur'an's historical context. Perhaps the Qur'an's author found it appropriate to conclude this short Sura (likely indeed written to be an "opening") with a supersessionist declaration. If the Jews are the object of divine anger and Christians are helplessly astray, then a new movement might make its case.

The Nativity of Jesus in Sura 19

A similar desire to set itself apart from Christians might be detected in the Qur'an's account of Jesus's birth in Sura 19. Here the Qur'an describes how Mary removes herself (v. 22) to a "distant [*qaṣiyy*] place" and there experiences birth pangs. The text does not clearly describe the birth of Jesus that follows. Instead, he abruptly appears on the scene two verses later, speaking (as a newborn) to Mary his mother: "But the one that was below her called to her, 'Nay, do not sorrow; see, thy Lord has set below thee a rivulet'" (Q 19:24).[19] The God-given rivulet that appears is only one part of the miracle. The voice continues (Q 19:25–26):

> 25 Shake also to thee the palm-trunk, and there shall come tumbling upon thee dates fresh and ripe.
>
> 26 Eat therefore, and drink, and be comforted; and if thou shouldst see any mortal, say, "I have vowed to the All-merciful a fast, and today I will not speak to any man."

There are two remarkable points about this version of the birth of Jesus (one might say, of Christmas). First is the setting in a remote location, not in the town of Bethlehem (as in the Gospels of Matthew [2:1] and Luke [2:4]). In this the Qur'an seems to be following a tradition (as it does in its allusions to the childhood of Mary in Sura 3) found in an early text known as the *Protoevangelium of James*, a Greek, Christian work written in the late second century and translated into Syriac by the fifth century. In this early text we read:

> And they came half the way, and Mary said to him: "Joseph, take me down from the ass, for the child within me presses me, to come forth." And he took her down there and said to her: "Where shall I take you and hide your shame? For the place is desert." And he found a cave there and brought her into it, and left her in the care of his sons and went out to seek for a Hebrew midwife in the region of Bethlehem. (Prot. Jas. 17:2–18:1)[20]

Although it is perhaps difficult to prove, it seems possible that the Qur'an is intentionally engaging with what had become an unorthodox account of the nativity of Jesus, namely his birth in a deserted place outside of Bethlehem and not in the town itself. Thereby the Qur'an might be intentionally challenging Christian claims to authoritative knowledge on Jesus. Yet there is a second point here as well. The miracle of the spring of water and the palm tree, with its provision of dates, is also known from a alternative Christian tradition, as recorded for example in the Latin *Gospel of Pseudo-Matthew* (likely written in the early seventh century).[21] However, in *Pseudo-Matthew* the miracle is associated with the flight of the holy family into Egypt, and not with the birth of Jesus:

> Now on the third day of their journey [to Egypt], as they went on, it happened that blessed Mary was wearied by too great heat of the sun in the desert, and seeing a palm tree, she said to Joseph, "I should like to rest a little in the shade of this tree." And Joseph led her quickly to the palm and let her dismount from her animal. And when blessed Mary had sat down, she looked up at the top of the palm tree and saw that it was full of fruits, and said to Joseph, "I wish someone would fetch some of these fruits of the palm tree." . . . Then the child Jesus, who was sitting with a happy countenance in his mother's lap, said to the palm, "Bend down your branches, O tree, and refresh my mother with your fruit." And immediately at this command the palm bent its head down to the feet of blessed Mary, and they gathered from it fruits with which they all refreshed themselves. . . . Then Jesus said to it, "Raise yourself, O palm, and be strong and join my trees which are in the paradise of my Father. And open beneath your roots a vein of water which is hidden in the earth, and let the waters flow so that we may quench our thirst from it." And immediately it raised itself, and there began to gush out by its root a fountain of water very clear, fresh, and completely bright. (Ps.-Mt. 20:1–2)[22]

This second point, namely the qur'anic association of the miracle of the palm tree with Jesus's nativity, was long a riddle. However, Stephen Shoemaker insightfully noted that the traditions of the palm tree and Jesus's nativity do indeed come together before the Qur'an in a very specific place: the Kathisma Church on the road south of Jerusalem on the way to Bethlehem.[23] The Kathisma Church (which seems to have served as the model for the Dome of the Rock and thus to have been of great interest to the earliest Muslim community in Palestine) was a site where (in competition with the Church of the Nativity in Bethlehem) the birth of Jesus was commemorated *along with* the miracle of the palm tree and spring given to Mary during the flight to Egypt. Thus it seems likely (as no other pre-qur'anic text or tradition combines the nativity of Jesus with the miracle of the palm tree and the spring) that the Qur'an was influenced by the popular Palestinian traditions surrounding the Kathisma Church. Why would the Qur'an follow this alternative nativity tradition, if not to challenge the dominant narrative of Christmas that is so central to the Christian liturgical calendar?[24]

The Miracles of Jesus

The Qur'an shows an exceptional interest in the miracles performed by Jesus. Indeed, only rarely does it refer to miracles accomplished by other prophets. In the Qu'ran Moses turns his staff into a snake (Q 7:107–17, 20:69, 26:32–45, 27:10, 28:31) and splits the sea with the same staff (Q 26:63); David defeats Goliath (Q 2:251); and Solomon has control over animate and inanimate objects (Q 34:12–13). However, for the most part prophets perform no miracles, even if God might give to them miraculous signs (like Ṣāliḥ's camel) or save them from a calamity (as with Noah and the flood or Abraham and the furnace). Jesus, however, performs a long list of miracles, as God retrospectively recounts to him in Sura 5:

> When God said, "Jesus Son of Mary, remember My blessing upon thee and upon thy mother, when I confirmed thee with the Holy Spirit, to speak to men in the cradle, and of age; and when I taught thee the Book, the Wisdom, the Torah, the Gospel; and when thou createst out of clay, by My leave, as the likeness of a bird, and thou breathest into it, and it is a bird, by My leave; and thou healest the blind and the leper by My leave, and thou bringest the dead forth by My leave; and when restrained from thee the Children of

> Israel when thou camest unto them with the clear signs, and the unbelievers among them said, 'This is nothing but sorcery manifest.'" (Q 5:110; cf. 3:49)

It is notable that this list includes miracles known from the canonical Gospels, such as the healing of the blind or leprous or the raising of the dead, along with miracles known from noncanonical Gospels, such as speaking as a newborn or bringing a clay bird to life. However, I especially draw attention to the two other features of this list: first, that it includes the very miracles used in Christian sources to portray the divinity of Christ, and second, that the Qur'an repeatedly has God declare that Jesus performed these miracles only "by My leave" (*bi-idhnī*).

The miracle of Jesus's raising of Lazarus in John's Gospel (John 11) points to Jesus's power over life and death. This much is taught by the dialogue between Lazarus's sister Martha and Jesus that immediately precedes the miracle:

> [24]Martha said to him, "I know that he will rise again in the resurrection at the last day." [25]Jesus said to her, "I am the resurrection and the life; he who believes in me, though he die, yet shall he live, [26]and whoever lives and believes in me shall never die. Do you believe this?" [27]She said to him, "Yes, Lord; I believe that you are the Christ, the Son of God, he who is coming into the world." (John 11:24–27)

This conversation is missing from the Qur'an, as are all of the details of the story. Instead, the Qur'an simply declares, "and thou bringest the dead forth by My leave." Thereby the Qur'an does not set aside the figure of Jesus, or the miracles that Christians associate with him. It redefines them and undermines the use to which Christians (including John the Evangelist) put them.

In a way, the story of the clay bird illustrates this point even more dramatically. In the second-century Greek-language *Infancy Gospel of Thomas* Jesus creates twelve birds from clay, on the Sabbath. When he is caught violating the Sabbath in so doing Jesus brings them to life. The lesson of the story is clear: Jesus (who is only a young boy at the time) is the author of life and is not bound by the law as all other humans (even prophets) are:

> This little child Jesus when he was five years old was playing at the ford of a brook: and he gathered together the waters that flowed there into pools, and made them straightway clean, and commanded them by his word alone. And having made soft clay, he fashioned thereof twelve sparrows. And it was the Sabbath when he did these things (or made them). And there were also many other little children playing with him.
>
> And a certain Jew when he saw what Jesus did, playing upon the Sabbath day, departed straightway and told his father Joseph: Lo, thy child is at the brook, and he hath taken clay and fashioned twelve little birds, and hath polluted the Sabbath day. And Joseph came to the place and saw and cried out to him, saying: Wherefore doest thou these things on the Sabbath, which it is not lawful to do? But Jesus clapped his hands together and cried out to the sparrows and said to them: Go! and the sparrows took their flight and went away chirping. And when the Jews saw it they were amazed, and departed and told their chief men that which they had seen Jesus do.[25]

One can see the profoundly Christian nature of the miracle in a detail preserved even in the Qur'an. In Q 3:49 Jesus declares how he will bring the bird to life by breathing into it (*anfukhu fīhi*). Thus a direct parallel appears with the way that God (in the Qur'an, as in Genesis) creates Adam by forming him from dirt (*turāb*) or clay (*ṭīn*) and breathing into him, something alluded to a few verses after the reference to Jesus and the bird (Q 3:59). And yet this dramatic parallel between Jesus and God in the Qur'an (the only two characters to whom the verb "create," *khalaqa*, is attributed) is no less dramatically undermined by the Qur'an's insistence (in Q 3:49 as in Q 5:110) that Jesus brought the bird to life only through God's permission, a detail missing from the *Infancy Gospel of Thomas*. Notably, with the miracles of Jesus the Qur'an repeatedly adds this detail. Other prophets (at least Moses, David, and Solomon) also carry out miracles, but only once (Q 34:12) does the Qur'an add "by God's permission." *It is with Jesus alone* that the Qur'an is particularly solicitous to add this phrase. Why would that be, if there were not Christians around whose views about Jesus needed to be anticipated?[26]

Allah, Good News, and Parables

In other cases the Qur'an seems not to react against Christian teaching but rather to use Christian ways of speaking, perhaps with an eye toward supersession. Yet even here one detects a polemical edge. In Sura 3 the angels speak to Mary of her conception of Jesus: "Mary, God gives thee good tidings for a Word from Him whose name is Messiah, Jesus, son of Mary" (Q 3:45). The Arabic behind "gives thee good tidings" is *yubashshiruki,* from the root *b-sh-r.* This root is related to Hebrew *b-s-r,* which in the Old Testament is used to give good tidings (e.g., for victory in war in 2 Sam 18:19). The New Testament *euangelion* ("good news," "Gospel") is presumably a sort of calque on the Hebrew root. Matthew describes Jesus's proclamation (Matt 4:23, 9:35, 11:5, 24:14) as the "good news" (*euangelion*) of the kingdom of God (cf. Mark 1:1, 14, 15; 8:35; 10:29; 13:10; 14:9; 16:15; Luke 3:18, 4:18, 9:6, 20:1, passim). The Acts of the Apostles regularly refers to the apostles' preaching the "good news" of Jesus (Acts 5:42, 8:35, 11:20). Paul speaks of the *euangelion* as the message (about the Son of God), which is the "power of God for salvation to every one who has faith" (Rom 1:16; cf. 1:2, 3, 9, 15; 2:6; 11:28; 15:16, 19, 20; 16:25; 1 Cor 1:17, 21; 4:15, passim).

The Syriac Peshitta uses a transliterated version of Greek *euangelion* to refer to this "good news" or "Gospel." However, as Arthur Jeffery notes, Christian Palestinian Aramaic uses instead *basūrā,* cognate with qur'anic Arabic *bushrā* (Syriac does have a version of this in the verb *saber,* "to hope," "to announce," with metathesis).[27] Thus it seems possible that the root *b-sh-r* was known to Christians as an allusion to the saving proclamation about Jesus.

It is notable, then, that the Qur'an uses *b-sh-r* to refer not only to the message that God gives to Mary, but also to the nature of its own proclamation. The Qur'an regularly describes itself as a *bushrā:*

> Say: "Whosoever is an enemy to Gabriel—he it was that brought it down upon thy heart by the leave of God, confirming what was before it, and for a guidance and good tidings [*bushrā*] to the believers." (Q 2:97)

> God wrought this not, save as good tiding [*bushrā*] to you, and that your hearts might be at rest; help comes only from God the All-mighty, the All-wise. (Q 3:126)

> God wrought this not, save as good tidings [*bushrā*] and that your hearts thereby might be at rest; help comes only from God; surely God is All-mighty, All-wise. (Q 8:10)

> And the day We shall raise up from every nation a witness against them from amongst them, and We shall bring thee as a witness against those. And We have sent down on thee the Book making clear everything, and as a guidance and a mercy, and as good tidings [*bushrā*] to those who surrender. (Q 16:89)

> Say: "The Holy Spirit sent it down from thy Lord in truth, and to confirm those who believe, and to be a guidance and good tidings [*bushrā*] to those who surrender." (Q 16:102)

> . . . a guidance, and good tidings [*bushrā*] unto the believers. (Q 27:2)

> Yet before it was the Book of Moses for a model and a mercy; and this is a Book confirming, in Arabic tongue, to warn the evildoers, and good tidings [*bushrā*] to the good-doers. (Q 46:12)

There are also secular uses of *bushrā* in the Qur'an. It is used for the "good tidings" given to Abraham and his wife of a son to be born to them in their old age (Q 29:21) and for the discovery of Joseph in a pit by the travelers headed to Egypt (Q 12:19; cf. 12:96). It is also used to refer to the comforting message that the blessed will receive in paradise (Q 10:64, 57:12; and which the damned will not receive in hell, Q 25:22). In a few cases the *bushrā* is specifically the heavenly book given to Muhammad. Qur'an 2:97 and 16:102

both allude to the agent of revelation (Gabriel in 2:97 and the "Holy Spirit" in 16:102) and speak of his message as "guidance" (*hudan*) and "good tidings" (*bushrā*). Qur'an 3:126 ("God wrought this not, save as good tiding [*bushrā*] to you, and that your hearts might be at rest; help comes only from God the All-mighty, the All-wise") and Q 8:10 are a doublet; both describe the revelation as a *bushrā* for the believers ("you" in Q 3:126 is plural). Qur'an 46:12 is particularly intriguing, as it compares the new revelation to that of Moses. It speaks of the book of Moses as "a model and a mercy" (*imām wa-raḥma*) and of itself as a warning and "good tidings" (*bushrā*). Elsewhere other forms of *b-sh-r* are used to speak of the revelation given to Muhammad (Q 17:105, 25:56, 33:56, 48:8).

To this same end it is intriguing that the Qur'an too has Jesus "give good news," but not of the kingdom as he does in the Gospels. Instead, he preaches the "good news" of Muhammad (referred to as *aḥmad*): "And when Jesus son of Mary said, 'Children of Israel, I am indeed the Messenger of God to you, confirming the Torah that is before me, and giving good tidings [*mubashshiran*] of a Messenger who shall come after me, whose name shall be Ahmad.' Then, when he brought them the clear signs, they said, 'This is a manifest sorcery'" (Q 61:6). The use of the expression "giving good tidings" may be related to Greek *euangelion* (or more directly Christian Palestinian Aramaic *b-s-r*). This verse thus transforms, or co-opts, the image of Jesus in the Gospels as a figure bringing good news of salvation. In Q 61:6 he comes to bring good news instead of Muhammad, whose revelation is itself "good tidings" (*bushrā*). Muhammad himself is elsewhere called "bearer of good tidings" (*bashīr*): "We have sent thee with the truth, good tidings to bear, and warning. Thou shalt not be questioned touching the inhabitants of Hell" (Q 2:119; cf. 7:188, 11:2, 34:28, 35:24). In one place (Q 41:4) the Qur'an is said to be a *bashīr.* In another place Muhammad is specifically said to be a *bashīr* (and a "warner," *nadhīr*) for the People of the Book: "People of the Book, now there has come to you Our Messenger, making things clear to you, upon an interval between the Messengers lest you should say, 'There has not come to us any bearer of good tidings [*bashīr*], neither any warner.' Indeed, there has come to you a bearer of good tidings and a warner; God is powerful over everything" (Q 5:19). Now, all of the prophets, and not only Muhammad, are presented by the Qur'an as offering "good tidings" (Q 2:213, 4:165, 6:48, 18:56). In this (among other things), pre-Muhammadan prophets play a clear role in the qur'anic script. But their parts are written to make the case that Muhammad belongs among them. Indeed one could even say that the particular quality of these prophets, including Noah, Abraham, Moses, and Jesus, as warners, and bearers of good tidings, is another way in which the Qur'an engages with Christianity. The Qur'an makes claims on the prophets of the Bible precisely because it is operating in a Christian context. Its ultimate claim, of course, is that Muhammad is the culmination of this biblical salvation history. He is the one whom Jesus announced as "good tidings," and whom Jews and Christians will find in their scriptures (Q 7:157).

That the Qur'an speaks intentionally in Christian modes is suggested by a second example, that of the proverb or parable (*mathal;* pl. *amthāl*). Mathias Zahniser offers a list of twenty-eight different *mathal*s in the Qur'an, including the following:[28]

> The likeness [*mathal*] of them is as the likeness of a man who kindled a fire, and when it lit all about him God took away their light, and left them in darkness unseeing. (Q 2:17)
>
> . . . or as a cloudburst out of heaven in which is darkness, and thunder, and lightning—they put their fingers in their ears against the thunderclaps, fearful of death; and God encompasses the unbelievers. (Q 2:19)
>
> The likeness [*mathal*] of those who expend their wealth in the way of God is as the likeness [*mathal*] of a grain of corn that sprouts seven ears, in every ear a hundred grains. So God multiplies unto whom He will; God is All-embracing, All-knowing. (Q 2:261)

As these examples show, the Qur'an uses *mathal* to speak about both believers and unbelievers. The final example above is an agricultural metaphor. The Qur'an picks up this thread a few verses later:

> O believers, void not your freewill offerings with reproach and injury, as one who expends of his substance to show off to

> men and believes not in God and the Last Day. The likeness [*mathal*] of him is as the likeness of a smooth rock on which is soil, and a torrent smites it, and leaves it barren. They have no power over anything that they have earned. God guides not the people of the unbelievers. (Q 2:264)

This is one of the parables in the Qur'an that resembles a parable from the Gospels (see Matt 13:1–9; Mark 4:1–9; Luke 8:4–8). There are a number of other such cases, as earlier scholars have shown.[29] One might note, for example, Q 57:13: "Upon the day when the hypocrites, men and women, shall say to those who have believed, 'Wait for us, so that we may borrow your light!' It shall be said, 'Return you back behind, and seek for a light!' And a wall shall be set up between them, having a door in the inward whereof is mercy, and against the outward thereof is chastisement." As Rudi Paret has argued, the Qur'an here seems to develop the parable of the foolish virgins (Matt 25:8–9: "And the foolish said to the wise, 'Give us some of your oil, for our lamps are going out.' But the wise replied, 'Perhaps there will not be enough for us and for you; go rather to the dealers and buy for yourselves'").[30]

Now, it is important to note that in late antiquity Christians did not have a monopoly on parable-making. Parables are prevalent in the literature of various contexts of the late antique Near East, and they had a long history. As A. Tarasenko writes: "All ancient Mediterranean societies developed parables as a product of human consciousness, and these later began to form human consciousness. . . . In Near-Eastern culture, however, where mythological consciousness co-existed with Egyptian medicine and Babylonian astronomy, the parable had a particular significance."[31]

Although the parable (*mashal*) is not a significant part of the Hebrew Bible/Old Testament, it is prominent in later Jewish literature. Moreover, Menahim Kister asserts convincingly that even if Tannaitic and talmudic rabbinic literature date later than the composition of the New Testament, both corpora manifest an earlier oral rabbinic culture with which the New Testament is also engaging.[32] Thus parables in the New Testament seem to reflect an earlier (and ongoing) Jewish tradition of parable-making. Indeed, it has been (persuasively) argued that the nature of the New Testament parables (or to be more specific, those in the synoptic Gospels), and the way they are employed, clearly reflects Palestinian Jewish culture, and not Greek "philosophical" culture.[33] The parables of Matthew, Mark, and Luke tend to employ images that would be common in Palestine, and they tend to use techniques similar to the parables in the Mishnah and the Talmud.

For our purposes the ongoing nature of this Jewish tradition of parable-making is of course what matters, since the composition of the Talmud (Palestinian first, and then the Babylonian) in the centuries immediately preceding the Qur'an shows that parables continued to be an element of Jewish culture.[34] The point here is that both Jews and Christians in the Qur'an's context likely used, and recognized the use of, parables in religious teaching, although it is interesting that Jewish rabbinic sources are not unanimous regarding the appropriateness of parables.[35]

One passage suggests that the Qur'an associates parables specifically with the biblical tradition:

> Muhammad is the Messenger of God, and those who are with him are hard against the unbelievers, merciful one to another. Thou seest them bowing, prostrating, seeking bounty from God and good pleasure. Their mark is on their faces, the trace of prostration. That is their likeness in the Torah [*mathalahum fī l-tawrāh*], and their likeness in the Gospel [*mathaluhum fī l-injīl*]: as a seed that puts forth its shoot, and strengthens it, and it grows stout and rises straight upon its stalk, pleasing the sowers, that through them He may enrage the unbelievers. God has promised those of them who believe and do deeds of righteousness forgiveness and a mighty wage. (Q 48:29)

After describing a mark of prostration as the "likeness" (*mathal*) of believers in the Torah, Q 48:29 presents the "likeness" of believers in the Gospel as a plant that grows "stout" and "straight" (that God might "enrage the unbelievers" through them). This is most likely connected to the parable of the sower in Matt 13:1–9 (cf. Mark 4:26–29):

> [1]That same day Jesus went out of the house and sat beside the sea. [2]And great crowds gathered about him, so that he got into a boat and sat there; and the whole crowd stood on the beach. [3]And he told them many things in parables, saying: "A sower went out to sow. [4]And as he sowed, some seeds fell along the path, and the birds came and devoured them. [5]Other seeds fell on rocky ground, where they had not much soil, and immediately they sprang up, since they had no depth of soil, [6]but when the sun rose they were scorched; and since they had no root they withered away. [7]Other seeds fell upon thorns, and the thorns grew up and choked them. [8]Other seeds fell on good soil and brought forth grain, some a hundredfold, some sixty, some thirty. [9]He who has ears, let him hear."

The qur'anic verse above is important not simply because it offers an example of a parallel between the New Testament and the Qur'an, but for our purposes because it speaks explicitly of a parable (*mathal*) in the "Torah" and the "Gospel." That is, the Qur'an's author clearly sees the *mathal* as a way of speaking associated with scripture, and Jewish/Christian scripture in particular. The Qur'an's author might have assumed that to speak in a "scriptural" mode one *must* use parables.[36] Angelika Neuwirth argues that the use of parables itself is a sort of signal: "The form of the parable . . . was considered a charismatic privilege, a symbol of power of the prophets—despite the problem of it being not immediately comprehensible."[37]

To this it is important to add that the Qur'an does not simply have God speak in parables; *it also speaks about God's ability to speak in parables.* Perhaps the most famous example of this is the Light Verse:

> God is the Light of the heavens and the earth; the likeness of His Light is as a niche wherein is a lamp (the lamp in a glass, the glass as it were a glittering star) kindled from a Blessed Tree, an olive that is neither of the East nor of the West whose

> oil wellnigh would shine, even if no fire touched it; Light upon Light. (God guides to His Light whom He will.) (*And God strikes similitudes for men,* and God has knowledge of everything.) (Q 24:35; italics added)

In this verse the Qur'an first describes God as "light" and then offers a "likeness" (*mathal*) of his light. Finally, and notably, the Qur'an adds a sort of exegetical comment on what has preceded (which Arberry rather helpfully puts in parentheses, marking it as a sort of meta-textual speech): "God strikes similitudes [*yaḍribu allāhu al-amthāla*] for men." Thus the Qur'an is concerned both with a lesson about God's nature (the parable itself) and with an argument about God's speaking in parables (the commentary that follows).

Elsewhere the Qur'an seems to respond to an objection regarding the sort of parables it has been telling: "God is not ashamed to strike a similitude even of a gnat, or aught above it" (Q 2:26). As this verse continues, parables are presented as a manner by which the Qur'an's God distinguishes between believers and unbelievers: "As for the believers, they know it is the truth from their Lord; but as for unbelievers, they say, 'What did God desire by this for a similitude?' Thereby He leads many astray, and thereby He guides many; and thereby He leads none astray save the ungodly." This, as I discuss below, is quite close to the function of Jesus's parables in the Gospels.

In this regard one might note a curious turn of phrase in Q 30:27, *lahu l-mathalu l-aʿlā fī l-samāwāti wa-l-arḍi,* rendered by Arberry as "His is the loftiest likeness in the heavens and the earth," but which might be translated more literally as "God has the highest parable [*mathal*] in the heavens and the earth." What this "highest parable" might be is not clear. Ibn al-Jawzī comments on this phrase: "*mathal al-ʿalā:* the commentators say that it means 'He has the highest attribute . . . for there is no god but Him.'"[38] It is not obvious, however, that *mathal* is the same as "attribute" (*ṣifa*), and it is notable that the very next verse includes a *mathal* *and* a comment in which God announces that he explains things ("signs") for humans: "He has struck for you a similitude [*mathal*] from yourselves; do you have, among that your right hands own, associates in what We have provided for you so that you are equal in regard to it, you fearing them as you fear each other? So We distinguish [*nufaṣṣil*] the signs for a people who understand" (Q 30:28). Perhaps the reference to the "highest" (or "best") parable in the previous verse is to present God as the master teller of parables, and consequently, the Qur'an as God's word par excellence.

All of this seems to match very closely the discourse around Jesus and parables in the Gospels. The Gospel authors do not simply have Jesus speak in parables. They have Jesus discuss his use of parables, and on occasion offer interpretations of them. In some ways parabolic speech is paradigmatic of Jesus's discourse in the Gospels. In Matthew 13 (cf. Mark 4; Luke 8:10) the author writes, "he told them many things in parables" (Matt 13:3). After reporting Jesus's parable of the sower, the author continues:

> [10]Then the disciples came and said to him, "Why do you speak to them in parables?" [11]And he answered them, "To you it has been given to know the secrets of the kingdom of heaven, but to them it has not been given. [12]For to him who has will more be given, and he will have abundance; but from him who has not, even what he has will be taken away. [13]*This is why I speak to them in parables, because seeing they do not see, and hearing they do not hear, nor do they understand.* (Matt 13:10–13; cf. Mark 4:10–12; Luke 8:9–10; italics added)[39]

In this passage parables are presented as the sort of speech that separates believers from unbelievers. Discipleship, belief in Jesus, allows one to access their inner meaning and, ultimately, to attain salvation. Moreover, Jesus's discourse in parables bespeaks his authority. His use of parables is a way by which he separates faithful believers from the unfaithful, those who "do not see" or "understand" (Matt 13:13). It allows him to carry out his role as one who divides the righteous from the unrighteous, both in this life (Matt 10:35; Luke 12:53) and in the eschaton (Matt 25:31–46). Matthew 13:13 ("seeing they do not see, and hearing they do not hear, nor do they understand") is a paraphrase of God's words to Ezekiel regarding the rebellious people among the Israelites: "Son of man, you dwell in the midst of a rebellious house, who have eyes to see, but see not, who have ears to hear, but hear not" (Ezek 12:2; cf. Jer 5:21). Thus Jesus's commentary on parable-making in Matthew has him speak in a divine mode, akin to that used by God in Ezekiel.

As with the case of language surrounding "good news" or "Gospel," with its discourse on parables the Qur'an means to supersede Christian claims and make itself a new authority. That the Qur'an tells so many parables, and that it so often speaks about the way that it tells parables, suggests that it does not mean simply to teach lessons through its parables (although it certainly means to do that too). Parable-telling *itself* matters to the Qur'an. The Qur'an means to signal that it is engaging in a rhetorical tradition that its audience would recognize as properly scriptural. Indeed in one place the Qur'an comes close to boasting of the capaciousness of its parabolic language, even as it alludes (like Jesus in the passage from Matthew above) to resistance to its message: "We have indeed turned about for men in this Koran every manner of similitude [*mathal*]; man is the most disputatious of things" (Q 18:54).

"Thine It Is Only to Deliver the Message"

A number of qur'anic passages have God counsel Muhammad that his role is only to "deliver the message" (*al-balāgh*). Qur'an 64:12 declares, "And obey God, and obey the Messenger; but if you turn your backs, it is only for the Messenger to deliver the Manifest Message [*al-balāgh al-mubīn*]." Qur'an 42:48 relates: "But if they turn away, We sent thee not to be a guardian over them. It is for thee only to deliver the Message [*al-balāgh*]." Qur'an 24:54 communicates a similar message, but it is phrased as Muhammad's speech to his audience: "Say: 'Obey God, and obey the Messenger; then, if you turn away, only upon him rests what is laid on him, and upon you rests what is laid on you. If you obey him, you will be guided. It is only for the Messenger to deliver the manifest Message'" (cf. also Q 16:35, 82; 21:106; 29:18; 36:17; 46:35; 72:23). Qur'an 13:40 includes a note that God will judge those who reject the message: "Whether We show thee a part of that We promise them, or We call thee to Us, it is thine only to deliver the Message, and Ours the reckoning." Qur'an 5:92 is similar, although the threat is veiled: "And obey God and obey the Messenger, and beware; but if you turn your backs, then know that it is only for Our Messenger to deliver the Message Manifest" (cf. Q 3:20, 5:99).

These passages are related to others that emphasize how God alone guides and leads astray. Qur'an 6:39 insists: "And those who cry lies to Our signs are deaf and dumb, dwelling in the shadows. Whomsoever God will, He leads astray, and whomsoever He will, He sets him on a straight path." Qur'an 7:178 is similar: "Whomsoever God guides, he is rightly guided; and whom He leads astray—they are the losers." Many other passages could be cited. In certain places this sort of discourse is framed as a personal message to Muhammad. Notable is Q 10:99–100:

> 99 And if thy Lord had willed, whoever is in the earth would have believed, all of them, all together. Wouldst thou then constrain the people, until they are believers?
>
> 100 It is not for any soul to believe save by the leave of God; and He lays abomination upon those who have no understanding.

Walid Saleh (and he is not alone) sees this passage as a sort of divine counsel meant to address Muhammad's despair at the hardheartedness of the Meccans who have rejected his message: "The crux of this sura is verses Q 10:99–100, with its pointed dismay at Muhammad's desire to convert all of humanity."[40]

I would propose instead that we not link such passages too closely to Muhammad's psychology, but instead see them as the development of a motif found also in the Gospels, namely that of insiders-outsiders, and the notion that believers are elected by God. As Laura Sweat has insightfully described, this message is at the heart of the discourse in Mark 4, where it is related to Jesus's choice to teach in parables. After offering the parable of the sower, Jesus goes on to quote Isa 6:9: "And he said to them, 'To you has been given the secret of the kingdom of God, but for those outside everything is in parables; so that they may indeed see but not perceive, and may indeed hear but not understand; lest they should turn again, and be forgiven" (Mark 4:11–12). Sweat comments:

> . . . Claiming that everything happens under God's control releases the community from the sole responsibility for its struggles (particularly in proclaiming 'the word,' as implied by 4.14–20). To this end, the community could have confidence that all things are in God's hands. The latter conclusion is supported by an interpretation of this passage that emphasizes a motif of fulfilment from prophecy: as God willed obduracy through Isaiah's prophetic proclamation [Isa 6:9, which is quoted in Mark 4:12], so God has done again through Jesus' parables.[41]

In other words, determinism in the Qur'an, especially as it is manifested in passages about Muhammad's responsibility only to deliver the message (since everything else is in God's hands), develops a Christian motif about insiders and outsiders. It is notable that in Mark 4 this motif is specifically connected to Jesus's choice to teach in parables. Again, it is worth recalling how Q 2:26 connects God's choice to speak in parables with his will to divide believers from unbelievers: "But as for those who disbelieve, they say, 'What did Allah mean by this parable?' He misleads many by it, and He guides many by it, but He misleads none but the wrongdoers."

To this observation one might add how Muhammad, whose job is only to deliver the message (*al-balāgh*), seems in the Qur'an to play the role of the apostles in the Gospels. The qur'anic passages with this motif might be compared to Matt 10:14 (cf. Mark 6:11; Luke 9:5). Here Jesus counsels the twelve that they should simply leave a house or town that will not accept their words (*logous;* Syriac *mellē*): "And if any one will not receive you or listen to your words, shake off the dust from your feet as you leave that house or town." The parallel is even more interesting as Jesus goes on to warn of eschatological punishment against that town (much as God, in the passages cited above, warns of divine judgment against those who ignore Muhammad's message): "Truly, I say to you, it shall be more tolerable on the day of judgment for the land of Sodom and Gomor'rah than for that town" (Matt 10:15). Thus the role of Jesus in Matthew, who counsels the apostles only to deliver their words since judgment is in God's hands, is played by God in the Qur'an.

Fear of God and Eschatological Piety

A further instance of the Qur'an's engagement with Christianity is found in the nature of its eschatological language, and more generally in the language surrounding the fear of God (inevitably connected to notions of divine judgment on the last day). In a work written initially in German, and later translated into French as *Les origines de l'Islam et le Christianisme,* the Swedish scholar Tor Andræ notes the commonalities between language on fear of God in the Syriac works of Eastern Christians and in the Qur'an. At the heart of the spirituality of the Syriac fathers, he maintains, is the notion of the fear (Syriac *deḥlā*) of divine punishment. Andræ finds this very similar to the Qur'an's emphasis on judgment, and the corresponding human disposition of pious fear.[42] He notes to this end a passage in Qur'an 76. In Q 76:8 the Qur'an explains how the faithful feed "the needy, the orphan, the captive." It then quotes these believers speaking to those whom they have fed (Q 76:9–10):

> 9 We feed you only for the Face of God; we desire no recompense from you, no thankfulness;
>
> 10 for we fear from our Lord a frowning day, inauspicious.[43]

In this passage the charitable deed by the believers of feeding the hungry is inspired by a fear of the "frowning" Day of Judgment. Andræ comments: "Here the motif of the love of God is surpassed in a very characteristic manner by the motif of fear."[44]

Andræ goes on to argue, with reference to the early Syriac text known as the *Didascalia Apostolorum* ("Teaching of the Apostles"; see more below), that this sort of sober piety, marked by a constant awareness of the threat of divine punishment, is an important element of spirituality in the late antique Syriac church. He notes how the *Didascalia* counsels Christians to celebrate even their feast days with "fear and trembling":

> We must conduct our festivals and our rejoicings, then, with fear and trembling; for a faithful Christian, it saith, must not

> sing the songs of the heathen, nor have anything to do with the laws and doctrines of strange assemblies; for it may happen that through (their) songs he will make mention also of the name of idols, which God forbid that it should be done by the faithful.[45]

Andræ writes, "Tears and sadness take a preponderant place in the piety of the Syrian church among Christian virtues."[46] He even argues—perhaps with some exaggeration—that the Syriac fathers focus in their spirituality on the individual rigors taken up by each believer, to the detriment of an evangelical sense of the grace won by Christ and shared with believers: "The pious man must merit forgiveness by his own works, by a disposition throughout his life through the macerations that he inflicts upon himself."[47] To this end as well Andræ notes that one of the Syriac words used by the church for monks (or nuns) is simply *abīl,* "weeper."[48] This weeping is provoked by eschatological dread, regret for sins, fear of individual judgment, and fear of hellfire.

However, it is important to emphasize that the notion of fear before divine judgment hardly exhausts the spirituality of the Syriac-speaking church. Ephrem, for example, emphasizes not only God's justice, but also his otherness, his sublimity. Those who enter deeply into this contemplation are often overwhelmed not only by a feeling of fear, but also by a feeling of wonder; they are reduced to silence before God. In his *Hymns on Faith,* Ephrem uses the language of the sea (in the passage below, the "dreadful sea") to speak of the majesty, vastness, and ultimate incomprehensibility of the divine essence:

> You are a complete marvel,
> On all the sides into which we search for you.
> You are near and far
> And who can arrive at you?
> Investigation's reach
> Is unable to come to your side.
> Whenever it has reached out to come [to you],
> It was cut off and fell short.
> It stands beneath your mountain.

Faith reaches [you]
And love, with prayer.
It is easier for us to think
Than to speak a word.
Thinking—which is able to stretch out everywhere—
Whenever it sets off
On your road, toward your investigation,
Its path disappears in front of it.
It becomes confused and stalls.
If thinking is so defeated.
How much more a word,
Whose path [lies] amidst confusion?
It is fitting for the mouth
To give praise, and then to be quiet.
And when it refuses to rush,
It takes refuge entirely in silence.
Therefore, one can understand
If one has not hurried to understand.
The one who is quiet has greater understanding
Than the hasty one who hurries.
The ignorant one, who has investigated,
Look: that weak one toils,
For the dreadful sea is treacherous.[49]

All of this language on the majesty of God, and the silence that it instills in the heart of the worshipper, is close to the language of *taqwā,* a pious fear of God, in the Qur'an, and the remarkable emphasis of the Qur'an on repentance as well as love of God.[50] I have argued elsewhere that the Qur'an expects all humans to be attentive to their sinfulness and live with a penitential disposition: "The God of the Qur'an does not expect humans to be perfect or sinless. He expects them instead to be repentant (*tā'ibūn* or *tawwābūn;* see Q 2:222; 9:112; and 66:5, where *tā'ibāt* is among the aspirational virtues of the Prophet's wives). All humans sin, and all are called to repent."[51]

Beyond these general observations on the spirituality of the Syriac fathers and the Qur'an, one might also note the commonalities between the eschatological vocabulary in the Qur'an and Syriac literature. In the chapter on the "Meccan" Qur'an in *The Qur'an: A Historical-Critical Introduction,* Nicolai Sinai writes, "The dominant theme of the early Meccan surahs is arguably the announcement of a divine reckoning that will take place at the end of the world."[52] As Sinai notes, the qur'anic demand that its audience repent in light of this reckoning rests on the reality of the resurrection of the body, the necessary condition for individual human judgment in the eschaton. Sinai goes on to note that not only this general scenario, but even the particular elements of the Qur'an's eschatological scenario seem to reflect the imagery and ideas found among Christians:

> The early Qur'an's eschatological kerygma displays manifold parallels to Christian eschatological discourse. Most obviously, the Qur'anic announcements of an eschatological earthquake (for example, Q 73: 14, 79: 6–7, and 99: 1), of a darkening and scattering of the celestial bodies (for example, Q 81: 1–2 and 82: 2), of a trumpet blast triggering the Resurrection (Q 69: 13, 74: 8, and 78: 18), of a displacement or destruction of the mountains (for example, Q 69: 14, 70: 9, and 101: 5), and of the opening of record books in preparation for the Last Judgement (Q 81: 10) all have patent counterparts in the New Testament. One can moreover discern a number of phraseological parallels; for example, the Qur'anic affirmation that God's 'affair' will transpire 'in the blink of an eye' (Q 54: 50) is very similar to a Pauline metaphor (1 Corinthians 15: 52), the designation of the end of the world as 'the Hour' harks back to passages like Matthew 24: 36 and 25: 13, and the frequent Qur'anic 'on that day' (*yawma'idhin*) also has a New Testamental equivalent (see Matthew 7: 22).[53]

To this we might add that the Qur'an also speaks of a "Beast" (*dābba*) that will come from the earth on the Day of Judgment (Q 27:82) as the Book of Revelation speaks of a beast emerging from the ground (Rev 13:11). The Qur'an also speaks of the sky being rolled up "as a scroll" (Q 21:104; cf. 39:67). Such imagery is found in Isaiah ("All the host of heaven shall rot away, / and the skies roll up like a scroll"; Isa 34:4) and is taken up again in the Book of Revelation ("the sky vanished like a scroll that is rolled up"; Rev 6:14).

As Sinai notes, the eschatological parallels are not limited to the Qur'an and the New Testament, but are especially salient between the Qur'an and late antique Christian homilies in Syriac, notably with Ephrem (d. 373), Narsai (d. 503), and Jacob of Serugh (d. 521). Sinai suggests the following historical scenario for the transmission of this material to the Qur'an: "Our best hypothesis is that the early Meccan surahs arose from and spoke to a cultural habitat that had for some time been exposed to Christian missionary preaching yet had so far proved largely impervious to it. This preaching, probably delivered in Arabic, would have drawn inspiration from Syriac homiletic literature in stoking fear of eternal damnation."[54]

One might think again of the Companions of the Cave story (see Chapter 2) in this regard. In his homily on the topic Jacob of Serugh has the "Sleepers of Ephesus" declare, "For your sake has Christ our Lord awoken us / so that you might see . . . that the resurrection truly exists."[55] The Qur'an for its part has God relate, "And even so We made them stumble upon them, that they might know that God's promise is true, and that the Hour—there is no doubt of it" (Q 18:21).

Indeed as David Bertaina has convincingly argued, Syriac texts of late antiquity are particularly interested in the theme of the resurrection of the body, a theme that is likewise found throughout the Qur'an's eschatological material.[56] This concern appears in the second century CE work 2 Baruch, which, in its Syriac version, became part of the West Syrian Miaphysite lectionary.[57] Bertaina notes a parallel between the way Baruch asks God about the resurrected body (2 Bar. 49:1–3: "In what form will those living live in your day?" [v. 2]) and the way Abraham, in the Qur'an, says to God, "show me how Thou wilt give life to the dead" (Q 2:260).[58]

Bertaina illustrates another remarkable parallel around this theme in the writings of the fourth-century Syriac author Aphrahat. In his *Demonstrations,* Aphrahat (d. 345) notes (quoting 1 Cor 15:35) how some doubt the power of God to raise a body when it is reduced to dust: "For the body wears out and is destroyed; as the time lengthens, the bones also are reduced to a powder and are unrecognizable."[59] Now, Aphrahat's opponents do not deny the afterlife; they deny only that the body will be raised. In response Aphrahat argues that God will bring forth a new body from the old, as seed decays and forms new grain or as Adam was originally created from dust.[60] Qur'an 22:5 refers directly to the creation of the first man from dust as a sort of argument for God's ability to raise dead bodies: "O men, if you are in doubt as to the Uprising, surely We created you of dust then of a sperm-drop, then of a blood clot, then of a lump of flesh, formed and unformed that We may make clear to you" (cf. Q 21:104, 30:27, 36:79, 50:15).

Bertaina also notes the arguments of a figure contemporary to the emergence of the Qur'an, Babai the Great (d. 628), directed against a fellow Church of the East theologian named Ḥenana of Adiabene (d. 610). Ḥenana argued that the resurrected body is not the same as one's body in this world. Babai responded that Ḥenana's view is tantamount to a denial of the resurrection (and accuses him of teachings close to those of Origen, who was likewise accused of denying the resurrection of the body).[61] Babai writes:

> However all of these followers of Ḥenana even in our day rise up for their destruction. These people deny not only the resurrection of the body of our Lord, but also the general resurrection of the bodies of all men. They believe in the redemption of all souls in the future and they believe that their redemption is when they are freed from the prison of the body in which they are confined. But in truth the bodies of these evil ones will rise in the resurrection of judgment and they will be handed over to eternal punishment with Satan their father, whose deception they have accepted.[62]

That the Qur'an is so concerned with resurrection deniers has often seemed curious to observers. The so-called *mushrikūn* ("associators"), the opponents of Muhammad in many Meccan Suras, seem to accept that Allah is God and the creator of the cosmos. They acknowledge that the natural order, including the subservience of the sun and the moon

(Q 29:61), is all due to God. The problem is that they deny the resurrection of the body. One wonders, considering the range of religious actors in late antiquity, what, or who, is behind the *mushrikūn* of the Qur'an. Many scholars, including Patricia Crone and Nicolai Sinai, have attempted to identify the *mushrikūn* as, alternatively, aberrant monotheists or Judaizing (or Christianizing) polytheists. Sinai argues that the *mushrikūn* were indeed pagans but had "appropriated elements of Christian ritual practice," as monotheistic traditions were "increasingly seeping into the Arabian interior."[63] He writes the following (after discussing a pilgrimage at Mamre, in Byzantine Palestine, which involved both monotheists and pagans in late antiquity):

> Unlike Mamre, Mecca was not subject to any external authority interested in, and capable of, enforcing "the worship of god according to the law of the church," allowing for an entirely uncontrolled fusion of pagan and Judaeo-Christian components. Most likely, it is such a milieu that yielded the religion of the Qur'anic Associators, polemics against which take up so much of the Islamic scripture.[64]

An alternative view is that proposed by Patricia Crone, that the *mushrikūn* were Jews (or Christians) who might have worshipped angels and whom the Qur'an caricatures as polytheists in the course of its religious polemics.[65] Still another perspective is offered by Valentina Grasso:

> Although I agree with Hawting's suggestion that the Qur'ānic *mushrikūn* are not polytheists, I argue that these were not Jews or Christians and that the Qur'ānic idols were not angels. . . . I argue that the *mushrikūn* were sympathizing monotheists who venerated Allāh. This was a pagan god who assumed biblical character due to the intense proselytizing activity of monotheistic communities active in Arabia.[66]

I would put things a bit differently. The evidence of late antique Syriac homilies suggests that scholars need not imagine that the qur'anic *mushrikūn* were some unique and idiosyncratic hybrid of paganism and monotheism. Indeed one does not need to be an especially aberrant Christian to be caricatured as a heretic. Babai makes Ḥenana, who was not simply a faithful member of the Church of the East but a bishop of that same community (!), into a heretic for his particular understanding of the resurrection. Indeed he deems him liable to final condemnation in hellfire for his understanding: "But in truth the bodies of these evil ones will rise in the resurrection of judgment and they will be handed over to eternal punishment with Satan their father, whose deception they have accepted."[67] It is important to learn from such cases that it was the nature of late antique religious actors to engage in hyperbolic and polemical rhetoric in order to advance a particular doctrinal or sectarian cause. The Qur'an is no different.[68]

Intriguingly, Bertaina also carefully discusses the rise of a significant controversy among non-Chalcedonians in the late sixth century (that is, right before the rise of Islam) around teachings attributed to the Jacobite/Miaphysite John Philoponus (d. 570); Conon, bishop of Tarsus (fl. 601); and Eugenius, bishop of Seleucia, all of whom were accused of tritheism (essentially, that the three persons of the Trinity also have three natures, although one will).[69] The accusation of tritheism appears to be a second case of a theological caricature of one's opponent with a (significant) echo in the Qur'an.

It seems particularly telling that the charge the Qur'an makes against the *mushrikūn* (in addition to the principal charge of *shirk* or association) is the denial of the resurrection, and the resurrection of the body in particular. As Bertaina has shown, this is a principal issue of contention in late antique Christian texts. This explains the popularity of the Seven Sleepers of Ephesus tale, which makes its way into the Qur'an as the Companions of the Cave narrative.[70] Moreover, it was an issue of contention (as evidenced by Babai's writing against Ḥenana) precisely at the time that Muhammad (at least according to the traditional dates) was preaching in Mecca and Medina. In other words, all of this invites us to see the Qur'an's concern with the resurrection of the body on the last day, along with the question of association (or "tritheism" in the Jacobite debates), as its own engagement with key questions in Christian religious polemics of the day. The Qur'an, with its portrayal of the *mushrikūn*, enters into the fray of this debate.

We saw in Chapter 3 that there is no clear evidence at all in the epigraphic record for the continued existence of idolatrous pagans in the qur'anic milieu.[71] Accordingly, perhaps we should not identify the *mushrikūn* with pagans. Perhaps we should not identify them as an historical group at all. Rather, we might appreciate the literary function that the *mushrikūn* play in the Qur'an, as representatives of odious views that the Qur'an foregrounds in order to advance its own doctrines of monotheism and the resurrection of the body.

Martyrs

A final example of the manner in which the Qur'an engages implicitly with Christianity has to do with what it promises martyrs in the holy war.[72] In Sura 2 the divine voice of the Qur'an tells the believers, "And say not of those slain in God's way, 'They are dead'; rather they are living, but you are not aware" (Q 2:154). In this verse the Qur'an seems to be saying something specifically about those "slain in God's way," regarding martyrs of the holy war. The martyrs, and the martyrs alone, are "living" after their deaths.

In Sura 3 the Qur'an comforts the believers regarding the fate of the martyrs in a similar manner: "Count not those who were slain in God's way as dead, but rather living with their Lord, by Him provided" (Q 3:169). The last phrase, "by Him provided," renders Arabic *'inda rabbihim yurzaqūn,* an expression that is key to understanding the Qur'an's doctrine on the martyrs. This expression is more literally rendered by Yusuf Ali as, "Nay, they live, finding their sustenance in the presence of their Lord." The Arabic root *r-z-q* has to do with sustenance or food. Thus the passive verb *yurzaqūn* in this verse implies that the martyrs, even now (that is, before the Day of Judgment), not only are alive but also are being provided with food in the garden of paradise. This, in turn, implies that they have bodies, with hands, with which they eat.

At first glance this sort of passage may seem to follow naturally from the qur'anic idea of paradise as a physical place, indeed the very garden of Eden in which Adam and his wife, Eve, were created (the Qur'an refers to the "garden of Eden" or "gardens of Eden" in Q 9:72, 13:23, 16:31, 18:31, 19:61, 20:76, 35:33, 38:50, 40:8, 61:12, 98:8). However, the disruptive nature of Q 3:169 is seen when it is appreciated that the Qur'an elsewhere denies immediate retribution. The typical description of things after death implies that reward in the garden of paradise (or punishment in hellfire) will unfold only after the raising of bodies on the Day of Judgment. A number of qur'anic passages imply as much, namely that recompense is dealt out only after the "trumpet" is blown (Q 27:87–90):

> 87 On the day the Trumpet is blown, and terrified is whosoever is in the heavens and earth, excepting whom God wills, and every one shall come to Him, all utterly abject;
>
> 88 and thou shalt see the mountains, that thou supposest fixed, passing by like clouds—God's handiwork, who has created everything very well. He is aware of the things you do.
>
> 89 Whosoever comes with a good deed, he shall have better than it; and they shall be secure from terror that day.
>
> 90 And whosoever comes with an evil deed, their faces shall be thrust into the Fire: "Are you recompensed but for what you did?" (cf. Q 18:99–105, 20:100–104, 23:101–3, 39:68–74, 69:13–16, 78:18–24)

The normal sequence by which humans are judged and sent to reward or punishment is developed in more detail in Qur'an 50: angels record the merits and faults of humans during their lives (vv. 16–18), humans die (v. 19), the trumpet of the Day of Judgment is sounded (v. 20), at which "every soul shall come, and with it a driver and a witness" (v. 21), to be judged and rewarded or punished (v. 22–35). Although Sura 50 does not say so explicitly, it mentions nothing about reward or punishment between the death of humans (v. 19) and the Day of Judgment (v. 20). On the basis of such verses, Islamic tradition would develop the idea of *barzakh* (a term that appears in the Qur'an but in a different sense), according to which the dead fall into a sort of sleep after their death, when the soul is separated from the body, until the Day of Judgment (although according to some traditions God will give bodies the ability to experience suffering in the tomb as they are questioned by angels during this period).[73]

This doctrine of "soul sleep" is illustrated elsewhere in the Qur'an by the Companions of the Cave narrative (Qur'an 18) and by the story of the man and his donkey (Q 2:259). In the former story the companions "awake" from their sleep with no sense of how much time has passed ("We have tarried a day, or part of a day"; Q 18:19). In Q 2:259 the man declares similarly, "I have tarried a day, or part of a day." God informs him, "Nay; thou hast tarried a hundred years" (Q 2:259).

So what does the Qur'an mean when it affirms (Q 3:169) that even now those "slain in God's way" are alive and being sustained or fed by God? Evidently this verse speaks of a special favor or grace given to war martyrs, that they have an immediate reward in the heavenly garden (see also Q 3:195, 9:111, 47:4–6).[74] In Q 3:195 the Qur'an explains that this is possible because God forgives martyrs for their sins. Qur'an 9:111 makes the reward of the garden part of a transaction: a payment to the believers for offering their lives and their property to the cause of holy war. The idea that the martyrs go to heaven immediately upon their deaths left interpreters with a problem, however. It is clear from the Qur'an (and from the tombs in which the dead were buried) that the bodies of the dead remain in this world. How, then, could the martyrs enjoy the pleasures of the garden (generally understood to be a physical garden)? One creative answer is that God provides for their souls the bodies of green birds. Thus the martyrs fly around the garden of paradise and eat of its fruit until the Day of Resurrection when they are reunited with their human bodies. In this way they are provided with sustenance (*yurzaqūn*). This view appears already in the commentary attributed to Muqātil b. Sulaymān (d. 150 AH/767 CE).[75] It is cited again by Ṭabarī (d. 310 AH/923 CE), Zamakhsharī (d. 538 AH/1144 CE), and Ibn Kathīr (d. 774 AH/1373 CE), among others.[76]

Yet how does the Qur'an come to distinguish so sharply between the eschatological fate of the martyrs and that of all other believers? In my opinion the notion of the martyr in the Qur'an reflects generally an engagement with the Christian idea of martyrs. It is worth noting (although this point is not really key to the argument) that the Arabic word for martyr (*shahīd*) is likely a calque (possibly through Syriac *sāhdā*) on the Greek term *martyr*.[77] The Greek, Syriac, and Arabic forms alike have the dual meaning of "witness" and "sacrificial victim for one's faith."

The context of the East Syrian Church is particularly important here. Many early thinkers in the East Syrian Church held the doctrine of "soul sleep."[78] The soul of the dead will be awakened only when the body is raised. Soul and body will be joined together, judged, and sent to their reward or punishment. Tor Andræ sees this doctrine as a reflection of a larger conviction among Semitic cultures that the soul could have only a shadowy existence (such as the biblical Sheol), if any, before the resurrection of the body.[79] Thus standard eschatological teaching of the East Syrian Church was precisely that suggested by the Qur'an: the soul will not be rewarded (or punished) before it is reunited with the body.[80] Aphrahat (who lived before Chalcedon but was from Iran, in the East), for example, taught that the soul is buried with the body and is awakened only on the Day of Judgment; notably it is awakened (as in the Qur'an) by the blast of a trumpet.[81] On the general use of sleep for death, from which God will awaken the righteous, Aphrahat writes the following:

> But receive this explanation from me, that a sinner, while he is living, is dead unto God; and a righteous man, though dead, is alive unto God. For such death is a sleep, as David said, I lay down and slept, and awoke. Again Isaiah said, They that sleep in the dust shall awake (Isaiah 26:19). And our Lord said concerning the daughter of the chief of the synagogue, the damsel is not dead, but sleeping a slumber (Matthew 9:26). And concerning Lazarus, He said to His disciples: Our friend Lazarus has fallen asleep; but I go to waken him (John 11:11). And the Apostle said: We shall all sleep, but we shall not all be changed (1 Corinthians 15:51). And again he said: Concerning those that sleep, be not grieved (1 Thessalonians 4:13).[82]

This same doctrine of "soul sleep" is taught by Aphrahat's younger contemporary from Mesopotamia, Ephrem (d. 373), and by the aforementioned Babai the Great (d. 628). Babai, as we have seen, tells the story of the Seven Sleepers (or Youths) of Ephesus in order to defend this doctrine.[83]

However, as argued by Andræ the East Syrian fathers often made one exception to the rule that the dead will sleep until the resurrection. He writes, "None of those who have left this life will dwell immediately with the Lord, if he has not obtained through martyrdom the privilege of residing in paradise and not in hell."[84] A clear witness to this teaching is found just before the emergence of the Qur'an in the thought of the East Syrian theologian Mar Ishai (d. late sixth century), who wrote, concerning the martyrs: "People believed that they are dead. But their death killed their sin and they are living in the presence of God [*be-ḥayyē lewāt alāhā*]."[85] One might compare this to Q 3:169: "Count not those who were slain in God's way as dead, but rather living with their Lord [*aḥyā'un 'inda rabbihim*], by Him provided."[86]

The teaching on the glory earned by martyrs is widespread in the early church. It is nevertheless telling to find the way it is emphasized in the third-century Christian text the aforementioned *Didascalia Apostolorum,* originally written in Greek but preserved in Syriac.[87] The *Didascalia* clearly teaches that the martyrs will have a privilege above other faithful believers:

> If then He raises up all men,—as He said by Isaiah: *All flesh shall see the salvation of God* [Isa 40.5; 52.10],—much more will He quicken and raise up the faithful; and (yet more) again will He quicken and raise up the faithful of the faithful, who are the martyrs, and establish them in great glory and make them His counsellors. For to mere disciples, those who believe in Him, He has promised a glory as of the stars [Dan 12.3]; but to the martyrs He has promised to give an everlasting glory, as of the luminaries which fail not, with more abundant light, that they may be shining for all time.[88]

The *Didascalia* is also clear, as is the Qur'an, that martyrs enjoy a special grace through the forgiveness of sins that their deaths have earned for them:

> But again, sins are *forgiven* by baptism also to those who from the Gentiles draw near and enter the holy Church of God. Let us inquire also, to whom sins are *not imputed*. To such as Abraham and Isaac and Jacob and all the patriarchs, as also to the martyrs. Let us hear then, brethren, for the Scripture saith: Who shall boast himself and say: I am clear of sins? Or who shall be confident and say: I am innocent? [Prov 20.9]. And again: There is no man pure of defilement: not though his life be but one day [Job 14.4–5 LXX]. To everyone therefore who believes and is baptized his . . . former sins have been forgiven; but after baptism also, provided that he has not sinned a deadly sin nor been an accomplice (thereto), but has heard only, or seen, or spoken, and is thus guilty of sin. But if a man go forth from the world by martyrdom for the name of the Lord, blessed is he; *for brethren who by martyrdom have gone forth from this world, of these the sins are covered.*[89]

We might compare Q 3:195: "'And those who emigrated, and were expelled from their habitations, those who suffered hurt in My way, and fought, and were slain—them *I shall surely acquit of their evil deeds,* and I shall admit them to gardens underneath which rivers flow.' A reward from God! And God with Him is the fairest reward" (italics added). In other words, the Qur'an seems to be well aware of Christian devotion to the martyrs. Yet it does not simply borrow or copy this devotion.[90] Instead, it develops its own teaching on the martyrs. It reshapes the Syriac Christian notion of martyrs as those innocently slain in persecution to a notion of those who die while fighting in God's way against the unbelievers. Notably, when Q 3:195 speaks of martyrdom, it first refers to persecution ("those who suffered hurt in My way") but then adds the qur'anic innovation by making reference to the participation of believers in the holy war ("and fought, and were slain"). Thus the Qur'an speaks of its notion of martyrdom in a way that is comprehensible to an audience familiar with the Christian concept but, with the use of prophetic authority, also offers its unique idea that martyrdom (and consequently, the heavenly garden) is rightly won through participation in the military campaigns of the new Prophet.

A Final Thought

The literary and historical evidence suggests that the Qur'an emerged from a Christian context. Traditionally, academic scholars have considered the Qur'an and Christianity only when the Qur'an explicitly engages with Christian characters such as Jesus, John, or Mary; with Christian stories such as the Seven Sleepers of Ephesus; or with Christians (*naṣārā*) themselves. Here we have suggested that even in those places where the Qur'an is not explicitly engaging with Christians or Christian traditions, it is attentive to the Christian nature of its context. The Qur'an is eager to express its arguments in ways that will be recognizable and meaningful to Christians, and above all in ways that will persuade them to accept a new prophet.

It is important to be clear here regarding what I am *not* arguing. There is a significant tradition of Christian scholars, both medieval and modern, who have argued that the Qur'an, properly understood, agrees with and endorses Christian teaching. In 1977 the Italian Franciscan scholar Giulio Bassetti-Sani published *The Koran in the Light of Christ*, in which he argues that the church (and he means the Catholic Church in particular) holds the key that unlocks the true meaning of the Qur'an, much as (according to his understanding) it holds the key that unlocks the true, Christological meaning of the Hebrew scriptures.[91] In 1985 the Protestant scholar Georges Tartar offered his own Christianizing reading of the Qur'an in his work *Connaître Jésus-Christ: Lire le Coran à la lumière de l'Évangile.*[92]

Although neither Bassetti-Sani nor Tartar has much to say about the earlier legacy of this argument, it is in fact not particularly new. Most famously Paul of Antioch (d. early thirteenth century) argued at length for a Christian reading of the Qur'an in *Risāla ilā baʿḍ aṣdiqāʾihi alladhīna bi-Ṣayḍā min al-muslimīn* ("Letter to a Muslim Friend in Sidon"). Paul already made the argument that Muhammad was sent only to the pagan Arabs (not Christians) and that the Qur'an has latent Christian meaning (e.g., and as mentioned above, he held that the *basmala* points to the Trinity).[93] Paul, apparently, was not an outlier in this regard, because the Muslim Muʿtazilī scholar ʿAbd al-Jabbār (d. 415 AH/1025 CE) expressed concern a few centuries earlier about Christians who argued for a Christian interpretation of the Qur'an. He wrote in *Tathbīt dalāʾil al-nubuwwa* that Christians in his day claimed that "Muḥammad conveyed Christianity and our teachings, but his companions did not understand him."[94]

The argument of this chapter, and of the present book generally, is fundamentally different. Indeed in some ways it is perfectly contrary to that proposed by the tradition of Christianizing readings of the Qur'an. The point about the Qur'an's engagement with Christianity is that it is fundamentally a polemical engagement. The Qur'an is not a Christian text and it does not have Christian meanings, either latent or manifest. The Qur'an offers its own teaching, and above all offers arguments for the legitimacy of its new prophet. It is this highly polemical concern that, finally, explains the remarkable density of self-referential and metatextual language in the Qur'an, as has been well argued by Anne-Sylvie Boisliveau.[95]

There is much more to be said, perhaps in another work, about the way in which the Qur'an positions itself polemically vis-à-vis the Christianity of its context. The evidence presented in this work (principally in Chapter 3) suggests that Christianity was spreading in Arabia in part through scripture and liturgy in non-Arabic (principally Syriac/Aramaic) languages. This corresponds perfectly with the Qur'an's repeated and insistent declarations of its own Arabic language. The Prophet was giving his people a scripture in their own language.

Of course, what was at stake was not only a new language, but above all a new prophet. In order to advance its claims of a new prophet, the Qur'an engages with Christian modes of religious expression and theological language, including an interest in parables and parable-making, in the fear of God, and in the special privilege of martyrs. In each case, however, the Qur'an presents itself as an alternative. It is the Qur'an's parables that matter, it is the Qur'an's God who is to be feared, and it is the Qur'an's own martyrs who enjoy a special privilege in the heavenly garden.[96]

Notes

Abbreviations

BSOAS	*Bulletin of the School of Oriental and African Studies*
CdH	Amir-Moezzi and Dye, eds., *Coran des historiens*
CSCO	*Corpus Scriptorum Christianorum Orientalium.* Edited by Jean Baptiste Chabot et al. Paris, 1903
EI2	*The Encyclopaedia of Islam,* 2nd ed. Leiden: Brill, 1954–2006
EQ	*The Encyclopaedia of the Qurʾān.* Edited by J. McAuliffe. Leiden: Brill, 2001–2006
JAOS	*Journal of the American Oriental Society*
JIQSA	*Journal of the International Qurʾanic Studies Association*
JNES	*Journal of Near Eastern Studies*
JQS	*Journal of Qurʾanic Studies*
JSAI	*Jerusalem Studies in Arabic and Islam*
QB	Reynolds, *The Qurʾan and the Bible*
QBS	Reynolds, *The Qurʾān and Its Biblical Subtext*
QHC	Reynolds, ed., *The Qurʾān in Its Historical Context*
QSC	Azaiez, Reynolds, Tesei, and Zafer, eds., *Qurʾan Seminar Commentary*

ONE Traditional Ideas About Christianity in Muhammad's Arabia

1. On this term see Kister, "*ʾAl-Taḥannuth,*" who notes that the term is regularly glossed with *tabarrur* ("piety") or *taʿabbud* ("worship"). Ibn Isḥāq's report of the Prophet's *taḥannuth* explains that this monthly sojourn was a practice of the Quraysh generally in the time of ignorance (*jāhiliyya*) and that Muhammad brought with him food, which he would distribute to the poor who called on him on the mountain. Ibn Isḥāq

mentions that Muhammad's family (meaning, apparently, Khadīja) was with him. He does not mention a cave. See Ibn Hishām, *Sīrat Rasūl Allāh,* English trans.: Ibn Isḥāq, *Life of Muḥammad,* 105. Cf. the version in Bukhārī, according to which instead Muhammad practiced *taḥannuth* alone in a cave because he liked solitude; see *Ṣaḥīḥ*, 1, Kitāb Bad' al-Waḥy, #3 (numbering of hadith in Bukhari's *Ṣaḥīḥ* is according to the Arabic/English edition of M. Muhsin Khan [Riyadh: Darussalam, 1997]). As Kister (ibid., 229) explains, H. Hirschfeld proposed that *taḥannuth* was an Arabization of a cognate Hebrew word meaning prayer. See Hirschfeld, *New Researches,* 2. He imagines that Muhammad heard this word in Medina and used it to recount his experience on Mount Ḥirā' to his followers. Others (see Kister, ibid., 228–30) have followed the traditional Arabic etymology, noting that *ḥinth* could mean "sin" and consequently that *taḥannuth* might mean the absolving of sin. Bell ("Mohammed's Call," 16) argues that the story is a myth developed on the basis of "Christian ascetic practice" (in part since fasting, such as the sort attributed to Muhammad, was not practiced by the early Muslims until after the hijra). Kister (ibid., 236) argues, after a meticulous examination of traditions, that Muhammad really sojourned on Ḥirā', which was a regular place of solitude for the Quraysh connected somehow to the Ka'ba, and that a sojourn there was connected to doing "charitable deeds towards one's fellow men."

2. Translations of the Qur'an in the present book are from Arthur J. Arberry, *The Koran Interpreted* (London: George Allen & Unwin, 1955). Translations of the Bible are from the Revised Standard Version, copyright 1952 by the Division of Christian Education of the National Council of the Churches of Christ in the United States of America. Used by permission.

3. Ibn Hishām, *Sīrat Rasūl Allāh,* 153; Ibn Isḥāq, *Life of Muḥammad,* 106 (henceforth referred to as "Ibn Isḥāq," followed by page numbers from the Arabic and/or English translation [indicated by "trans."]).

4. Ibn Isḥāq, trans. 106–7. This statement is found in the version of Ibn Isḥāq's account preserved in Ṭabarī's history and is not found in the version preserved in Ibn Hishām's history. See Ṭabarī, *Ta'rīkh,* ed. M. J. de Goeje (Leiden: Brill, 1878–1901), 1150.

5. Ibn Isḥāq, 153; trans. 107.

6. Bukhārī, *Ṣaḥīḥ*, 1, Kitāb Bad' al-Waḥy, #3. Note that Juan Cole (*Muhammad,* 44) describes Zayd b. Ḥāritha as a Christian (before his conversion to Islam).

7. Lammens, "Chrétiens à la Mecque," 218. Ibn Isḥāq relates that Waraqa studied Christian scriptures until he "became skillful in Christianity and followed the scriptures from their community" (*istaḥkama fī l-naṣrāniyya wa-ittaba'a l-kutub min ahlihā*). Ibn Isḥāq, 143 (my translation).

8. Waraqa's effective disappearance from the later sections of the Prophet's biography is indeed curious. The biographical historian Ibn Ḥajar al-'Asqalānī (d. 852 AH/1449 CE) includes an entry (almost two pages in the modern edition) on Waraqa in his work *K. al-Iṣāba fī tamyīz al-ṣaḥāba* and focuses almost exclusively on his initial reaction to Muhammad's first experience of revelation. Ibn Ḥajar notes that the classical Muslim authorities were divided over whether Waraqa ever embraced Islam. In order to address this matter Ibn Ḥajar relates an account according to which Khadīja (presumably after

the death of Waraqa) asked Muhammad about his fate. The Prophet responded, "I saw him wearing a white robe and I figure that if he were among those condemned to hell he would not be wearing a white robe." *K. al-Iṣāba* (Cairo: Maṭbaʿat al-Saʿāda, 1328 [1910]), 3:635. Azzi (*Le prêtre et le prophète,* 46) points to a tradition recorded in the *Ṣaḥīḥ* of Bukhārī (d. 870) regarding Waraqa that makes him an "old man" who had "lost his eyesight" at the beginning of Muhammad's revelation. This tradition mentions that Waraqa died a few days after confirming Muhammad's revelation and that "divine inspiration also paused for a while [*fatara al-waḥy*]." See Bukhārī, Kitāb Badʾ al-Waḥy, #3.

9. The pseudonym is a play on words from the author's actual name (which indeed appears in the French translation): Joseph Azzi. Arabic *qazz* (pronounced *azz* in Lebanese dialect) means "silk," as does *ḥarīr.*

10. In the French translation the opening lines of the introduction relate, "This work seeks to illuminate the identity and the personality of the priest Waraqa ibn Nawfal and to determine his connections with the prophet Mohammed ibn Abdallah, in order to reveal what has been hidden historically of the truth of Islam and its relationship with Nazoreanism [Arabic: *nasrânîya,* the name of the Christianity of Mecca]." Azzi, *Prêtre et le prophète,* 17, my translation (from the French). The Arabic original is Abū Mūsā al-Ḥarīrī, *Qass wa-nabīy: baḥth fī nashʾat al-Islām* (Beirut: Diyār ʿAql, 1979, 2005). On the possible role of Waraqa in mentoring Muhammad, see now El-Badawi, *Queens and Prophets,* 202–5.

11. In Acts 24 a certain Tertullus, making an argument before the Roman governor against the apostle Paul, speaks of him as "ringleader of the sect of Nazarenes" (Greek *nazōraiōn;* Syriac Peshitta *nāṣrāyē*). On this question, see further Griffith, "*Al-Naṣārā* in the Qur'an."

12. Notably the *Panarion* of Epiphanius of Salamis (d. ca. 403). See further de Blois, "Elchasai–Manes–Muḥammad." Griffith ("*Al-Naṣārā* in the Qur'an," 303) writes the following about the use of the term Nazorean: "In his *Onomasticon,* the church historian, Eusebius of Caesarea (d. ca. 340) remarked in connection with his entry on the name of the village of Nazareth that 'From it, Christ was called a "Nazorean," and we too early on [were called] "Nazarenes," who are now Christians.'" In his Latin translation of this passage, St. Jerome (ca. 342–420) adds a note that "we were called Nazarenes *quasi pro obprobrio* [almost out of contempt]'" (Griffith, ibid.).

13. Azzi (*Prêtre et le prophète,* 19) writes: "The first [Waraqa] inspires, professes, forms, and provides the foundations. The second [Muhammad] listens, learns, studies, and constructs the edifice. The merit of the first in respect to the second is like that of an educator in respect to an apprentice" (my translation). Azzi, it might be added, not only argues that the historical role of Waraqa in the foundation of Islam has largely been forgotten; he also thinks that the version of the Qur'an known to us (which he refers to as the Qur'an of [the third caliph] ʿUthmān) does not correspond to the original Qur'an proclaimed by Muhammad.

14. Ibn Isḥāq, 143; trans. 99. For further references to traditional reports on the *ḥanīf*s, see Rubin, "*Ḥanīfiyya* and Kaʿba." Rubin defends the historicity of the *ḥanīf*s and argues that they connected themselves with "the religion of Abraham" and had a special

devotion to the Kaʿba as the house of Abraham (see esp. 97). There is some controversy regarding the background of this term, cognate to Syriac *ḥanpā,* which means instead "pagan." Jeffery (*Foreign Vocabulary,* 115) explains: "This word [i.e., Syriac *ḥanpā*] was commonly used with the meaning of *heathen,* and might well have been known to the pre-Islamic Arabs as a term used by the Christians for those who were neither Jews nor of their own faith." This explanation might account for Q 3:65–67. Jeffery also notes there the view that there may be a connection to Paul's arguments in Romans 4 that Abraham was counted righteous before the law, that is, before Judaism.

15. Ibn Isḥāq (144; trans. 99) includes a report that after his conversion to Christianity ʿUbaydallāh boasted to his former Muslim coreligionists, "We see clearly, but your eyes are only half open."

16. Ibn Isḥāq's report suggests that Zayd, the last of the four "*ḥanīfs*" to be mentioned (and the one described in the greatest detail), never met Muhammad but nevertheless anticipated the coming of a new prophet (thereby modeling the "proper" disposition of other monotheists). He relates that Zayd, in his old age, would lean against the Kaʿba and say: "O Quraysh, By Him in whose hand is the soul of Zayd, not one of you follows the religion of Abraham but I . . . O God, if I knew how you wished to be worshipped I would so worship you; but I do not know." Ibn Isḥāq subsequently relates, "Then he prostrated himself on the palms of his hands." Ibn Isḥāq, trans. 99–100. Later Zayd leaves Mecca and travels to Mesopotamia and Syria where he finally meets a man who indeed promises him that a new prophet will arise, "sent with the Ḥanīfiyya," in Zayd's own country. However, Zayd is murdered before he can return. Ibn Isḥāq, 148–49; trans. 103.

17. For a different interpretation (but still one that takes the narratives about these men as historical reports), see Maxime Rodinson (*Mohammed,* 64): "There must have been some at least who thought in this way and yet did not become either Christians or Jews. We have seen the considerations of national pride which prevented many Arabs from accepting such a conversion. Perhaps they were already becoming known as *ḥanīfs* towards Allah—a word derived, most probably, from a misinterpretation of an Aramaic word meaning 'unbelievers.'" Montgomery Watt dedicates an "Excursus" in his book *Muhammad at Mecca* to the *ḥanīfs*, noting that other authors add more examples of them to the four mentioned by Ibn Isḥāq. He (*Muhammad at Mecca,* 162) argues that the early sources apply the name *ḥanīf* to these men on the basis of the Qur'an and that "none of these persons named would have called himself a *ḥanīf* or said he was in search of the *ḥanīfiyah.*" Nevertheless, Watt continues by speculating that these men might really "have been feeling their way towards monotheism" and arguing that they are collectively "an additional illustration of the way in which monotheism was permeating the environment in which Muḥammad grew up" (ibid).

18. Qur'an 2:135; 3:67, 95; 4:125; 6:79, 161; 10:105; 16:120, 123; 30:30. The exceptions are Q 10:105 and Q 30:30. The plural *ḥunafāʾ* occurs on two occasions: Q 22:31 and Q 98:5. It is perhaps even more important to note that the term *ḥanīf* is never specifically applied to a figure other than Abraham in the Qur'an. See further, *QBS,* 71–87.

19. On *ḥanīf,* see now Goudarzi, "Unearthing Abraham's Altar."

20. "It is said that everyone who leaves a religion for another religion is a *ṣābi'*." Al-Rāghib al-Iṣfahānī, *Mufradāt alfāẓ al-Qur'ān*, 475.

21. The claims made by Jews and Christians in this regard have been discussed extensively in recent literature, in part by those who seek to show the problems inherent in the category of "Abrahamic religions." See *QB*, 127–28 (with references to Romans, Galatians, and Eusebius); see also Levenson, *Inheriting Abraham*, Introduction and chap. 6. Levenson writes: "The rise of Christianity in the first century of the Common Era posed a different sort of challenge to Judaism and elicited a different sort of response. In this case, the central issue was twofold: Which community today can lay just claim to the promises made to Abraham's descendants, and what is that community obligated to practice?" (ibid., 6). Later, criticizing the notion of Abrahamic religions, he adds: "Earlier, we also saw that the idea of three equally Abrahamic religions fails in its naïve attempt to move from a historical observation to a normative claim—from the observation that the three traditions speak of Abraham in ways that resonate across communal boundaries to the claim that the communal boundaries have no ultimate significance. Ironically, this misses one of the most salient historical characteristics of all three Abrahamic traditions—their disbelief in the very proposition that each is equally as Abrahamic as the other two" (ibid., 213–14). See, for a similar argument, Hughes, *Abrahamic Religions.*

22. On this see also Watt, *Muhammad at Mecca*, 163. Earlier, Watt (ibid., 24–25) speaks of the "decadence" of the old pagan religion, which had lost its force and appeal to the Arabs (in his estimation) despite the pagan ceremonies that continued to linger. Watt also believes that the old "humanism" of the tribes had likewise declined because of a growth of "individualism." Together these religious/social phenomena, along with economic questions centering around the concentration of wealth with the leaders of the Quraysh, made for fertile ground for a new religious movement. Watt was picking up on an earlier trend of psychological/sociological arguments for Islam's origins. Note, for example, Hurgronje (*Mohammedanism*, 35–36), who in his 1916 work seems to have a remarkable knowledge of Muhammad's inner state: "In the materialistic commercial town of Mecca, where lust of gain and usury reigned supreme, where women, wine and gambling filled up the leisure time, where might was right, and widows, orphans, and the feeble were treated as superfluous ballast, an unfortunate being like Mohammed, if his constitution were sensitive, must have experienced most painful emotions. . . . Mohammed felt his misery as a pain too great to be endured; in some way or other he must be delivered from it. He desired to be more than the greatest in his surroundings, and he knew that in that which they counted for happiness he could never even equal them. Rather than envy them regretfully, he preferred to despise their values of life, but on that very account he had to oppose these values with better ones."

23. Bell, *Origin of Islam*, 57.

24. Bell, *Origin of Islam*, 57. Bell is largely right in this assessment regarding the Qur'an's tendency to assume, rather than to argue for, the existence of only one God. There are some exceptional verses, however, that offer arguments for the logical problems with polytheism. See Q 21:22, 23:91.

25. Lammens, "Chrétiens à la Mecque," 196.

26. "[Muhammad] must, I think, have adopted [*ḥanīf*] because he found it in use, applied to a class of men who, turning away from idolatry, cherished some such idea of what the true religion was." Bell, *Origin of Islam,* 59.

27. Bell, *Origin of Islam,* 1.

28. None other than Theodor Nöldeke (also a Protestant) inclined to this view as well: "What Muḥammad knew of Christianity he had partly from his own experience in Syria, whose language was foreign to him, partly from the needy recollections of such people as those discussed above, and finally partly through Jewish mediation. The latter may have taught him the idea of the three Christian gods and the goddess Mary, which, by the way, can easily be explained in terms of the religious condition of the oriental Christians at that time." T. Nöldeke, "Hatte Muhammad christliche Lehrer," *Zeitschrift der deutschen morgenländischen Gesellschaft* 12 (1858): 699–708, 707. One wonders how Bell and Nöldeke would square this with the continued waves of conversion to Christianity in other areas within and bordering the Byzantine Empire in late antiquity (including, as we will see, among Arabic speakers). For a similar and more recent (also Protestant) perspective on the state of Christianity in pre-Islamic Arabia, see Trimingham, *Christianity Among the Arabs.*

29. Bell, *Origin of Islam,* 2.

30. Bell, *Origin of Islam,* 59.

31. See the long account in the *Panarion* (sect 19) of Epiphanius (d. 403), 48–51.

32. Bell, *Origin of Islam,* 61.

33. Sprenger (*Leben und die Lehre,* 93–102) cautiously suggests that the qur'anic wisdom figure Luqmān (see Qur'an 31) might be connected to Elkesai. For a much later argument regarding the Elkesaites and the Qur'an, see Roncaglia, "Éléments Ébionites."

34. A. von Harnack, *Lehrbuch der Dogmengeschichte* (Tübingen: Siebeck, 1909–1920), 2:537. Other advocates for the Jewish Christian origins of Islam include Rudolph, *Die Abhängigkeit;* Schoeps, *Theologie und Geschichte,* see 334–43; Yūsuf Durra al-Ḥaddād, *Al-Qur'ān da'wa naṣrāniyya* (Jounieh: Librairie pauliste, 1969), and *Al-Injīl fī-l-Qur'ān* (Jounieh: Librairie pauliste, 1982); more recently, see de Blois, "*Naṣrānī* and *Ḥanīf*"; Gallez, *Messie et son prophète;* Gnilka, *Nazarener und der Koran;* Youssef, *Moine de Mahomet.*

35. Tor Andræ (*Origines de l'islam*) was skeptical of this idea. A 2018 work is dedicated to the discussion of the idea of Jewish Christian influence on Islam's origins (del Río Sánchez, ed., *Jewish Christianity*). Sidney Griffith (*Bible in Arabic,* 13) expresses the reservation of many contemporary scholars regarding Jewish Christianity when he writes: "There is no indisputable documentary evidence for the presence of any notable Jewish Christian group thriving in Arabia in this period. Modern scholars who have postulated such a presence have done so, we shall argue, on the basis of extrapolations from their theological interpretations of certain passages in the Arabic Qur'ān."

36. Among the resolutions of the Lucknow conference (Wherry, ed., *Lucknow,* 37) was the following: "URGENCY OF THE MUHAMMADAN PROBLEM: That this

conference, in view of the steady advance of Islam, not only among various animistic tribes and other peoples, but also to some extent among historic Christian Churches and recently Christianized pagans, expresses the conviction that it is absolutely necessary that Christendom at large, and more especially the missionary boards and committees of the churches, which we represent, should forthwith take practical measures for a more comprehensive and systematic prosecution of the work among Muslims."

37. Speer, "Attitude of the Evangelist," 233. A still more dramatic manifestation of this disposition is found in a comment by the Protestant translator (identified only as E.T.) of the German Jewish scholar Gustav Weil's work on the Bible and the Qur'an (Weil, *Bible, Koran, Talmud,* 250). He writes, regarding the church of Muhammad's day: "Many heresies respecting the Trinity and the Savior, the worship of saints and images, errors on the future state of the soul, etc., had so completely overrun the nominal church of that country, that it is difficult to say whether one particle of truth was left in it. More especially the worship of Mary as the mother of God, whom the Marianites considered as a divinity, and to whom the Collyridians even offered a stated sacrifice, was in general practice round Mohammed; and it is as curious as it is sad to observe how this idolatry affected him."

38. See, for example, Parrinder, *Jesus in the Qur'an,* 134–37. Just before the section on Q 5:116 Parrinder comments: "It has often been thought that the Qur'ān denies the Christian teaching of the Trinity, and commentators have taken its words to be a rejection of orthodox Christian doctrine. However, it seems more likely that it is heretical doctrines that are denied in the Qur'ān" (133). Note the more dramatic statement of the (Protestant) Christian apologist Samuel Zwemer (*Cradle of Islam,* 306–7): "Not only was religious life at a low level in all parts of Christendom but heresies were continually springing up to disturb the peace or to introduce gigantic errors. Arabia was at one time called 'the mother of heresies.' The most flagrant example was that of the Collyridians, in the fourth century, which consisted in a heathenish distortion of mariolatry. Cakes were offered to the Holy Virgin, as in heathen times to Ceres."

39. For more, see *QB,* 121–22 (on bringing a clay bird to life), 476–78 (on speaking in the cradle).

40. On this idea, see Bell, *Origin of Islam,* 154. The idea of docetic influence is also entertained by Parrinder (*Jesus in the Qur'an,* 110–12). Cragg (*Jesus and the Muslim,* 173–74) mentions the idea but is cautious.

41. Gibb, "Pre-Islamic Monotheism," 270–71. However, note that even the Catholic (priest) Lammens ("Chrétiens à la Mecque," 223) writes: "Ne l'oublions pas, les communautés chrétiennes dans l'Arabie anarchique, ennemie de la contrainte, se répartissaient entre les diverses fractions hétérodoxes du christianisme oriental; elles se trouvaient fatalement soustraites, en vertu de leur situation excentrique, à l'opportune surveillance d'une hiérarchie ecclésiastique organisée."

42. Reynolds, "On the Presentation of Christianity," 42–54.

43. This saying is quoted several times, but without attribution, in Shahîd, *Byzantium and the Arabs,* 28, 201, 278, 563. One might also note the use of this phrase by Zwemer in the quotation above at note 38. It is also alluded to by Bell (*Origin of Islam,*

20), who writes: "Arabia (by which probably is meant the Roman province of Arabia, not the land of the nomads) had a reputation in the early Church as a source of heresies. That is perhaps not to be wondered at if we remember that in these regions the Greek and the Semitic mind were in contact, and in a manner in conflict. For the Semitic elements of the Church all along had difficulty in following the subtleties of the Greek intellect." One of the anonymous reviewers of the present book pointed out to me that the expression ("Arabia haeresium ferax") appears already in the 1651 work *Historia Orientalis* of the Protestant scholar Heinrich Hottinger. On Hottinger, see J. Loop, *Johann Heinrich Hottinger: Arabic and Islamic Studies in the Seventeenth Century* (Oxford: Oxford University Press, 2013).

44. From Greek *kolluris,* meaning a circular loaf of bread. Bell (*Origin of Islam,* 20) writes the following: "Our information about [the Collyridians] is very meagre, if indeed what we have is not due to Ephiphanius' imagination."

45. On the anticlerical motif in the Qur'an, see El-Badawi, *Qur'an and the Aramaic Gospel Traditions,* 114–43.

46. Bell, *Origin of Islam,* 4.

47. Bell, *Origin of Islam,* "tradition and fanaticism," 4; "self-proud prelates," 5; "shuttlecock," 5–6.

48. Bell, *Origin of Islam,* 13.

49. Bell, *Origin of Islam,* 68–69.

50. Bell (*Origin of Islam,* 69) writes, "As regards Christianity, his own direct knowledge of it was to begin with, I believe, just such knowledge as we might expect in a caravan trader who had been to Syria and seen Christian churches, and perhaps Christian services."

51. Al-Azmeh, *Emergence of Islam,* 2.

52. Al-Azmeh, *Emergence of Islam,* 39.

53. Al-Azmeh, *Emergence of Islam,* 40.

54. For a classic articulation of this idea, see Watt, "Qur'ān and Belief"; before this Watt wrote "Belief in a 'High God.'"

55. "It may or may not have been the case that the Arabs of the Ḥijāz, and reputedly elsewhere, would appeal to a certain Allāh in situations of special distress. One would interpret this, if true, in line with the aggregative nature of pagan divinities implied in syncretism, as the appeal to multiple deities in case of need, and to a vaguer being [Allāh] for good measure and added value." Al-Azmeh, *Emergence of Islam,* 302. Here Al-Azmeh's perspective has some commonality with that of Marshall Hodgson (*Venture,* 155), who wrote: "Back of these active divinities was a vaguer figure, Allāh, 'the god' par excellence, regarded as a creator god and perhaps as guarantor of rights and agreements which crossed tribal lines. But, as with many 'high gods,' he had no special cult." See this quotation also in Hawting, *Idea of Idolatry,* 31. It is true, as we will see in Chapter 3, that the divine name *allāh* appears relatively infrequently in pre-Islamic Arabian inscriptions.

56. Al-Azmeh, *Emergence of Islam,* 295. Earlier Al-Azmeh (ibid., 282) writes the following about the accomplishment of Muhammad in elevating Allah: "Ultimately,

this development involved the promotion, by a political and social process, of one divinity to a position of exclusive dominance in the mundane and the divine realms, and to a position of transcendence and primacy that precludes reciprocity. This was accomplished ultimately by replacing the horizontal transference of names, functions, attributes and locations between gods, familiar in syncretism, with a vertical transference of epithets, location and capacities, concentrated in the indivisible divine remit enjoyed by Allāh and his Meccan, later his cosmic, abode."

57. While Al-Azmeh of course recognizes that the Qur'an uses the word *ilāh* to refer to a "god" in a general sense, and its plural *āliha* to refer to false gods, he does not think that Allah was a title created by combining the Arabic article *al* and the word *ilāh*. This he refers to as "the retrospective morphological craft of grammarians" (*Emergence of Islam,* 286).

58. Al-Azmeh, *Emergence of Islam,* 284. Al-Azmeh (ibid., 244) speculates that *rabb* could also have been associated with Muhammad: "It is not entirely inconceivable that the term *rabb* may have referred, in the form of *Rabb al-Ka'ba,* to Muhammad."

59. Al-Azmeh, *Emergence of Islam,* 286.

60. Al-Azmeh (*Emergence of Islam,* 287–93) quite carefully discusses a wide range of Safaitic (and South Arabian) inscriptions and considers their possible relationship (which, for him, is in fact nothing of substance) with Allah.

61. Robin ("*Al-'Ilāh* et *Allāh,*" 93) concludes his study with the observation, "Allāh a d'abord été le nom du Dieu des Arabes chrétiens avant d'être celui de l'islam."

62. Al-Azmeh, *Emergence of Islam,* 350–51. He continues (ibid., 351): "Biblical narratives in the Qur'ān have little formal self-sufficiency, deploying motifs rather than themes, used as secondary narrative mythopoeia, in narratives continually intruded upon by a stylistically disruptive rhetoric subordinating Biblical themes to Qur'ānic motifs." Al-Azmeh (ibid., 397) notes in a footnote that the "only relative exception is the story of Joseph."

63. *QBS,* 87–96.

64. Durie, *Qur'an and Its Biblical Reflexes,* 118.

65. Durie, *Qur'an and Its Biblical Reflexes,* 256.

66. Al-Azmeh, *Emergence of Islam,* 349.

67. Al-Azmeh, *Emergence of Islam,* 350.

68. The earliest lives of Simeon (d. 459), including that of his contemporary Theodoret (d. 457), do not mention this. According to Theodoret (and the Syriac *Life of Simeon*) he was from Ṣīṣ in northern Syria and presumably a native Syriac speaker. See C. C. Torrey, "The Letters of Simeon the Stylite," *JAOS* 20 (1899): 253–76.

69. In fact John of Ephesus (d. 589) describes in his *Ecclesiastical History* how the non-Chalcedonian bishop of Antioch Paul the Black found refuge (possibly in 566) among the Jafnids, under the protection of al-Ḥārith, when he was threatened with dissent from those who supported Jacob Baradaeus (d. 578), who had previously consecrated Paul. He writes: "The course taken by the Arabs of the desert was the only one marked by any degree of moderation." See John of Edessa, *Ecclesiastical History,* trans. R. Payne Smitch (Oxford: Oxford University Press, 1860), 295.

70. Bell, *Origin of Islam,* 33.

71. On the story of the *wafd* (or "deputation") of Najran as a manner of explaining this qur'anic verse, see (for example) Ibn al-Jawzī, *Zād al-Masīr,* 1:399.

72. "That [Christianity] established itself far in the heart of the country we cannot say." Bell, *Origin of Islam,* 26.

73. "No doubt, too, as at the present day, camel riders and caravans continually visited centres of population." Bell, *Origin of Islam,* 42. On the next page (ibid., 43): "The Christian dealer, with his supplies of wine, penetrated far into Arabia."

74. Bell, *Origin of Islam,* 49–50. In fact, and as Sinai (*Rain-Giver*) has shown, Allah is indeed frequently mentioned in "pre-Islamic" poetry, unlike the pagan gods.

75. See also Cheiko, *al-Naṣrāniyya wa-adabuhā bayna ʿarab al-Jāhiliyya.* On the complicated legacy of Cheikho, see N. K. Schmid, "Louis Cheikho and the Christianization of Pre-Islamic and Early Islamic Ascetic Poetry," *Philological Encounters* 6 (2012): 339–73. Regarding "pre-Islamic" poetry, see also, and more recently, Hainthaler, "ʿAdī ibn Zayd al-ʿIbādī"; Horovitz, "ʿAdi ibn Zeyd"; Dmitriev, "Early Christian Arabic Account"; Sinai "Religious Poetry"; Sinai, *Rain-Giver.*

76. On this, see Margoliouth, "Origins of Arabic Poetry," 440–43. See the response by N. Miller, "Tribal Poetics in Early Arabic Culture: The Case of Ashʿār al-Hudhaliyyīn," PhD diss., University of Chicago, 2016.

77. Huart, "Une nouvelle source."

78. "He is rather uncritical," writes Bell (*Origin of Islam,* 50) of Cheikho. Those interested in a robust challenge to the skepticism of the previous paragraph in regard to pre-Islamic poetry might read Sinai, *Rain-Giver;* see esp. 22–26 where Sinai establishes certain criteria for distinguishing between authentic and inauthentic elements in the poetry. He (*Rain-Giver,* 26) also argues that the presentation of God/Allah among the poets essentially matches that attributed to the "associators" by the Qur'an: "Poetry supplies us with glimpses of an understanding of Allāh that generally matches or credibly complements that held by the quranic Associators, except for a limited number of aspects that will be duly pointed out." This, however, is perhaps what one would expect if the poetry reflects the vision of the "associators" held by the Muslim authors in whose works the *jāhilī* poetry is found.

79. For "in vogue," see Sinai, *Rain-Giver;* Lindstedt, *Muḥammad and His Followers,* 111–18; and now Miller, *Emergence of Arabic Poetry.*

80. Lammens, "Chrétiens à la Mecque," 225.

81. F.-C. Muth, "Reflections on the Relationship of Early Arabic Poetry and the Qur'ān: Meaning and Origin of the Qur'ānic Term *Ṭayran Abābīla* According to Early Arabic Poetry and Other Sources," in *Results of Contemporary Research on the Qur'ān: The Question of a Historio-Critical Text of the Qur'ān* (Würzburg: Ergon, 2007), 147–56.

82. T. Nöldeke, "Umaija b. AbiṣṢalt," *Zeitschrift für Assyriologie* 27 (1912): 159–72, 163.

83. And at which Lammens ("Chrétiens à la Mecque," 225) adds, "Allons-nous nous montrer plus crédule que Dhahabī?"

84. See my assessment in *QB,* 5–6. For a robust defense of the authenticity of pre-Islamic poetry with reference to the oral-formulaic theories of the anthropologists M. Parry and A. Lord, see Monroe, "Oral Composition." See also, more recently, Montgomery, "Empty Ḥijāz." It is interesting to note that the absence of references in this poetry to pagan gods and religious practices became something of a riddle to the early orientalists. As Hawting notes (*Idea of Idolatry,* 29), Theodor Nöldeke explained that the difficult life of a Bedouin impeded the rise of any true religious sentiment (although one might ask why other cultures in similar circumstances were religious). Others, notably J. W. Hirschberg, took this as a sign of the debased state of paganism right before the rise of Islam. See Nöldeke, "Arabs (Ancient)," 1:659b; Hirschberg, *Jüdische und christliche.* Hirschberg (ibid., 13) argues that the absence of real meaning in paganism made the conversion to Islam simply one of political calculation: "Besonders zur Zeit Mohammeds war das Heidentum derart jeden positiven Inhalts bar, dass der Übertritt der Araber zum Islam in erster Linie ein Akt politischer Berechnung war." He also argues (ibid., 12) that very little influence from Christianity or Judaism can be found in pre-Islamic poetry (without considering whether that poetry is authentic): "Wenn wir aber in der Poesie der Beduinen nach religiösen Meinungen und Anschauungen suchen, die von einer Beeinflussung seitens des Christentums oder Judentums zeugen würden, so werden wir in diesen Erwartungen arg enttäuscht."

85. "By the sixth century the pagan gods had completely disappeared from the inscriptions of North Arabia." Al-Jallad, "Pre-Islamic *Basmala,*" 17. As Al-Jallad ("Linguistic Landscape," 122) has observed, this development took place somewhat earlier in South Arabia: "By the fourth century CE, references to the pagan gods disappear almost entirely from the inscriptions, ushering in what scholars have termed the 'monotheistic period.'" For an example of a pre-Islamic Arabic-language Christian inscription from northwest Arabia, see Nehmé, "New Dated Inscriptions."

86. "The religion represented by the monks and hermits scattered along the trade-routes and in the fixed monastic centres could excite little more than a passing interest in the Arabs since it had no relationship to the family or clan life of either nomad, oasis-dweller, or townsman." Trimingham, *Christianity Among the Arabs,* 250.

87. Those readers curious about the considerable number of traditional Islamic reports of Christians in or around Mecca might consult Lammens, "Chrétiens à la Mecque."

88. One might compare also the summary assessment of Michael Lecker ("Muhammad," 159): "Muḥammad's tribe, Quraysh, lived in Mecca which for centuries had been a cultic center for Arabian polytheists before becoming the holy city of Islam. The Arab idol-worshippers were polytheists, but they also believed in a High God, Allāh, whose house was in the Ka'ba and who was supreme to the tribal deities. There was much diversity in the forms of Arabian idol worship, but on the whole it was a common characteristic of pre-Islamic society. In the centuries preceding the advent of Islam, Christianity and Judaism were struggling with each other in the Yemen to win over its people. Medina had a large and dominant Jewish population, while Yamama (near Riyadh) and

settlements in eastern Arabia and in the Gulf had a large Christian one. . . . On the whole, however, idol worship prevailed, with the prominent exception of the Yemen."

89. Bell, *Origin of Islam*, 57. The convictions of Bell (and indeed of Rodinson, Watt, and a number of other twentieth-century scholars) are well summed up by Hawting (*Idea of Idolatry*, 20): "Attention has focused on what might be called a strong element of monotheism in the predominantly pagan religion of the Arabs of central and western Arabia. However it has been accounted for, this has often been used in explanations of the appearance of Islam and of its success."

90. He is not alone in this. One might compare the comments of the Swedish Protestant scholar Tor Andræ (*Origines de l'islam*, 99), who combines social and psychological causes to explain Muhammad's zeal: "Certainement ce sont les circonstances de la Mekke, peut-être aussi les expériences d'une jeunesse sans joie, qui ont surtout engagé d'abord le Prophète à l'acceptation enthousiaste de tous ces points de vue et au mépris prétentieux de tout ce qu'il appelle 'le clinquant de la vie terrestre.'" "Clinquant ['flashiness'] de la vie terrestre" is an allusion to passages such as Q 6:130 that speak of the seduction of the "lower life."

91. See Hawting, *Idea of Idolatry*. An alternative to the "evolutionary" model for Arabian religious development is that entertained by Carl Brockelmann, in part (according to Hawting) under the influence of earlier scholars of comparative religion. Brockelmann ("Allah und die Götzen") held that even at a "primitive" stage the Arabs had a vague idea of a "high god" behind the active gods. However, this "high god"—sometimes labeled *deus otiosus* (lit. an "idle god")—was not the special object of worship or considered to be responsible for the daily welfare of humans.

92. "Consequently the idea was suggested that Arab religion was undergoing a fundamental evolution which might have been completed even without Muḥammad's intervention." Hawting, *Idea of Idolatry*, 26. As Hawting notes, some scholars imagined that foreign (by which he presumably means Jewish and Christian, and at any rate non-Arabian) influences had a factor in this progression, while others held that this progression was natural and "inevitable." The classical articulation of this idea, as explained by Hawting (ibid., 26), is the work of Wellhausen, *Reste arabischen Heidentums*, especially the section "Der Polytheismus und seine Auflösung" (215–24). There, Wellhausen speaks of the Arab religion as "syncretism," which, he holds, is "in truth the dissolution of polytheism" ("eine Auflösung des Polytheismus"). Wellhausen saw as a key element of this process the decline or decay of particular devotions among different ethnic groups (which he names "der Verfall des religiösen Ethnicismus") (217).

93. Hawting, *Idea of Idolatry*, 33.

94. Ibn Isḥāq, 821; trans. 552. Later on this same page a second report of Ibn Ishāq describes Muhammad's discovering a drawing in the Kaʿba of Abraham divining with pagan arrows (*azlām*), at which he exclaims, "May God fight them!"

95. "In the present work, I intend firstly to establish the semantic emptiness of the pre- and early Islamic Ḥijāz, a semiotic evacuation effected by the Qur'anic event, a religious, linguistic, cultural, social and spiritual eruption which led to the almost total obliteration of anything extra-Islamic (though not necessarily anything extra-

Qur'anic)—with one major and, I submit, profoundly significant exception: the *qaṣīda* poetry of the *Jāhilīya*." Montgomery, "Empty Ḥijāz," 42.

96. Montgomery, "Empty Ḥijāz," 43.

97. See also the references to Arabian deities in the context of Noah in Q 71:23.

98. See Lammens, "Qoran et tradition."

99. On the topic of Muhammad and eschatological reward and punishment, Bell (*Origin of Islam,* 90) writes: "It was different, I think, with the concrete conceptions of the Judgement Day, and of the Paradise and the Fire which lay beyond it. These were not in his mind to begin with, and it was after he had begun to deliver the Qur'ān that they wove themselves into the texture of his thought. They came to him from without, but none the less they made a tremendous impression upon him personally. The agitated, semi-poetical character of his early descriptions of the End of all things shows how the Prophet himself was moved."

100. In her 2008 book *The First Muslims* Asma Afsarrudin writes, "From all accounts, Muhammad was an unpretentious and self-effacing young man who was given to introspection and long periods of meditation before his call to prophethood" (1).

101. "The challenge of the Qur'ānic text to scholarship, therefore, is not to reduce it to a coherent whole through the vehicle of history, but to celebrate the ways in which the text disturbs the reader's sense of coherence. This is not a matter of opposing an assumed sense of textual coherence, as the goal of the scholarly endeavor, with a notion of incoherency, which seems to be the fear of those who see newer methods of approaching literature as destroying any standards for interpretation. . . . The works of Wansbrough and Arkoun have already been mentioned as forerunners of this tendency." Rippin, "Reading the Qur'an," 646–47.

102. Indeed, he explicitly denies seeking "to say anything about the actual religious situation" in seventh-century Arabia (Hawting, *Idea of Idolatry,* 20). It is on this point that the present book especially departs from Hawting. Like Hawting we call into question traditional ideas regarding nascent Islam's polemical world, but unlike Hawting we offer alternative ideas.

103. Hawting, *Idea of Idolatry,* 74, 85.

104. Hawting, *Idea of Idolatry,* 64.

105. Hawting, *Idea of Idolatry,* 47.

106. Wansbrough (*Qur'anic Studies,* 20) writes, "But taken together, the quantity of reference, the mechanically repetitious employment of rhetorical convention, and the stridently polemical style, all suggest a strongly sectarian atmosphere, in which a corpus of familiar scripture was being pressed into the service of as yet unfamiliar doctrine." Hawting's (*Idea of Idolatry,* 20) observation in his opening chapter regarding the tendencies of earlier scholarship on nascent Islam is worth quoting: "In general it will be argued that questionable theoretical presuppositions have been combined with a less than critical approach to the information provided by Muslim tradition to produce explanations of the origins of Islam in Arabia which have been remarkably tenacious, repeated in general works and textbooks as if established facts." One might say, to paraphrase Hawting, that the standard portrait of pre-Islamic Arabia was more imagined than reconstructed.

107. Kister, "'Labbayka." Hawting (*Idea of Idolatry,* 32) contrasts the perspectives of these scholars with that of traditional Islamic reports: "Where traditional scholarship saw Muḥammad as sent to restore what had once existed in Arabia [with Abraham and Ishmael], modern scholars have tended to portray him as a part of the evolutionary process."

108. "The traditional Muslim exegetes supplied interpretations of individual verses by telling us why they were revealed: the verses were referred to incidents in the life of the Prophet, to customs of the pre-Islamic Arabs, to accusations levelled at the Prophet by his opponents, etc. In this way difficult and often obscure koranic passages were provided with a meaning and, at the same time, the milieu in which the Koran was revealed was established and depicted." Hawting, *Idea of Idolatry,* 33.

109. Hawting, *Idea of Idolatry,* 22–23; Ibn Isḥāq, 53; trans. 36–37. In Wüstenfeld's edition of the *sīra* the name of the god is vocalized as 'Ammu Anas.

110. On this, see Reynolds, "'Killers of the Prophets.'" For further examples of this charge, see Q 2:61, 87; 3:21, 112, 183; 4:155; 5:70.

111. Ibn al-Jawzī, *Zād al-Masīr,* 1:514. He attributes this report to Ibn 'Abbās, adding that Mujāhid, 'Ikrima, al-Suddī, and Muqātil report something similar. Ibn al-Jawzī adds a second report, which attributes the saying generally to the Jews. Cf. the longer account related by al-Wāḥidī (d. 468 AH/1075 CE), *Asbāb al-Nuzūl,* 45. Wāḥidī relates a second, shorter story (on the authority of Mujāhid) that likewise makes Finḥāṣ culpable for the sacrilege.

112. Ibn al-Jawzī, *Zād al-Masīr,* 3:116; cf. al-Wāḥidī, *Asbāb al-Nuzūl,* 79.

113. See *QBS,* 19, n. 70. Al-Ṭabarī, *Jāmi' al-bayān fī ta'wīl al-Qur'ān,* 1:86–96.

114. On self-referentiality and the Qur'an, see Madigan, *Qur'an's Self-Image;* Wild, ed., *Self-Referentiality;* Boisliveau, *Coran par lui-même.* See also now Loynes, *Revelation in the Qur'an.*

115. Bell, *Origin of Islam,* 90. It is perhaps worth noting that *qeryānā* is not a standard manner of referring to the Bible in Syriac texts (which is rather *ktābē* or *seprē*). Instead it refers specifically to the book for public scriptural recitation in a liturgical setting. I am grateful to Jack Tannous for this point.

116. "Having started to produce these oracles or *qeryānē,* Muhammad devoted a great deal of pains to the composition of them." Bell, *Origin of Islam,* 96.

117. It is worth adding here that the equivalent word in Christian Palestinian Aramaic is *qeryan* or *qeryān.* See F. Schulthess, *Lexicon Syropalaestinum* (Berlin: Reimer, 1903), 183. Schulthess defines *qeryan* as "lectio."

118. See Sokoloff, *Syriac Lexicon,* 1409b.

119. Sokoloff, *Syriac Lexicon,* 1286b; Jeffery, *Foreign Vocabulary,* 198.

120. Payne Smith (3524) defines *qām b-ṣlōtā* as "he began to pray." Cf. also (Payne Smith, 3528) the expression *aqīmat anīn b-slōtā,* "She commanded them to stand in prayer." See R. Payne Smith, *Thesaurus Syriacus* (Oxford: E Typographeo Clarendoniano, 1879 [Tome 1]; 1901 [Tome 2]). By way of comparison the standard Biblical Hebrew root used for prayer is *p-l-l.* This point is made already by Brockelmann, "Iqāmat aṣ-ṣalat." I am grateful to Nicolai Sinai for this reference.

121. In the reading traditions of the Qur'an the *wāw* is considered only a *mater lectionis* for the sound *ā*, but this is possibly a later adjustment. C. Segovia (*CdH*, 2:68) writes, "Très tôt, les chercheurs contemporains, notamment Nöldeke (*Geschichte*, vol. 1, p. 255; *Neue Beiträge*, p. 29–30), Mingana ('Syriac Influence,' p. 86, 91), Jeffery (*Foreign Vocabulary*, p. 197–199), Spitaler (*Schreibung*, p. 217), Bell (*Origin*, p. 91) et Lüling (*Challenge*, p. 470–71) ont interprété le *ṣlwt* coranique, à cause de son orthographe, comme un emprunt au syriaque ou à l'araméen (d'après *ṣlwt-ṣlōtā*, 'prière')."

122. Lindstedt, *Muḥammad and His Followers*, 3.

123. "The tradition of prophecy associated with Muhammad is a specific one: he is portrayed as one of a series, in which his forerunners were mainly figures known in the Jewish and Christian scriptures. When he is referred to as a prophet, it is not meant merely that he had powers or gifts that were 'prophet-like,' but that he was the heir of a tradition of prophecy that was centuries old and was shared, mutatis mutandis, by Jews and Christians. Accordingly, terms used in connection with prophets in that tradition are attached to him, notably *nabī* (= Greek *prophetes*), the Arabic form of the common Semitic word for 'prophet,' and *rasūl* (= Greek *apostolos*, Hebrew *mal'akh*, *shalīaḥ*), 'messenger.'" Hawting, "Were There Prophets?," 186.

124. On this see D. E. Aune, *Prophecy in Early Christianity and the Ancient Mediterranean World* (Grand Rapids: Eerdmans, 1983); Cook, *On the Question*. Hawting ("Were There Prophets?," 188) writes that the view that prophecy had ceased at "some relatively remote time" was "a view accepted by the rabbis and by the Church." While this is certainly the case for Judaism, it was more complicated for Christians. The early church fathers certainly accepted that prophecy continued in the sense of the affirmations of the Gospel made by those inspired by the Holy Spirit, but they also held that there was no new public revelation to come after the apostolic age. This distinction is found, for example, in Irenaeus (d. 202), *Against Heresies* (*Ante-Nicene Fathers*, vol. 1, ed. A. Roberts, J. Donaldson, and A. Cleveland Coxe [Buffalo, NY: Christian Literature Publishing, 1885], III:1, IV:35). As Jack Tannous has pointed out to me, Ephrem (*Saint Ephrem's Commentary*, 58) names John the Baptist "the last of the prophets."

125. On this topic, see Hawting, "Were There Prophets?"

126. One might note that the term *ummī* in this respect overlaps with the term *ḥanīf*, discussed above, that is usually applied to Abraham. Abraham is celebrated for coming to belief in the one God naturally. In Q 6:75–79 we see him come to that belief through the observation of celestial objects, a passage we discuss in Chapter 2. At the end of that process of observation he declares, "I have turned my face to Him who originated the heavens and the earth, a man of pure faith [*ḥanīf*]; I am not of the idolaters" (Q 6:79). The point for Abraham is that he has come to faith without the benefit of earlier scriptures (since, as the Qur'an says [Q 3:65], the Torah and the Gospel were revealed after him). There is thus a similarity with the Qur'an's use of *ummiyyūn* for the Arabs, who have not had a scripture revealed to them. This point comes to greater clarity when it is shown (see Chapter 3) that the Bible had not been translated into Arabic before Islam. For an alternative opinion of *ummiyyūn*, one that possibly lies behind Arberry's translation of the term as "common folk," see Reissner, "Ummī Prophet." Reissner writes, "The

ummī prophet was to be the leader of the masses against privileged minorities of wealth and sophistication. His message addressed itself to *ummiyyūn* comprising as the case might be, Arabs and Non-Arabs, monotheists and heathens, literates and illiterates, nomads and oasis dwellers" (ibid., 278). For a more recent study of this question, which engages with the apologetic view of *ummī,* see Günther, "Illiterate Prophet." See also Sinai's discussion of *ummī* (which he translates as "unscriptured") in *Key Terms,* 94–99.

127. Droge (*The Qur'an,* 102, n. 152) continues: "Ar. *ummī* means something like 'gentile' in the sense of those who do not have a written scripture and thus refers to the gentile Arabs. . . . That is, instead of sending the Arabs a missionary from the Jews or Christians ('those who already had a Book'), God chose to send them a prophet from among themselves."

128. Bell (*Origin of Islam,* 96) seems to have grasped this when he writes: "To him the knowledge of the revealed secrets was just as real as the knowledge of Nature which was already open to those who had eyes to see. To put that knowledge in Arabic form for those who, strangely, had not before received it, was probably what he conceived his function to be."

129. The classic critiques of their authenticity are those of Margoliouth, "Origins of Arabic Poetry," and Ṭāhā Ḥusayn, *Fī al-shi'r al-jāhilī* (Cairo: Dār al-Nahr, 1995; originally published in 1926). For more recent attempts at identifying authentic elements in the poetry, see Dmitriev, "Early Christian Arabic Account," regarding ʿAdī; and Sinai, "Religious Poetry," regarding Umayya (d. early seventh century), generally understood to be neither a Christian nor a Jew; see also Sinai, *Rain-Giver,* 19–26.

130. Tannous ("Arabic as Christian Language," 15–16) writes: "One way pre-Islamic Syriac authors referred to Arabs was to call them *Ṭayyāyē,* and BL Add. 12, 155 contains a Syriac treatise written by a certain Sergius, from the 'Monastery of the Ṭayyāyē,' perhaps in the late sixth century. Apart from this, we have several sixth-century Syriac references to a Monastery of the Ṭayyāyē, and John of Ephesus (d. 589) refers at one point to two 'Ṭayyāyē monks.'"

131. Tannous, "Arabic as Christian Language," 14.

132. On Arab conversion to Christianity before Islam, see also Fisher and Wood, "Arabs and Christianity," 307–8, and the response by El-Badawi (with reference to the Tanukhid ruler Mavia), *Queens and Prophets,* 167.

133. This situation can be recognized from what we know of the Jafnids. While the most common spoken language in their territories was certainly Arabic, Jafnid correspondence was often carried out through Syriac letters. See van Roey and Allen, *Monophysite Texts.* I am grateful to David Bertaina for this point and the above reference.

134. Tannous, "Arabic as Christian Language," 45.

135. Arberry's translation correctly (in my opinion) renders *'ālamīn* as "beings" and not as "worlds."

136. My critical comments on Bell here are completely in debt to the insights of Andrew Rippin, "Reading the Qur'ān."

137. Quoted by W. Montgomery Watt and Richard Bell, *Introduction to the Qur'an,* 2nd ed. (Edinburgh: Edinburgh University Press, 1977; 1st ed. 1970), 175. The

original 1856 Latin work was titled *De origine et compositione Surarum Qoranicarum ipsiusque Qorani*. See Nöldeke, *Geschichte des Qorāns*.

138. See Gabriel Said Reynolds, "The Qur'ānic Doublets: A Preliminary Inquiry," *JIQSA* 5 (2020): 5–39; Reynolds, "Intratextuality," 513–42; and perhaps most important, Reynolds, "Their Very Words?"

139. Nicolai Sinai, *Fortschreibung und Auslegung: Studien zur Frühen Koraninterpretation* (Wiesbaden: Harrassowitz, 2009); Sinai, "The Unknown Known: Some Groundwork for Interpreting the Medinan Qur'an," in *Mélanges de l'Université Saint-Joseph* 66 (2015–2016): 47–96; Sinai, "Processes of Literary Growth and Editorial Expansion in Two Medinan Surahs," in Carol Bakhos and Michael Cook, eds., *Islam and Its Past: Jāhiliyya, Late Antiquity, and the Qur'an* (Oxford: Oxford University Press, 2017), 106–22; Sinai, *The Qur'an*.

140. It is important to note here as well the substantial (statistical) case that Andrew Bannister makes for an oral model of the Qur'an's formation in his book *An Oral-Formulaic Study of the Qur'an*. See my assessment of that model in light of the presence of "doublets" in the Qur'an in Reynolds, "Intratextuality," 530–35.

141. The classical work on this idea is Goldziher, "Die Ginnen."

142. Jones, "Oral and the Written," 58.

143. Jones, "Oral and the Written," 64.

144. R. Fortna, "Redaction Criticism," in Keith Crim, ed., *Interpreter's Dictionary of the Bible Supplement* (Nashville: Abingdon, 1962), 733–735, at 733.

145. As does Bell (*Origin of Islam*, 102) when he speculates on the origin of the qur'anic punishment stories: "It is natural to suppose that on some caravan journey to Syria the vestiges of a vanished civilization which still remain at Meda'in Salih, and perhaps even those at Petra, had been seen by Muhammad, and that he had brooded over the meaning of them."

TWO Christian Material in the Qur'an

1. This passage might be compared with Q 7:157, which insists that the qur'anic prophet is mentioned in both the Torah and the Gospel. See further the discussion below.

2. On this, see, for example, Baumstark, "Eine altarabische Evangelienübersetzung"; A. Guillaume, "The Version of the Gospels Used in Medina Circa 700 A.D.," *Al-Andalus* 15 (1950): 289–96; Griffith, "Arguing from Scripture," 36–45; and most recently Anthony, "Muḥammad."

3. See my discussion in *QB*, 826, and Anthony, "Muḥammad," 273–76, in which Anthony argues for a reading of *aḥmad* as an elative adjective, thus suggesting the translation "his name is most praised" (276).

4. Arabic *iṣr* seems to mean more literally "rope," but its use in the Qur'an may reflect the biblical sense of "load," such as Greek *zugos* (Syriac *nīrā*) in Matt 11:30.

5. There are a variety of interpretations of this verse and its grammar (e.g., whether the first word should be read *lama, limā*, or *lamma*). One interpretation of its

meaning is that each prophet, in his lifetime, is asked whether he would accept the prophet to follow him, or, alternatively, Muhammad. Still, it seems to me more likely (note that the Qur'an has God address all of the prophets and all of the prophets respond collectively) that the Qur'an imagines the prophets speaking in a primordial moment (as with Q 7:172) or during the "interval" (see Q 5:19) between Jesus and Muhammad, that is, either before the births or after the deaths of earlier prophets. See Ibn al-Jawzī, *Zād al-Masīr,* 1:414–16.

6. The term *ummī* as used for the Prophet identifies him as one who is not part of *ahl al-kitāb* ("People of the Book"), those (both Jews and Christians) upon whom an earlier scripture was bestowed. The plural *ummiyyūn* accordingly represents in the Qur'an those who are "unscriptured." In Islamic tradition *ummī* is often understood to mean illiterate, but this understanding is likely an apologetic construction meant to enable an argument that Muhammad could not have learned about salvation history by reading books. On this question (and, more or less, this perspective) see Sinai, *Key Terms,* 94–99. Sinai does not like the translation "gentile" for *ummī,* in part because "gentile" might refer to any non-Jew (including a Christian).

7. Thus, even if Q 7:157 does not appeal to Jews and Christians in a second-person address (as do passages such as Q 3:64 and 4:171), it implies that there were Christians and Jews around who are being directly invoked by the Qur'an.

8. Lane (*Arabic-English Lexicon,* 2278b) writes for *ghull* (sing. of *aghlāl*), "A ring, or collar, of iron, which is put upon the neck." Cf. Ambros and Procházka, *Concise Dictionary,* 203.

9. In several places (other than Q 7:157) the Qur'an insists that it reduces the burden imposed by Jewish law. Cf. Q 4:160 and 6:146, two verses which declare that God imposed particularly harsh laws on the Jews because of their disobedience (on this, cf. Gal 3:19, as suggested by an anonymous reviewer of the present book).

10. Ibn al-Jawzī (*Zād al-Masīr,* 2:463) reports that there are two opinions regarding the "time" (*zaman*) of this statement in Q 5:116: first, that it will take place on the Day of Resurrection (Ibn ʿAbbās, Qatāda, Ibn Jurayj), and second, that it took place immediately after God raised Jesus to heaven (see Q 4:158; Suddī). He adds that the first is "more correct" (*aṣaḥḥ*).

11. Reynolds, "Biblical Turns of Phrase."

12. On this matter, see Obermann, "Koran and Agada"; and Witztum, "Syriac Milieu," 22–23.

13. Key here is 2 Cor 3:15, which speaks of "a veil . . . over their [the Jews'] minds" during the reading of the Torah. As Jack Tannous has suggested to me, of particular importance might be Jacob of Serugh's *Homily on the Veil on Moses' Face,* much of which is taken up with alternating affirmations of the Christological meaning of Old Testament passages and reprimands of the Jews for missing this. For example: "Their heart is darkened, being covered by the veil [*taḥfītā;* cf. 2 Cor 3:15, Peshitta], and they grope after the symbols and their explanations as if it was night; because their heart is not illumined by the Sun of righteousness, they do not understand how to read the prophets with clarity." See Jacob of Serugh, *Homily,* 54.

14. See Reynolds, "Biblical Turns of Phrase," 53.

15. See Ibn al-Jawzī, *Zād al-Masīr,* 1:113. Ibn al-Jawzī notes that some commentators read *ghuluf,* a plural noun meaning "containers," for *ghulf,* an adjective meaning "covered." Those who read *ghuluf* understand the sentence to mean "our hearts are containers of knowledge" and consequently "we have no need of your teaching." Thus Abdullah Yusuf Ali (*Holy Quran*) translates, "Our hearts are the wrappings (which preserve God's Word; We need no more)." See also the discussion in *QBS,* 149–51. The biblical subtext here and the prominent place of the metaphor of "circumcision [or uncircumcision] of the heart" makes the reading of *ghulf* more attractive.

16. As Witztum ("Syriac Milieu," 35–36) has pointed out, the expression "mustard seed" is also found in rabbinic sources, namely Mishnah Nazir 1.5 and Mishnah Nidda 5.2. However, in Mishnah Nazir the reference is to mustard seeds in the plural ("We regard the basket as though it were full of mustard seed, and he becomes a Nazirite for the whole of his life"). *Soncino Talmud, Seder Nashim* (London: Soncino, 1936), 3:23. The parallel in Mishnah Nidda is to a single seed: "and the discharges convey uncleanness, however small the quantity, even if it is only of the size of a mustard seed or less." *Soncino Talmud, Seder Ṭohoroth,* 276. Although it is true (as Witztum points out) that these references show that "mustard seed" seems to have been a common expression in Semitic languages to refer to something small, it is also arguably the case that the New Testament references (which deal with God in one way or another) are much closer to those of the Qur'an (which also deal with God) than are those in the Mishnah (which deal with two different ritual questions).

17. Cf. also the use in the Qur'an of *ba'ūḍa,* "gnat" (Q 2:26), for a very small thing. However, the point in Q 2:26 is the range of things with which God might coin a parable.

18. "One hundred" is used in a symbolic sense in Q 2:259, 261; 8:65, 66; "one thousand" is used in symbolic sense in Q 2:96; 8:9, 65; 22:47; 29:14; 32:5; 97:3.

19. See A.-L. de Prémare, "'Comme il est écrit': l'histoire d'un texte," *Studia Islamica* 70 (1989): 27–56; Clivaz and Schulthess, "Source and Rewriting"; and more recently Lange, "'What No Eye Has Seen.'" The connection of Q 32:17 to 1 Cor 2:9 is mentioned by Jan Van Reeth in *CdH,* 2:1115. Van Reeth refers to C. Gilliot, "Une reconstruction critique du Coran," in *Results of Contemporary Research on the Qur'an,* ed. M. Kropp (Beirut: Ergon, 2007), 33–137, at 78. In the verse of 1 Corinthians Paul is quoting an earlier text ("as it is written"), possibly Isa 64:4, "From of old no one has heard / or perceived by the ear, / no eye has seen a God besides thee, / who works for those who wait for him." For further discussion of the source of Paul's statement, see J.-M. Sévrin, "'Ce que l'oeil n'a pas vu . . .': 1 Co 2:9 comme parole de Jésus," in *Lectures et relectures de la Bible: Festschrift P.-M. Bogaert,* ed. J.-M. Auwers and A. Wénin (Leuven: Leuven University Press, 1999), 307–24. For the hadith *qudsī,* see Bukhārī, *Ṣaḥīḥ,* K. al-Tawḥīd, #7498.

20. Jeffery, *Foreign Vocabulary,* 71–72; Ambros and Procházka, *Concise Dictionary,* 314.

21. Jeffery, *Foreign Vocabulary,* 115–16; Ambros and Procházka, *Concise Dictionary,* 308.

22. A motif that seems to match more the militant context of Muhammad's Medinan period than the context of Jesus the itinerant Palestinian preacher in the Gospels; Jeffery, *Foreign Vocabulary*, 255–56; Ambros and Procházka, *Concise Dictionary*, 261.

23. On this question, see Griffith, *Bible in Arabic*. Griffith reviews the relevant earlier literature in chap. 1 (esp. 41ff.). Note also the work of Kashouh, *Arabic Versions*. Griffith (ibid., 52) argues regarding the absence of an Arabic Bible in Muhammad's Arabia: "Perhaps the best evidence in support of this hypothesis is the Arabic Quran itself, in which, as we shall see in the next chapter, detailed knowledge of biblical and ecclesiastical narratives is evident, along with an almost complete lack of textual detail in the form of direct quotations or even substantial retellings of the biblical stories; the focus being instead on the patriarchal and prophetic *dramatis personae*." As Norman Stillman notes, the Jews of Arabia from Muhammad's time left behind no literature. See N. Stillman, "The Judeo-Arabic Heritage," in Z. Zohar, ed., *Sephardic and Mizrahi Jewry* (New York: New York University Press, 2005), 40–54, at 42–43. Griffith (*Bible in Arabic*, 53) writes: "It may well have been the case that the appearance of the collected, written Quran in the second half of the seventh century provided the impetus for the first written translations of the Bible into Arabic." In addition, see Witztum, "Ibn Isḥāq and the Pentateuch." Witztum argues, on the basis of citations from Abū Jaʿfar al-Ṭabarī, that Ibn Isḥāq had access to an Arabic translation of the Peshitta in the second (AH)/eighth (CE) century. See also Ronny Vollandt, *Arabic Versions of the Pentateuch* (Leiden: Brill, 2015), esp. chap. 3.

24. "Therefore We prescribed for the Children of Israel that whoso slays a soul not to retaliate for a soul slain, nor for corruption done in the land, shall be as if he had slain mankind altogether; and whoso gives life to a soul, shall be as if he had given life to mankind altogether." Cf. m. Sanhedrin 4:5: "For this reason man was created one and alone in the world: to teach that whosoever destroys a single soul is regarded as though he destroyed a complete world, and whosoever saves a single soul is regarded as though he saved a complete world."

25. I encourage readers to consult my book *The Qur'an and the Bible* for a more comprehensive discussion of Christian material in the Qur'an.

26. On the Qur'an's engagement with legal material in the Hebrew Bible, see now Zellentin, *Law Beyond Israel*. On the Qur'an and poetry, see Hoffman, *Poetic Qur'ān*, and esp. Kermani, *God Is Beautiful*, chap. 2.

27. Acts does of course largely consist of stories. The absence of references to Acts in the Qur'an is better explained by the qur'anic rejection of Christian ecclesiology.

28. One might compare the Qur'an's interest in stories with the study of storytelling in the Hebrew Bible by Licht, *Storytelling in the Bible*. Note also the study on storytelling in early Christianity and Islam by R. Durmaz, *Stories Between Christianity and Islam* (Berkeley: University of California Press, 2022), esp. chap. 3.

29. This material has been a favorite topic of Western scholarship on the Qur'an, so it is difficult to offer a comprehensive bibliography of it. However, see, for example, E. Beck, "Iblis und Mensch, Satan und Adam: Der Werdegang einer koranischen Erzählung," *Le Muséon* 89 (1976): 195–244; A. Neuwirth, "Negotiating Justice: A Pre-

Canonical Reading of the Qur'anic Creation Accounts (Part I)," *JQS* 2, no. 1 (2000): 1–18; Neuwirth, "Negotiating Justice (Part II): A Pre-Canonical Reading of the Qur'anic Creation Accounts," *JQS* 2, no. 2 (2000): 1–28; Neuwirth, "Qur'ān, Crisis, and Memory: The Qur'ānic Path Towards Canonization as Reflected in the Anthropogonic Accounts," in *Crisis and Memory in Islamic Societies*, ed. A. Neuwirth and A. Pflitsch (Beirut: Ergon, 2001), 113–52; *QBS*, 39–63; N. Sinai, *Fortschreibung und Auslegung: Studien zur frühen Koraninterpretation* (Wiesbaden: Harrassowitz, 2009), 86–96; W. Bodman, *The Poetics of Iblīs: Narrative Theology in the Qur'an* (Cambridge, MA: Harvard University Press, 2011); Pohlmann, *Die Entstehung des Korans*, 81–146; Joseph Witztum, "Variant Traditions, Relative Chronology, and the Study of Intra-Quranic Parallels," in *Islamic Cultures, Islamic Contexts, Essays in Honor of Professor Patricia Crone*, ed. B. Sadeghi, A. Ahmed, R. Hoyland, and A. Silverstein (Leiden: Brill, 2014), 1–50. See also the corresponding passages in Reynolds, *QB* and *CdH*.

30. Pohlmann, *Entstehung*, 114.

31. As Witztum ("Variant Traditions," 24–28) shows, Beck makes the version of Qur'an 20 later than the version of Qur'an 7, whereas Neuwirth sees things the other way around. Witztum agrees with Beck, although with a new argument (namely that the word *mulk* in Q 20:120 is a play on *malakayni* in Q 7:20). Witztum holds that the version in Qur'an 2 is later still than the version in Qur'an 20.

32. The other occurrences are Q 9:114 (Abraham's father), Q 20:39 (Pharaoh), Q 26:77 (pagan gods), Q 28:19 (Moses and man quarrelling), and Q 43:67 (the condemned on the Day of Judgment).

33. As Nicolai Sinai (*Key Terms*, 7–8) points out, there are some pre-Islamic Arabian inscriptions which suggest that this use of the root *kh-l-f* was current in the Qur'an's context. He refers to the work of Ruben Schenzle, who notes that in a 548 CE inscription the South Arabian king Abraha (Abraham) uses the corresponding Sabaic word for *khalīfa*, and a verb related to Arabic *istakhlafa*, with the meaning of "viceroy" (or, in the case of the verb, "to appoint a viceroy"). See Schenzle, "If God Is King," 141–42. On this, see now Hussain, "Adam and the Names."

34. On this, note the argument of Rahman (*Major Themes*, 18) that the devil in the Qur'an is more an "anti-man force" than an "anti-God principle."

35. It seems to me that the correspondence between God's description of man in the Talmud as made "in our image" and God's description of man in the Qur'an as a *khalīfa* further helps clarify the meaning of this latter term. The Qur'an (which says regarding God, "like Him there is naught") does not follow the Bible (Gen 1:26) in speaking of humanity created "in the image of God" (although it is found in a well-known hadith; see Melchert, "'God Created Adam'"). It seems to me that the Qur'an is reshaping the idea of *imago Dei* by speaking of Adam as a "viceroy" (*khalīfa*) in Q 2:30. The subsequent prostration of the angels shows that this description still points to a divine dignity in Adam, although the Qur'an assiduously avoids the language of divine "image."

36. See *QB*, 35–36.

37. For the range of Christian accounts, see Minov, "Satan's Refusal," and now Minov, *Memory and Identity*.

38. See *QB*, 51–52. For the original Syriac text and French translation see, *Caverne des tresors* (fourth to early seventh centuries CE) = CSCO 486 (Syriac text) and 487 (French trans.), ed. and trans. S.-M. Ri (Louvain: Peeters, 1987), chap. 3:1–2.

39. See Anderson and Stone, *Synopsis*. For an analysis of this account and its relation to other similar Jewish and Christian accounts, see Minov, "Satan's Refusal," esp. 231–33.

40. This is the translation of the Armenian version found in Anderson and Stone, *Synopsis*.

41. Anderson, *Genesis of Perfection*, 27.

42. "Ambush" in Q 7:16 is literally "sit for them in your straight path." Cf. Q 9:5 where God instructs the believers to do the same to the unbelievers.

43. One might note that the Qur'an consistently uses the term Iblīs for the devil in the scenes involving the command to prostrate before Adam, and Satan (*shayṭān*) in the scenes involving the temptation of Adam and his wife in the garden.

44. Anderson, *Genesis of Perfection*, 32. For the passage from Genesis Rabbah, see *QB*, 251.

45. *Cave of Treasures* [Oc.], 2:12–13, 2:22–25. See *QB*, 252.

46. I have disputed the traditional notion that the Qur'an denies the death of Christ. See Reynolds, "Muslim Jesus." Nevertheless, at the very least one can affirm that the Qur'an (in Q 4:157 and elsewhere) shows no interest in any idea of the salvific meaning of the crucifixion.

47. On this, see Baynes, "*Enoch* and *Jubilees*."

48. On this, see W. Adler, "Jewish Pseudepigrapha in Jacob of Edessa's Letters and Historical Writings," in B. T. Haar Romeny, ed., *Jacob of Edessa and the Syriac Culture of His Day* (Leiden: Brill, 2008), 49–65. Note Adler's comment: "Although *Jubilees* was barely known to Christian authors of the first three centuries, quotations and traditions originating in that work turn up later in a wide array of sources" (55).

49. On the qur'anic phrase (e.g., Q 1:4) "Day of Judgment" (Arabic *yawm al-dīn*), compare the Syriac (Peshitta) of Matt 10:15 (and 12:36): "It shall be more tolerable on the day of judgment [*yawmā d-dīnā*]."

50. I am indebted to Jon Levenson for this idea. See Levenson, *Inheriting Abraham*, 136.

51. Levenson, *Inheriting Abraham*, 137.

52. See Kulik, *Retroverting*, esp. 1–7. In his study Kulik analyzes the Slavonic in order to discern ("retrovert") the wording of the earlier Greek, and when possible Semitic (Hebrew or Aramaic), texts. On this basis he offers a new translation of the text. Quotations below are from Kulik's translation.

53. Levenson (*Inheriting Abraham*, 137–38) insightfully depicts this scene as a revelation "crowning" Abraham's earlier rational search for the true God: "Abraham begins in philosophy, as it were, reasoning logically to the insight that his father's idols cannot be God. But then revelation crowns philosophy, as the true God whom he has been approaching intellectually reveals himself to him personally. Young Abraham's search

points him towards God, and God rewards him with a personal relationship and with deliverance from the idolatry he saw through."

54. Another important difference, which I have generally ignored here, is the name given to Abraham's father. In *Jubilees* and the *Apocalypse* he is named (following Genesis) Terah, but in the Qur'an (Q 6:74) he is named Āzar. All sorts of theories have been offered by Western scholars to explain the anomalous (historically speaking) name Āzar, some of which involve attempts to see it as a corruption of Hebrew *teraḥ* (*therra* in the Septuagint), through some sort of metathesis. Jeffery (*Foreign Vocabulary*, 53–55) argues that *āzar* more likely reflects a confusion with the Hebrew name of Abraham's servant *elīʿezer*.

55. Genesis Rabbah 38:13. Translation from *Midrash Rabbah*, vol. 1, trans. H. Freedman (London: Soncino, 1983), 1:310–11.

56. Meanwhile, Abraham's uncle Haran, who declares that he was on Abraham's side after seeing the latter saved from the fire, is also cast into the fire, but he is consumed by flames and dies. The whole account then serves as an explanation for Gen 11:28: "Haran died before his father Terah in the land of his birth, in Ur of the Chalde'ans."

57. This declaration caused no little consternation among the exegetes because it appeared to some to be a lie, something unthinkable for an impeccable prophet. On this, see the well-known article by Calder, "Tafsīr from Ṭabarī to Ibn Kathīr," 101–40.

58. On this, see Reynolds, "Noah's Lost Son"; and Reynolds, "Flawed Prophet?"

59. See Levenson's remarks, *Inheriting Abraham*, 141–42.

60. On this, see Seppälä, "Reminiscences of Icons?"

61. "The anachronistic iconographic symbols on the coins, however, were secondary in ideological terms and had to serve as recognizable marks to make the coins acceptable in circulation." Heidemann, "Evolving Representation," 170–71.

62. There are examples of early Islamic frescoes in houses, for example at Quṣayr ʿAmra. See G. Fowden, *Quṣayr ʿAmra: Art and the Umayyad Elite in Late Antique Syria* (Berkeley: University of California Press, 2004). Fowden (chap. 5) argues that one of the frescoes at Quṣayr ʿAmra alludes to the figure of Adam and is similar to Christian iconography of the time. I am grateful to one of the anonymous reviewers of the present book for this reference.

63. Note esp. M. R. Waldman, "New Approaches to 'Biblical' Materials in the Qur'ān," *Muslim World* 75 (1985): 1–16; Mir, "Qur'anic Story"; J. Hämeen-Anttila, "'We Will Tell You the Best Stories': A Study on Surah XII," *Studia Orientalia* 67 (1997): 7–32. For more references to the study of the Joseph story in the Qur'an, see the bibliography of the study on Sura 12 by J. Decharneux, *CdH*, 2:551–54.

64. Waldman, "New Approaches," 13.

65. Witztum ("Syriac Milieu," 188) mentions Geiger, *Was hat Mohammad*, trans. *Judaism and Islam*, 111–18; D. Sidersky, *Les origines des légendes musulmanes dans le Coran et dans les vies des prophètes* (Paris: Geuthner, 1933), 55–68; C. Torrey, *The Jewish Foundation of Islam* (New York: Jewish Institute of Religion, 1933), 109–13; M. S. Stern,

"Muhammad and Joseph: A Study of Koranic Narrative," *JNES* 44 (1985): 193–94; Roberto Tottoli, *Biblical Prophets in the Qur'ān and Muslim Literature* (Richmond, UK: Curzon, 2002), 31, 56–57; J.-L. Déclais, "Joseph," in *Dictionnaire du Coran*, ed. M. A. Amir-Moezzi (Paris: Laffont, 2007), 452–54. Witztum ("Syriac Milieu," 188, n. 2) goes on to mention that Schapiro (*Die haggadischen Elemente im Erzählenden Teil des Korans* [Leipzig: Gustav Fock, 1907]) mentions Syriac sources but "mainly as parallels to Muslim exegetical traditions." He also notes that H. Speyer (*Die biblischen Erzählungen*, 187–224) shows more interest in Syriac sources of the qur'anic Joseph story. Finally, Witztum (ibid.) mentions a work on the Joseph story in Syriac texts but that does not include an analysis of precise parallels with Qur'an 12: M. Tamcke, "Die Hymnen Ephraems des Syrers und ihre Verwendung im christlichen Gottesdienst unter besonderer Berücksichtigung der Josephtexte," in *Der Koran und sein religiöses und kulturelles Umfeld*, ed. T. Nagel (Munich: Oldenbourg, 2010), 173–95.

66. H. Näf, "Syrische Josef-Gedichte mit Uebersetzung des Gedichts von Narsai und Proben aus Balai und Jaqob von Sarug," PhD diss., Zürich, 1923.

67. Witztum ("Syriac Milieu," 191, n. 14) refers to Näf, "Syrische Josef-Gedichte," 85 and 87.

68. This point is made in several places by Witztum ("Syriac Milieu"). For example: "The two most central authors of early Syriac literature, Aphrahat and Ephrem, are well-known for sharing a stock of traditions with early Judaism and for displaying a deep interest in the Old Testament" (6; see also 43–44). Indeed Witztum's dissertation (which addresses only Hebrew Bible material in the Qur'an and not, for example, its Jesus material) is globally a vindication of the importance of the Old Testament to the Syriac fathers. For an eloquent reflection on Ephrem's method of reading the Old Testament (and the Bible generally) typologically, see S. Brock, "St. Ephrem."

69. Witztum ("Syriac Milieu") provides a precise description of the "state of the question" on the authenticity (or otherwise) of these attributions, and references to editions, translations, and studies. I will not repeat these here but refer the reader to Witztum, "Syriac Milieu," 188, n. 4; 189, nn. 5, 6, 7; 190, nn. 8, 9. Witztum also notes Ephrem's *Commentary on Genesis*, a Greek sermon attributed to Ephrem, and two texts by Romanos the Melodist (sixth century). See St. Ephrem the Syrian, *Selected Prose Works: Commentary on Genesis, Commentary on Exodus, Homily on Our Lord, Letter to Publius*, trans. E. G. Mathews and J. P. Amar, Fathers of the Church 91 (Washington, DC: Catholic University of America Press, 1994); P.-H. Poirier, "Le sermon pseudo-éphrémien *In pulcherrimum Ioseph*: typologie et midrash," in *Figures de l'Ancien Testament chez les Pères* (Strasbourg: Centre d'analyse et de documentation patristiques, 1989), 107–22; J. Grosdidier de Matons, ed., *Romanos le Mélode: Hymns I* (Paris: Cerf, 1964), 202–45 (*De Joseph*), 260–93 (*Tentation de Joseph*). For further references, see Witztum, ibid., 190 nn. 10, 11. See now as well K. Heal, *Genesis 37 and 39 in the Early Syriac Tradition* (Leiden: Brill, 2023). On the debate over a possible Syriac origin for Romanos's Greek texts, see Witztum, ibid., 41–43. For more on the relationship between Ephrem and Romanos, see S. P. Brock, "From Ephrem to Romanos," *Studia Patristica* 20 (1989): 139–151; and M. Papoutsakis, "The Making of a Syriac Fable: From Ephrem to Romanos," *Le Muséon* 120

(2007): 29–75. I am grateful to one of the anonymous reviewers of the present book for this reference.

70. Witztum, "Syriac Milieu," 190.

71. The following section is reliant on Witztum, "Syriac Milieu," 191–239, and the reader should refer to this section of his dissertation for a more robust discussion of the subtext to Qur'an 12.

72. Mir, "Qur'anic Story," 1.

73. Mir, "Qur'anic Story," 15.

74. Mir's claims seem to be predicated on a comparison with other qur'anic stories, in which case they are more defensible. In comparison to the Genesis story, however, one could argue that in the Qur'an the "variety of scenes and characters" is severely reduced, that the plot is less "tightly knit" (indeed some elements of the plot have serious holes without commentary), and that the tensions in the story, too, are reduced (as some of the imperfections of biblical characters are smoothed out in the Qur'an).

75. Haleem, *Understanding the Qur'an,* 154, 155, 156.

76. *Homiliae Mar-Narsetis in Joseph,* in P. Bedjan, *Liber Superiorum* (Paris: Harrassowitz, 1901), 522–23 (henceforth Ps-N). Translation Witztum, "Syriac Milieu," 193. For details on the dating of this text (based in part on K. S. Heal, "Tradition and Transformation: Genesis 37 and 39 in Early Syriac Sources," PhD diss., University of Birmingham, 2008), see Witztum, "Syriac Milieu," 189, n. 7. Now see K. S. Heal, *Genesis 37 and 39 in Early Syriac Tradition* (Leiden: Brill, 2023), 58–63.

77. Translation Witztum, "Syriac Milieu,"199; Ps-N, 523.

78. Witztum ("Syriac Milieu") argues that the reluctance of Jewish sources to connect the wild animal with a "wolf" is because Benjamin (Joseph's favorite brother, fellow son of Rachel) is named a wolf in Gen 49:27.

79. Ps-N, 524; Witztum, "Syriac Milieu," 202.

80. Ps-N, 526–27; Witztum, "Syriac Milieu," 204. See Heal, *Genesis 37 and 39,* 60. Witztum also finds here a sign of parallelism between the Daniel account (see Dan 6:22, where God is said to have sent an angel to Daniel in the lions' den) and the Joseph story.

81. See Bedjan, *Histoire complète,* 60–63. Witztum, "Syriac Milieu," 208–9. Witztum attributes these homilies to Balai. For his discussion of the manuscript evidence and scholarly debate of their authorship, see ibid., 189, n. 6.

82. Ps-N, 541–42; Witztum, "Syriac Milieu," 215–16. In Pseudo-Narsai, Potiphar's wife still manages to persuade her husband to throw Joseph into prison, which might explain (in part) Q 12:35.

83. Ps-N, 550–51; Witztum, "Syriac Milieu," 218–19. See Heal, *Genesis 37 and 39,* 61. Witztum, in thinking through why the Syriac authors (not only Pseudo-Narsai but also Balai and [the Greek] Ephraem Graecus) have Potiphar's wife reappear, proposes that they sought to develop a parallel between the Joseph story and the Book of Esther, in which Haman consults with his wife after Mordechai's rise to power (Esth 6:12–13).

84. See the lengthy discussion in Ibn al-Jawzī, *Zād al-Masīr,* 4:238–40.

85. Witztum, "Syriac Milieu," 223.

86. Thus Narsai has Jacob say (after looking at Joseph's garment; Syriac *kūtīn*), "Who extinguished his father's lamp [*shargā*] the light [*nūhrēh*] of which was beautiful / so that in my grief over him I stumble as if in darkness?" Trans. Witztum, "Syriac Milieu," 224, n. 135. Narsai, *Narsai Doctoris Syri Homiliae et Carmina*, ed. A. Mingana (Mosul: Typus Fratrum Praedicatorum, 1905), 2:274–75. Cf. Ps-N, 573. Witztum (ibid.) mentions a possible connection with the Book of Tobit, noting that scholars have argued that the plot of Tobit is shaped by the Genesis Joseph story. Tobit becomes blind when bird droppings fall in his eyes (Tob 2:10) and is later healed by his son Tobias when the latter rubs his eyes with the gall of a fish that the angel Raphael had prepared for him (Tob 11:11–14). Witztum writes, "It is possible that [Tobit] later influenced retellings of the Joseph story."

87. It is important to keep in mind here, however, that the Qur'an is up to much more than transforming this biblical idiom into a plot element. For example, by using the same word (*qamīṣ*) the qur'anic author suggests that the shirt of Joseph that the brothers show to Jacob (Q 12:18) is the same shirt that is ripped by Potiphar's wife from behind (Q 12:25–28) and that later heals Jacob (Q 12:93, 96). Thus the shirt becomes a linking feature of the three principal elements of the qur'anic story of Joseph.

88. The best-known case of this is Q 38:21–26, which represents the two characters from Nathan's parable to David (2 Sam 12:1–13) as "real" characters who meet David. I have argued ("Noah's Lost Son") that the son of Noah who is lost in the waves of the flood in the Qur'an (Q 11:42–47) is a representation of the hypothetical sinful son of Noah spoken about in Ezekiel (Ezek 14:13–20).

89. Ps-N 593; trans. Witztum, "Syriac Milieu," 233. See Heal, *Genesis 37 and 39*, 63.

90. See Witztum, "Syriac Milieu," 235–36.

91. Witztum, "Syriac Milieu," 237. See Bedjan, *Histoire complète*, 287–91.

92. Bedjan, *Histoire complète*, 295–96.

93. Witztum ("Syriac Milieu," 211) notes that there is a possible precedent for this in a Greek text attributed to Ephrem but nothing in the Syriac tradition.

94. On this motif and the particular case of Moses and Pharaoh, see Reynolds, "Moses."

95. For a discussion and analysis of these two points, see Witztum, "Syriac Milieu," 225–28 and 229–30.

96. Griffith, "Christian Lore." See also Massignon, "'Sept dormants'"; *QBS*, 157–84; *QSC*, 213–20; Archer, "Hellhound."

97. "It is hard to avoid the thought that not only is the Qur'an here using a familiar Christian narrative to enhance the understanding of the sense of the expression 'God's signs,' but that it is also proposing in the sequel that the true meaning of the Christian story corrects what the Qur'an considers to be one of the major errors of the Christian understanding. Namely, the doctrine that God has a son and that he is Jesus, the Messiah." Griffith, "Christian Lore," 118.

98. Griffith, "Christian Lore," 120. The earliest extant copies of the Seven Sleepers story are two *mēmrēs* (verse homilies) of Jacob of Serugh. See I. Guidi, "Testi Orientali Inediti sopra I Sette Dormienti di Efeso," *Reale Accademia dei Lincei* 282 (1884–1885)

(Rome: Tipografia della R. Accademia dei Lincei, 1885), 18–29. One of the versions is also published in H. Gismondi, *Linguae Syriacae Grammatica et Chrestomathia cum Glossario*, 4th ed. (Rome: De Luigi, 1913), 45–53. Both versions are translated into German by P. M. Huber, *Die Wanderlegende von den Siebenschläfern* (Leipzig: Harrassowitz, 1910). For more details on the relationship of the two recensions of Jacob's homily, see Griffith, "Christian Lore," 120–21; A. Vööbus, *Handschriftliche Überlieferung der Mēmrē-Dichtung des Ja'qōb von Serūg*, CSCO 344 and 345, 421 and 422 (Louvain: Secrétariat du CSCO, 1973 and 1980), 71–72. The legend of the "Youths of Ephesus" is also preserved in two other early texts: a Syriac translation of the Greek *Ecclesiastical History* of Zacharias of Mitylene (d. 536), and the Syriac *Ecclesiastical History* of John of Ephesus (d. 586), as quoted by the *Chronicle* of Dionysius of Tell Maḥrē (d. 845) in the *Chronicle* of Michael the Syrian (d. 1199) and also by the *Ecclesiastical Chronicle* of Bar Hebraeus (d. 1286). The *Ecclesiastical History* of Zacharias of Mytilene was translated, according to Griffith ("Christian Lore," 121), by "an anonymous monk at Amida in the year 569." It is published in *Historia Ecclesiastica Zachariae Rhetori, vulgo Adscripta II*, CSCO 84, ed. E. W. Brooks (Paris: E Typographeo Reipublicae, 1921), 106–22; and *Anecdota Syriaca* 3, *Zachariae Episcopi Mitylenes aliorumque Scripta Historica Graece plerumque Deperdita*, ed. J. P. N. Land (Leiden: Brill, 1870), 87–99; for an English translation, see F. J. Hamilton and E. W. Brooks, trans., *The Syriac Chronicle Known as That of Zachariah of Mitylene* (London: Methuen, 1899). On the *Ecclesiastical History* of John of Ephesus, see J. J. van Ginkel, "John of Ephesus: A Monophysite Historian in Sixth-Century Byzantium," PhD diss., Rijksuniversiteit Groningen, 1995; W. Witakowski, *The Syriac Chronicle of Pseudo-Dionysius of Tel-Maḥrē: A Study in the History of Historiography, Studia Semitica Upsaliensia* 9 (Stockholm: Almqvist & Wiksell, 1987). For the account of the "Youths of Ephesus" (here they are eight), see Guidi, "Testi Orientali Inediti," 35–44, and P. Bedjan, *Acta Martyrum et Sanctorum I* (Paris: Harrassowitz, 1890), 301–25.

99. On this, see Hoyland, "Language of the Qur'an."

100. Trans. Griffith, "Christian Lore," 123; Guidi, "Testi Orientali Inediti," 1:20.

101. Guidi, "Testi Orientali Inediti," 1:23.

102. In Q 7:176 an unbeliever is compared to a dog ("So the likeness of him is as the likeness of a dog; if thou attackest it, it lolls its tongue out, or if thou leavest it, it lolls its tongue out").

103. Guidi, "Testi Orientali Inediti," 1:19–20.

104. Griffith, "Christian Lore," 128.

105. Later, Griffith ("Christian Lore," 128) writes, "The step down from guardian angel to watch-dog is no doubt too steep a step to imagine the Arabic-speaking Christians in the Qur'ān's audience readily to have taken in translating the legend."

106. *The Pilgrimage of Theodosius*, trans. J. H. Bernard (London: Palestine Pilgrims Text Society, 1893), 16.

107. The Arabic term here is *wariq*, which corresponds in Modern Standard Arabic with "paper"; however, in the historical context of the Qur'an (when there was no paper money), it refers to a coin. Arberry appropriately translates the term as "silver."

108. *Historia Ecclesiastica Zachariae,* ed. Brooks, 121–2; Griffith, "Christian Lore," 129.

109. Griffith, "Christian Lore," 129.

110. Griffith, "Christian Lore," 129.

111. "O believers, do not say, 'Observe us' [*rāʿinā*], but say, 'Regard us' [*unẓurnā*]; and give ear; for unbelievers await a painful chastisement." *Rāʿinā* (cf. Q 4:46) is close to Hebrew *rāʿ*, "evil." Horovitz argues that through the influence of Jews in Medina this word must have taken on a secondary, pejorative sense because of its proximity to Hebrew *rāʿ* and accordingly that Muḥammad asked his followers to use *unẓurnā* ("Regard us") instead. See J. Horovitz, "Jewish Proper Names and Derivatives in the Koran," *Hebrew Union College Annual* 2 (1925): 145–227, at 204 (repr. Hildesheim: Georg Olms, 1964). This argument already appears with A. Geiger (*Was hat Mohammed,* 17; trans. *Judaism and Islam,* 12–13).

112. On this, see J. Kugel, *In Potiphar's House: The Interpretive Life of Biblical Texts* (San Francisco: Harper San Francisco, 1990), 30–46.

113. Tannous, "Arabic as Christian Language," 35. Here Tannous means to marshal the biblical material of the Qur'an to argue that the Bible was likely known and read in Arabic in that context.

THREE Christianity in the Qur'an's Historical Context

1. Tannous, "Arabic as Christian Language." See now as well P. Wood, "Christianity in the Arabian Peninsula and Possible Contexts for the Qur'ān," in G. Dye, ed., *Early Islam: The Sectarian Milieu of Late Antiquity?* (Brussels: Éditions de l'Université de Bruxelles, 2023), 225–48. Wood focuses on the boundaries of Arabia and does not argue for a robust Christian presence in the Hijaz.

2. The observation that the Arabs were largely Christian before Islam is not so much a radical new proposal as much as a resuscitation of an idea that had been proposed long ago but now can be proposed with more confidence and precision. In 1856 (!) the Austrian scholar Aloys Sprenger wrote (more or less accurately): "All the most powerful tribes of Arabia had embraced Christianity, as the Ghassanites, whose chief was king of Petra, the Lakhmites, whose representative was king of Hyrah, the Taghlibes, the Taym allat and most of the Arabs who were settled in towns and villages in Najran and other districts of Yaman. Only the wild sons of the Najd and of the depth of the desert resisted the progress of civilization. Yet even among them we find Christian priests and hermits, and numerous converts." A. Sprenger, "On the Origin and Progress of Writing Down Historical Facts Among the Musulmans," *Journal of the Royal Asiatic Society* 25 (1856): 303–29, 375–81; at 375.

3. Al-Jallad, "Linguistic Landscape."

4. Cf. Q 19:97, which declares that God has made the revelation "easy by thy tongue [or 'language'] that thou mayest bear good tidings thereby to the godfearing, and warn a people stubborn" (cf. Q 44:58). Hoyland ("Language of the Qur'an," 22) trans-

lates Q 12:2: "We have sent it down as/made it an Arabic Qur'an so that you [Hijazis] can understand."

5. I agree here with Nicolai Sinai that the word *'arabī* in the Qur'an means "Arabic" (as opposed to a non-Arabic language). This is in contrast to the ideas of Retsö and Webb, to be discussed below, that it refers in the Qur'an to a specific type of Arabic speech.

6. Readers should keep in mind that not all scholars will agree with my understanding of *'arabī* ("Arabic") and *a'jamī* ("barbarous"). Jan Retsö argues that in the Qur'an (unlike later Islamic texts), *'arabī* means specifically "pure Arabic" and accordingly *a'jamī* means something like "incorrect Arabic" (not a non-Arabic language). See Jan Retsö, "What Is Arabic?" *Oxford Handbook of Arabic Linguistics,* ed. J. Owens (Oxford: Oxford University Press, 2013), 433–50, esp. 434. I disagree with this reading for two reasons: First, the Qur'an closely links the importance of its *'arabī* language with the people of the region in which it is proclaimed ("*umm al-qurā*" and its surroundings; Q 42:7). It is *their* language, not some particular form of that language. Second, the Qur'an is attentive to diverse languages (see Q 30:22) and indeed marks itself off from other scriptures particularly on that basis (Q 14:4). See below for more comments on the arguments of Retsö and Peter Webb.

7. For a detailed discussion of this question, and a convincing argument that the *a'jamī* language alluded to here is likely Aramaic, see Hoyland, "*'Arabī* and *a'jamī.*"

8. Al-Jallad, *Psalm Fragment;* see pp. 60–62, where Al-Jallad highlights some of the features (e.g., the distal demonstrative pronouns *dhālika* and *tilka*) that distinguish the QCT from the grammatical and syntactical rules of Classical Arabic. See now also the work of Marijn van Putten (*Quranic Arabic*) in which the argument that the QCT reflects a Hijazi dialect is developed in great detail. See esp. his chap. 4, where van Putten adds further examples, such as the loss of a glottal stop (*hamza*) in certain places and the use of *zawj* ("pair") for both feminine and masculine.

9. See Al-Jallad, *Psalm Fragment,* 66.

10. Al-Jallad, *Psalm Fragment,* 72.

11. Al-Jallad, *Psalm Fragment,* 73.

12. See Retsö, *Arabs in Antiquity,* esp. 593. See also Webb, *Imagining the Arabs,* 115–16.

13. Al-Jallad, *Psalm Fragment,* 73.

14. David Marshall has noted that all of the references to the Qur'an's Arabic language are in "Meccan" Suras, suggesting that in earlier material the Qur'an's author was especially eager to announce the arrival of a revelation in the native language of Arabic speakers. See D. Marshall, "Revelation," in Reynolds, Klar, Sidky, and Sirry, eds., *Yale Dictionary of the Qur'an,* forthcoming.

15. This is essentially consistent with the position of Hoyland, "Language of the Qur'an," 22. Al-Jallad's comments on Q 41:44 are also pertinent here. We quoted Arberry's translation of this verse: "If We had made it a barbarous [*a'jamī*] Koran, they would have said, 'Why are its signs not distinguished [*fuṣṣilat*]? What, barbarous and Arabic?'"

Al-Jallad (*Psalm Fragment,* 76) sees the last bit not as a second question but as part of the original question. He translates: "and if we had made it a recitation in a foreign language they would have said, if only its verse were explained, foreign (language) and then Arabic." He then goes on to suggest that this verse might offer an insight into the mechanics of spontaneous translation during Jewish or Christian liturgies in the pre-Islamic Hijaz. He continues: "The expression *law-lā fuṣṣilat ʔāyātu-hū ʔaʕǧamiyyun wa-ʕarabiyyun* may indicate the way this was normally done. The speaker would give the verse in its original, such as Greek, Aramaic, or Hebrew, and then its explication in Arabic, thus 'foreign (language) and then Arabic.'"

16. Sinai, *Key Terms,* 513.

17. "Say: 'People of the Book! Come now to a word common between us and you, that we serve none but God, and that we associate not aught with Him, and do not some of us take others as Lords, apart from God.' And if they turn their backs, say: 'Bear witness that we are Muslims'" (Q 3:64). That the "People of the Book" are Jews *and* Christians is suggested by the following verse: "People of the Book! Why do you dispute concerning Abraham? The Torah was not sent down, neither the Gospel, but after him. What, have you no reason?" (Q 3:65).

18. Notable here is Q 3:20, which makes a clear distinction between the People of the Book and the *ummiyyīn,* making them essentially the two types of people around the Prophet: "So if they dispute with thee, say: 'I have surrendered my will to God, and whosoever follows me.' And say to those who have been given the Book and to the *ummiyyīn:* 'Have you surrendered?' If they have surrendered, they are right guided; but if they turn their backs, thine it is only to deliver the Message; and God sees His servant."

19. "Counterdiscourse" meaning rhetorical citations of its real or fictional opponents. See Azaiez, *Contre-discours coranique,* and now Reynolds, "Their Very Words?"

20. On this, see Hoyland, *Arabia and the Arabs,* 59–62.

21. See Al-Jallad, *Psalm Fragment,* 3–4; his translation of this key phrase is close to that of J. Bellamy, "A New Reading of the Namārah Inscription," *JAOS* 105 (1985): 31–51, at 46.

22. See A. Al-Jallad, "*ʿArab, ʾAʿrāb,* and Arabic in Ancient North Arabia: The First Attestation of *(ʾ)ʿrb* as a Group Name in Safaitic," *Arabian Archaeology and Epigraphy* 31 (2020): 422–35. I owe this reference to Sinai, *Key Terms,* 514.

23. "It has sometimes been argued that the rise of Islam—what we prefer to understand as the first appearance and expansion of the Believers' movement—was essentially an 'Arab' movement. The implication of such a view is that an 'Arab' political identity existed on the eve of Muhammad's preaching and that it was the powerful desire to realize this latent collective identity as 'Arabs' in political form that really generated the Believers' expansion and the creation of their empire. This view is, however, anachronistic and profoundly misleading. It usually represents the facile interpolation back into the seventh century C.E. of modern concepts of Arab nationalism that only came into existence in the late nineteenth century." Donner, *Muhammad and the Believers,* 218.

24. Hoyland, "Language of the Qur'an," 22.

25. Hoyland, "Language of the Qur'an," 22.

26. See Robert Hoyland, "The Jews of the Hijaz in the Qur'an and in Their Inscriptions," in *New Perspectives on the Qur'an: The Qur'an in Its Historical Context 2,* ed. G. S. Reynolds (London: Routledge, 2011), 95–96.

27. "We have to move away from the idea that we are dealing with only two languages—Arabic and Aramaic—and from the idea that these two labels represent uniform and homogenous categories. We need to accept that a much more complex linguistic situation prevailed in the pre-Islamic Near East." Hoyland, "Language of the Qur'an," 26–27.

28. Hoyland, "Language of the Qur'an," 39. Hoyland's argument is articulated in part to counter the ideas of Alphons Mingana and Christoph Luxenberg that much of qur'anic vocabulary is best explained with recourse to Syriac. Hoyland proposes that this vocabulary had already been adopted by a robust Arabic-speaking Christian culture. He concludes: "This would then open up a whole new avenue of research, namely the reconstruction of pre-Islamic theological discourse in Arabic" (ibid., 40).

29. By the sixth century the Jafnids had become Jacobite Christians, and their rulers left a number of Greek-language inscriptions, some of them explicitly Christian. A 559 inscription of the ruler al-Ḥārith in Qaṣr al-Ḥayr al-Gharbī, Syria, begins: "In the name of our father Jesus Christ, savior of the world, who erases the sin [of the world]." See Grasso, *Pre-Islamic Arabia,* 150.

30. See Grasso, *Pre-Islamic Arabia,* chap. 5, esp. 134–40.

31. Lindstedt, *Muḥammad and His Followers,* 102.

32. Al-Jallad, "Linguistic Landscape," 112.

33. As Lindstedt (*Muḥammad and His Followers,* 68) notes, it is curious that there are no references to a Jewish community in South Arabia in Jewish literature, but the epigraphic record from the region confirms a Jewish presence there in late antiquity. For example, a Sabaic inscription dated to 470 CE speaks of the help of God, "the Master of the heavens and of the earth, and with the help of their tribe/people of Israel" (ibid., 71).

34. Al-Jallad, "Linguistic Landscape," 122.

35. Lindstedt, *Muḥammad and His Followers,* 101; Segovia, "Abraha's Christological Formula."

36. Al-Jallad ("Linguistic Landscape," 114) insists that the difference in regard to the definite article should not be seen as a key factor in linguistic classification: "Semiticists have recognized that [the definite article] is a late feature which spread among the Central Semitic languages through contact or as the result of parallel development . . . , and therefore is an unsuitable feature for linguistic diagnosis."

37. One Nabataean Aramaic inscription, from Madā'in Ṣāliḥ, is Jewish (the author describes himself as a Jew—*yhwdy'*). JS nab4, in R. Savignac and A. Jaussen, *Mission archéologique en Arabie* (Paris: P. Geuthner, 1909–1922), 149 (drawing of inscription with Hebrew transliteration and French translation). See Grasso, *Pre-Islamic Arabia,* 200.

38. Al-Jallad, "Pre-Islamic *Basmala,*" 14.

39. On this, see Al-Jallad, "Linguistic Landscape," 117–18. He writes, referring to the earlier work of Michael Macdonald, "Arabic was used for spoken communication, religious liturgies, oral literary works, and face-to-face political administrative and legal activity, while Aramaic expressed these functions in written form." See also M. Macdonald, "Arabia and the Written Word," in M. C. A. Macdonald, ed., *The Development of Arabic as a Written Language: Papers from the Special Session of the Seminar for Arabian Studies Held on 24 July, 2009* (Oxford: Archaeopress, 2010), 103–12. On the possibility that the later uniformity of Islamic Arabic administrative language points to the pre-Islamic use of Arabic in this capacity, see Tannous, "Arabic as Christian Language," 24, n. 91.

40. "And We have sent no Messenger save with the tongue of his people, that he might make all clear to them" (Q 14:4).

41. In brief, Al-Jallad and Al-Manaser ("Pre-Islamic Divine Name," 123–29) argue that *ʿ-s-y* is related to Sabaic *ʿsy* ("to purchase") and Geʿez *ʿasaya* ("to repay") and thus has a meaning of "redeemer" that would be roughly equivalent to Greek *sōtēr* and Syriac *pārōqā*. Thus the Qur'an would have taken an epithet, "redeemer," and made it into a personal name, something that perhaps has a parallel in the qur'anic names *ṣāliḥ* (Salih) and *ṭālūt* (Saul).

42. Al-Jallad and Al-Manaser, "Pre-Islamic Divine Name," 129.

43. Robin, Al-Ghabbān, and Al-Sa'īd, "Inscriptions antiques"; Nehmé, "New Dated Inscriptions."

44. Although it is not directly connected to my argument, I would still like to note Al-Jallad's important observation that the move toward a cursive form of the script (that is, toward the Arabic script as we know it) would have been generated from writing on perishable materials (because it would be difficult, although not impossible, to inscribe the curves in this script on a rock), although none of these remain to us. This means, quite possibly, that Arabic (alongside Aramaic) was a language of administration (which would have been conducted on perishable materials such as papyrus and parchment) in the Nabataean area (even after it was administered by Rome) and that the inscriptions eventually began to use this cursive form as well. On this basis Al-Jallad ("Linguistic Landscape," 119) concludes: "Thus, the growing body of pre-Islamic evidence strongly indicates that the use of Arabic for administration in the early Islamic period does not reflect an ad hoc invention, but the continuation of an established tradition of administration in Arabic which must have its origins in North Arabian and Syrian scribal practices."

45. Al-Jallad, "Linguistic Landscape," 119–20; J. Blau, "The Beginnings of the Arabic Diglossia: A Study in the Origins of Neo-Arabic," *Afro-Asiatic Linguistics* 4, no. 4 (1977): 1–28, see esp. 11 and n. 52 for a detailed discussion of earlier studies of this inscription. See also Hoyland, "Epigraphy," 222–24; and Hoyland, "Language of the Qur'an," 19–20.

46. As Jack Tannous has pointed out to me, this expression resembles the wording of Ps 145:13, which in the Syriac Peshitta includes *malkūtek malkūt koll ʿālmīn*, "your kingdom is a kingdom of all ages."

47. Scholars of Arabian epigraphy frequently note the continued use of pagan names by Arabian monotheists (much as the names of Roman and Norse gods were used by Christians in Europe, and even for the days of the week).

48. Hoyland ("Epigraphy," 237) dates this inscription "2–3 Century AD"; Al-Jallad ("Linguistic Landscape," 119), to before 150 CE.

49. See Nehmé, ed., *Darb al-Bakrah,* 185. See also the discussion in Lindstedt, *Muḥammad and His Followers,* 60–61.

50. For the reading and the translation, see Fiema, Al-Jallad, Macdonald, and Nehmé, eds., "*Provincia Arabia,*" 410–11. The authors write of this inscription, "Thus the fact that the five men who are assumed to be donors, but who are not the donors mentioned in the Greek and Syriac texts, had their names carved in Arabic shows a strong desire to express their *cultural* identity, in addition to their political and religious allegiance" (ibid., 410). The Greek and Syriac texts are not identical either.

51. Macdonald (in Fiema, Al-Jallad, Macdonald, and Nehmé, eds., "*Provincia Arabia,*" 414) indicates that the Greek alone "reveals that the founder, Šaraḥīl son of Ẓālim/Saraēlos Talemou, was a phylarch, and that the martyrion was dedicated to St John."

52. See Macdonald (in Fiema, Al-Jallad, Macdonald, and Nehmé, eds., "*Provincia Arabia,*" 414). The lines "after the rebellion" are disputed (they are sometimes explained with reference to a tradition that the Jafnid/Ghassanid leader al-Ḥārith, mentioned again below, conquered Khaybar in 567 CE).

53. See Lindstedt, *Muḥammad and His Followers,* 107.

54. See Hoyland, "Epigraphy," 233–35.

55. Macdonald (in Fiema, Al-Jallad, Macdonald, and Nehmé, eds., "*Provincia Arabia,*" 416–17) refers to a number of further pre-Islamic inscriptions "possibly" in Arabic, including an inscription in a church in Umm al-Jimāl in northern Jordan.

56. See Villeneuve, "Greek Inscriptions."

57. Nehmé, "New Dated Inscriptions."

58. Nehmé, "New Dated Inscriptions," 129.

59. See Robin, Al-Ghabbān, and Al-Sa'īd, "Inscriptions antiques." See now as well Grasso, *Pre-Islamic Arabia,* 94–95.

60. Robin, Al-Ghabbān, and Al-Sa'īd, "Inscriptions antiques," label these Ḥimā-Sud PalAr 1–11.

61. Another sign of the presence of Aramaic/Syriac in southern Arabia is signaled by a Syriac inscription and a Syriac letter by Jacob of Serugh (d. 521) to the Christians of the region. See Jacob of Serugh, Letter 18 (G. Olinder, CSCO 110 [Leuven: Durbecq, 1952]); and for a study, Forness, *Preaching Christology,* 89–133. In addition, a Syriac inscription has been found in the same region; see F. Briquel Chatonnet et al., "A First Syriac Inscription from the Area of Ḥimā," *Wiener Zeitschrift für die Kunde des Morgenländisches Gesellschaft* 112, (2022): 37–49.

62. See Al-Jallad, "Linguistic Landscape," 119, n. 9.

63. "Il est manifeste que les textes de Ḥimà-Sud ne sont pas la signature de simples voyageurs circulant entre le Yémen et l'Arabie du Nord, au contraire de la plupart des très nombreux graffites de la région. On observera tout d'abord que deux textes sont

soigneusement gravés sur de grandes dalles avec, dans un cas, une esquisse de décor architectural. Par ailleurs, trois noms sont répétés plusieurs fois. Ces textes trahissent manifestement la présence d'une communauté chrétienne installée à demeure." Robin, Al-Ghabbān, and Al-Sa'īd, "Inscriptions antiques," 1052.

64. "Cette communauté affiche fortement son adhésion à la foi chrétienne, en flanquant chaque texte d'une croix." Robin, Al-Ghabbān, and Al-Sa'īd, "Inscriptions antiques," 1053. Robin et al. (ibid., 1053–54) argues there may have been a particular connection between this community and the Christian community of Hira in Iraq, noting traditions that Christianity was introduced to Najran by a man (Ḥayyān) who converted in Hira in the mid-fifth century.

65. One might also include here the report in medieval Islamic sources, including the *Muʿjam* of the geographer Yāqūt (d. 626 AH/1228 CE), of a pre-Islamic Arabic inscription that was once found on a monastery built by Hind, the Christian wife of the Lakhmid/Nasrid ruler Mundhir III (d. 554) in Hira, Iraq. See Tannous, "Arabic as Christian Language," 19, and for the Arabic text, Yāqūt, *Muʿjam al-buldān* (Beirut: Dār Ṣādir/Dār Bayrūt, 1955–1957), 2:542. See also the text and analysis of I. Shahid, *The Arabs in Late Antiquity: Their Role, Achievement, and Legacy*, ed. R. Baalbaki (Beirut: American University of Beirut, 2008), 11. Tannous ("Arabic as Christian Language," 22) notes that the inscription "mentions a bishop (*usquf*), asks God (*al-Ilāh*) to forgive the sin of Hind (*khaṭī'atahā*) and to have mercy (*yataraḥḥam*) on her and her son, and also uses the expression *dahr al-dāhir*, 'ages of ages.'" This last expression could reflect Christian liturgical language. Tannous argues for the authenticity of the medieval reports of this inscription ("The authenticity and reliability of these reports is likely," ibid., 19). Hind describes herself as *ammat al-masīḥ*, "the handmaiden of Christ" (see Luke 1:38; the Peshitta uses *amthā* for "handmaiden"). On this inscription, see also (for Arabic text and English translation) I. Shahid, "Arab Christianity Before the Rise of Islam," in *Christianity: A History in the Middle East*, ed. H. Badr, S. Abou el Rouss Slim, and J. Abou Nohra (Beirut: Middle East Council of Churches, 2005), 435–51, at 442.

66. Al-Jallad and Sidky, "Paleo-Arabic Inscription."

67. Grohmann, however, attempted to read the inscription on the basis of a photograph that cut off part of the text and obscured other parts. See Al-Jallad and Sidky, "Paleo-Arabic Inscription," 1.

68. One should keep in mind their particular caution in proposing the names Qurrah and Sd in light of the extremely weathered nature of these letters in the inscription. See Al-Jallad and Sidky, "Paleo-Arabic Inscription," 6–7.

69. Al-Jallad and Sidky, "Paleo-Arabic Inscription," 8.

70. Al-Jallad and Sidky, "Paleo-Arabic Inscription," 8–9.

71. "Paleographically, all three lines fit comfortably into the Paleo-Arabic category and seem to lie on a continuum between the Ḥimà Paleo-Arabic texts with which it shares the distinct compact shape of the *kāf* and the inscriptions of the region between Tabūk and al-Ḥijr published by *Farīq al-Ṣaḥrā*." Al-Jallad and Sidky, "Paleo-Arabic Inscription," 7. A bit farther down they add, "These palaeographic features—along with the

particular introductory formula—indicate that the Riʿ al-Zallālah inscription was not a product of the standardized Arabic of the early Islamic period" (ibid.).

72. Al-Jallad and Sidky, "Paleo-Arabic Inscription," 10.

73. M. A. Al-Hajj and A. A. Faqʿas, "Naqsh Jabal Ḏabūb: Naqsh jadīd bi-khaṭṭ al-zabūr al-Yamānī fī l-istiʿāna bil-Llāh wa-taqwiyat al-īmān," *Al-ʿIbar li-l-dirāsāt al-tārīkhiyya wa-l-āthāriyya* 2 (2018): 12–43.

74. Al-Jallad, "Pre-Islamic *Basmala,*" 8.

75. This idea is mentioned by Al-Jallad, "Pre-Islamic *Basmala,*" 1, who credits it to Neuwirth, *Qur'an and Late Antiquity,* 116–17. On this question, see also M. Kropp, "'Im Namen Gottes, (d.i.) des gnädigen (und) B/(b)armherzigen' Die muslimische Basmalah: Neue Ansätze zu ihrer Erklärung," in M. Kropp and H. Kaufhold, eds., *Oriens Christianus: Hefte für die Kunde des christlichen Orients* 97 (Wiesbaden: Harrassowitz, 2015), 190–201.

76. It might be compared to a still unpublished inscription known as the ʿAbd Shams inscription, written, however, in Paleo-Arabic, which includes the invocation *bismika llāhumma.* See Al-Jallad, "Pre-Islamic *Basmala,*" 14, n. 66.

77. Al-Jallad, "Pre-Islamic *Basmala,*" 14.

78. "In the mid-sixth century, between the years of 535 and 555 CE, South Arabia was ruled by a vicegerent of Aksūm, Abraha. He expanded the political borders of ancient Ḥimyar considerably, with military excursions reaching far into North Arabia. While in the earliest periods, Ḥimyar's religion reflected Aksūmite Christian dogma, later inscriptions appear to show a compromise, using neutral terms for Christ such as 'Messiah' rather than 'son.' Perhaps reflecting a similar spirit, the *basmalah* emerged as a compromise—both south and north Arabian terms are treated as equals, and would have been regarded as acceptable in the cosmopolitan landscape created by Abraha's expansions." Al-Jallad, "Pre-Islamic *Basmala,*" 16.

79. On this, see Grasso, *Pre-Islamic Arabia,* 123.

80. I am following Al-Jallad's ("Pre-Islamic *Basmala,*" 15–16) argument here; he refers also to Q 25:60.

81. Al-Jallad, "Pre-Islamic *Basmala,*" 17. See Neuwirth, *Qur'an and Late Antiquity,* 116–17.

82. Al-Jallad and Sidky, "Paleo-Arabic Inscription." In the article they also discuss a second inscription from the same site, the author of which identifies himself as ʿAbd al-ʿUzzē or ʿAbd al-ʿUzza. Both inscriptions refer to God as *llh* (unlike other Paleo-Arabic texts that use *al-ilāh*) and open with the invocation *b-sm-k rb'n* ("in your name, our Lord") and so appear to be monotheistic (but not Islamic, as no Muslim formulas are used).

83. Al-Jallad and Sidky, "Paleo-Arabic Inscription," 1.

84. One exception to this is the use here of *bn* for "son," as opposed to *br* (unlike a second inscription at the same site), although the authors suggest that *bn* might have been added later.

85. See Ibn Isḥāq, 411–12; trans. 278.

86. Ibn Isḥāq, 412; trans. 278.

87. Al-Jallad and Sidky, "Paleo-Arabic Inscription," 10–11.

88. One rather obvious problem with this association, or rather with the Islamic tradition, is that monks generally do not have sons. Moreover, the title *al-rāhib,* and the association of certain pious figures with monasticism, is something of a literary motif in Islamic biographies.

89. Al-Jallad and Sidky, "Paleo-Arabic Inscription," 9.

90. Tannous, "Arabic as Christian Language," 11. This is mentioned by Nehmé, "New Dated Inscriptions," 154–55.

91. Loreto, "Results," 161–62. See the photo of the bell on p. 162.

92. Loreto, "Results," 162.

93. Lammens ("Chrétiens à la Mecque," 198–200) gathers references in medieval Islamic literature to Christians in Mecca, mostly Ethiopian (including mercenaries known as Aḥābīsh). Perhaps, he speculates, they found their way to Mecca subsequent to the military campaigns of the Ethiopian ruler in South Arabia, Abraha, although some might have been taken as slaves. There is also a reference to a Christian cemetery in Mecca by Al-Azraqī (d. 250 AH/837 CE). See ibid., 214, and Shahîd, *Byzantium and the Arabs,* 387. I do not find such late, and unrelated, reports to be especially compelling. As for Medina, Lammens (ibid., 202) notes the Islamic tradition that says the Medinan Zayd b. Thābit studied Syriac there (hypothetically this would have been from a Christian).

94. Cf. the statement of Shoemaker (*A Prophet Has Appeared,* 206–7): "Although Christianity had literally encircled the Hijaz by Muhammad's lifetime, there is simply no evidence of a significant Christian community in either Mecca or Medina."

95. Shoemaker, *Creating the Qur'an.* Shoemaker provocatively argues that the Qur'an does not fit the context of the early seventh-century Hijaz, which he holds to have been both largely illiterate and bereft of settled Christian communities. He holds accordingly that much material in the Qur'an (especially that which engages with Christian traditions) reflects a context farther to the north (in greater Syria or Palestine), where the first believers or Muslims were interacting substantially with Christian communities. Shoemaker also argues against the early carbon-14 dating of Hijazi Qur'ans that would suggest the consonantal text of the Qur'an was formed quite early. The section that follows in the present book assumes that the Qur'an did form early and does reflect a Hijazi context (I contend that the development of Paleo-Arabic monotheistic inscriptions, some of which are explicitly Christian, and the disappearance of pagan inscriptions are sufficient evidence that Arabia had embraced monotheism, especially Christianity, by the seventh century). For a detailed analysis and critique of Shoemaker's arguments, see Sinai, "Christian Elephant." Cf. my own review of Shoemaker's work in *JAOS* 144 (2024), 699–702.

96. For a more recent articulation of Muhammad meeting Christians in Syria, see J. Cole, *Muhammad: Prophet of Peace amid the Clash of Empires* (New York: Nation Books, 2018), 32–34.

97. Ibn Isḥāq, 115–17; trans. 79–81.

98. On counterdiscourse, see Azaiez, *Contre-discours,* and now Reynolds, "Their Very Words?"

99. This argument might be a response to Jews claiming that Abraham was a Jew "before the law" and Christians claiming that he was a Christian by his faith (developing Romans 4 and Galatians 3). Eusebius (d. ca. 342) wrote: "It was by faith towards the Logos of God, the Christ who had appeared to [Abraham], that he was justified, and gave up the superstition of his fathers, and his former erroneous life, and confessed the God who is over all to be one; and Him he served by virtuous deeds, not by the worship of the law of Moses, who came later. . . . It is only among Christians throughout the whole world that the manner of religion which was Abraham's can actually be found in practice." Eusebius, *Ecclesiastical History,* trans. K. Lake and J. E. L. Oulton (Cambridge, MA: Harvard University Press, 1964), 1:45. Thus the appeal to Abraham in the context of religious competition itself follows earlier trends in Jewish-Christian polemics, seen already in Romans 4 and Galatians 3 and then picked up by a long tradition of Christian authors in late antiquity to whom Jews would respond. See *QBS,* 71–86, and more recently Levenson, *Inheriting Abraham,* chap. 6; Hughes, *Abrahamic Religions,* chap. 2.

100. The term for "tribes" is *asbāṭ,* from Hebrew *shebeṭ.* See Ambros and Procházka, *Concise Dictionary,* 307. A Jew could of course contend that the Israelite "tribes" were Jewish.

101. This story is told in Ibn Isḥāq's biography in a report that has the Christians secretly acknowledge that Muhammad is a prophet; in their stubbornness they do not convert, but they also do not agree to the challenge (afraid that they would be punished by God if they curse a true prophet). Ibn Isḥāq (410; trans. 277) concludes, "So they came to the apostle and told him that they had decided not to resort to cursing and to leave him in his religion and return home."

102. Still, it is perhaps worth noting that this verse was made into the central point of a dialogue proposed by a group of Muslim scholars, who wrote a 2007 document titled "A Common Word." The "common word" in that document, however, is not about the principles seen in the qur'anic verse, but rather about love of God and love of neighbor (a theme more prominent in the Gospels than in the Qur'an). See https://www.acommonword.com/.

103. Ambros and Procházka, *Concise Dictionary,* 296.

104. Cf. also Q 3:20, which likewise includes counsel on how to debate with the People of the Book (and the *ummiyyīn*), mentioning what to do *in tawallaw,* if they "turn their backs."

105. *Milla* is often translated "community," but if it indeed is related to Aramaic *melltā,* meaning "word" or "teaching," then Arberry's translation might be appropriate. Ambros and Procházka (*Concise Dictionary,* 259) write: "*milla(t)* < Syriac *melltā,* which basically means 'word,' but has undergone a complex semantic development esp. under the influence of Greek *logos.*"

106. And, of course, a *muslim,* often taken not simply as "submissive" but as a signal that Islam is a timeless religion (although, as an anonymous reviewer of the present book has pointed out, one might consider Q 6:14, which suggests that Muhammad was the first one who *aslama,* "submitted" or "became Muslim").

107. The Arabic behind "recite God's signs" is *yatlūna āyāti llāhi. Āyāt* here might be "verses," if this is a reference to Christians, perhaps monks in particular, reciting scripture (although "verses" was likely not a current concept in Eastern Christian thinking about the Bible at this time). Paret (*Der Koran*) translates (into German) "Verse"; Khalidi (*The Qur'ān*) translates "revelation." Rudolph (*Abhängigkeit,* 8) discusses this turn of phrase while considering whether an Arabic Bible would have been present in pre-Islamic Arabia. He (correctly) notes that *yatlūna* need not mean "read" but could mean "recite." Still, this verse could refer to Christians reciting scripture (presumably, the Psalms) in Aramaic or Greek, even if no Arabic Bible were available. On the Jews and Christians "reciting the Book," see Q 2:44, 113.

108. Again, in Q 3:112 the Qur'an accuses the Jews of killing the prophets and invokes God's wrath. In Q 5:60 the Qur'an seems to have the Jews in mind when it speaks of a people "whom Allah has cursed" and with whom he is wrathful. The Qur'an also has God warn the Israelites of his wrath if they disobey his commands (Q 20:81), and it speaks of God's wrath against them when they do so by worshipping the golden calf (Q 7:150, 152; 20:86; 58:14; 60:13). In Sura 20, the Qur'an has God give a warning to the Israelites that they should not violate the food laws God has imposed on them. By doing so they would anger God and put their lives at risk. The divine voice of the Qur'an declares: "Eat of the good things wherewith We have provided you; but exceed not therein, or My anger shall alight on you; and on whomsoever My anger alights, that man is hurled to ruin" (Q 20:81). On the qur'anic accusation against the Jews of "killing the prophets," see Reynolds, "On the Qur'an and the Theme."

109. That the Qur'an has the Jews themselves declare "our hearts are *ghulf*" suggests that the principal meaning of *ghulf* here is "covered," even if there is a play with the biblical metaphor of an uncircumcised heart. On this phrase, which is related to a web of qur'anic expressions involving the heart, and its biblical subtext, see Chapter 2 and *QB,* 58.

110. Blachère (*Le Coran* [Paris: Maisonneuve, 1957], 91) writes: "Peut-être faut-il songer aux Chrétiens, ce qui est très plausible à l'époque où nous sommes, alors que Mahomet est si déçu par l'hostilité d'Israël." Cf. Droge, *The Qur'an,* 40, n. 131.

111. Ali, *Holy Quran,* 156, n. 437. This is indeed one of the opinions, although not the only one, recorded by Ibn al-Jawzī (see *Zād al-masīr,* 1:441–44).

112. Nasr et al., eds., *The Study Quran,* 162–63.

113. A close parallel to this verse is Q 28:52–53: "Those to whom We gave the Book before this believe in it and, when it is recited to them, they say, 'We believe in it; surely it is the truth from our Lord. Indeed, even before it we had surrendered.'" The connection with Q 5:83 suggests that in the Sura 28 passage the Qur'an is again speaking of Christians.

114. Although this is not the place to develop the topic further, it is interesting that Q 17:110 immediately goes on to consider whether God can be referred to as both *allāh* and *al-raḥmān.* This might reflect the naming practices of Christian and Jewish Arabic speakers in North (*al-ilāh* or *allāh*) and South (*al-raḥmān*) Arabia. See the discussion of the Jabal Dhabūb inscription earlier in this chapter.

115. "Da wegen der erwähnten Prosternation mit dem 'Volk der Schrift' hier wohl die Christen gemeint sind, dürfen wir die 'stehende Gemeinde' vielleicht auf die Mönche deuten, die unter Körperbeugungen ihre Gebete rezitieren." Rudolph, *Abhängigkeit*, 8.

116. See *QB*, 766–67. Jack Tannous has pointed out to me that Matthew was generally more popular among late antique Eastern Christians.

117. The term *ṣalawāt* ("oratories") is occasionally imagined to mean "synagogues" (although it is simply a plural noun formed from the Arabic root associated with prayer—hence a nice use of "oratories" with its Latin root), presumably in order to supply a Jewish cultic space alongside the Christian cultic spaces mentioned in this verse; thus Droge (*The Qur'an*) and Paret (*Der Koran*), albeit the latter with a question mark, in his translation, although in his *Kommentar* he translates "kultische Gebete" (350). He then adds, "Die einzelnen der hier aufgeführten kultischen Bauten können übrigens nicht mit Sicherheit bestimmten Glaubensgemeinschaften zugewiesen werden." I would agree with this statement as regards *ṣalawāt* and *masājid*, but not as regards *ṣawāmiʿ* and *biyāʿ* (from Syriac *bīʿtā*). It seems to me that the only reason why the translation of "synagogues" is entertained is because of the conviction that there were Jews in the Hijaz and that this verse must mention their sanctuaries, as it mentions the sanctuaries of Christians. *Ṣawmaʿa* (sing. of *ṣawāmiʿ*) almost certainly derives from Ethiopic *ṣōmāʿt*, meaning "hermit's cell." Ambros and Procházka, *Concise Dictionary*, 165.

118. Rudolph, *Abhängigkeit*, 7.

119. Bell, *Commentary*, 1:601.

120. "Commemorated" (from Latin *commemorare*, "brought to remembrance") nicely reflects the Arabic root *dh-k-r*. Jack Tannous has pointed out to me that in Syriac tradition a church might be referred to as *bēt segdtā* (cf. Arabic *masjid*) and commemorations referred to as *dukrānē* (cf. the wording of Q 22:40 and 24:36, which employ the corresponding Arabic root *dh-k-r*).

121. Holger Zellentin has advanced the argument, in part because of the authority assigned to *ruhbān* in Q 9:31 and 34, that this word in fact refers to bishops. See H. Zellentin, "Ahbar and Ruhban: Religious Leaders in the Qur'an in Dialogue with Christian and Rabbinic Literature," in *Qur'ānic Studies Today*, ed. A. Neuwirth and M. Sells (London: Routledge, 2016), 258–89. Zellentin mentions the view of Geiger, who argues that the root of *rāhib/ruhbān*, even if it comes from the root *r-h-b* (which is related to "fear" of God), may be connected to the root *r-b-b* ("lordship"). Zellentin also argues specifically that the *ruhbān* of Q 5:82 are implied to have oversight of priests (*qissīsīn*), although this is not self-evident. I think the web of associations that we have shown here (including as well Qur'an 24) shows convincingly that *ruhbān* does refer to monks (and *rahbāniyya* to monasticism). See also on *ruhbān* generally, E. El-Badawi, "From 'Clergy' to 'Celibacy': The Development of Rahbānīyyah Between the Qur'ān, Ḥadīth and Church Canon," *Al-Bayan Journal of Quran and Hadith Studies* 11 (2013): 1–14.

122. *Qirṭās* comes ultimately from Greek *chartēs*, possibly through Syriac *karṭīsā* (see Ambros and Procházka, *Concise Dictionary*, 223). Greek *chartēs* is used for "papyrus," but it is uncertain that this is what is meant here. Payne Smith renders Syriac *kartīsā* as a page (charta and folium), small book (libellus), or tablet (tabula). See R. Payne

Smith, *Thesaurus Syriacus* (Oxford: E Typographeo Clarendoniano, 1879, 1901), 3743. Thus "page" or "pages" might be the best translation of the term in Q 6:7, 91.

123. On this, see Reynolds, "On the Qur'anic Accusation."

124. Tannous ("Arabic as Christian Language," 38) refers to these verses as part of his argument that an Arabic Bible translation (or at least a partial translation) likely existed in pre-Islamic Arabia. However, there is no indication that these writings were in Arabic, and indeed at least in the case of the Jews this would be unlikely.

125. It is possible that the Qur'an's use of *ṣuḥuf* is related to the South Arabian and Ethiopic root *ṣ-ḥ-f* (meaning "to write a document"). See Ambros and Procházka, *Concise Dictionary,* 158. Thus the Qur'an's use of *ṣuḥuf* in Q 20:133 would be indebted to South Arabia, while its use of *qirṭās/qarāṭīs* in Q 6:7, 91 would be indebted to North Arabia.

126. Ambros and Procházka, *Concise Dictionary,* 133.

127. Pace Droge (*The Qur'an,* 358, n. 2), who writes, "*on parchment unrolled:* i.e. in the form of a scroll rather than a codex." The word *raqq* may come from Ethiopic, meaning "parchment." Ambros and Procházka, *Concise Dictionary,* 116.

128. Droge (*The Qur'an*) translates more appropriately as "former pages." For a further reflection, see ibid., 205, n. 106.

129. On this see Reynolds, "Their Very Words?"

130. *The Study Qur'an* (Nasr et al., 685–86) refers to Zamakhsharī and Ibn Kathīr, who cite a tradition that the Meccan idolaters knew that Muhammad would stop and listen to a Christian blacksmith in Mecca who used to recite scripture in his native language. They consequently accused the Prophet of learning from him. This tradition is also found in Al-Waḥidī, *Asbāb al-Nuzūl,* 101–2 (who speaks of two Christian blacksmiths). *The Study Qur'an* also mentions a tradition that the figure is Salmān al-Fārisī (who, although by tradition was born a Zoroastrian, became a Christian before converting to Islam), but the authors explain that the Prophet met Salmān only in the Medinan period (whereas Sura 16 is thought to be "Meccan"). Ibn al-Jawzī (*Zād al-Masīr,* 4:492–94) includes nine different opinions on the identity of the anonymous figure alluded to in Q 16:103.

131. It should be noted, however, that some scholars hold that this verse (along with vv. 101–2) is a Medinan insertion. There is a bit of self-confirming, or unfalsifiable, logic here, however. Material in a "Meccan" Sura that does not fit the Meccan label is simply classified as a "Medinan" insertion, whereas it might lead one instead to question the larger framework of the text's formation.

132. C. Rabin, "'Arabiyya," *EI2,* 1:564. Quoted by Tannous, "Arabic as Christian Language," 20, n. 75.

133. R. Hoyland, "Two New Arabic Inscriptions: Arabian Castles and Christianity in the Umayyad Period," in *To the Madbar and Back Again: Studies in the Languages, Archaeology, and Cultures of Arabia Dedicated to Michael C. A. Macdonald,* ed. L. Nehmé and A. Al-Jallad (Leiden: Brill, 2018), 327–37, at 335. Quoted by Tannous, "Arabic as Christian Language," 20, n. 75.

134. Tannous, "Arabic as Christian Language," 20, n. 75.

135. Tannous, "Arabic as Christian Language," 25.

136. Tannous's arguments are the latest in a long back-and-forth among scholars on this question. Anton Baumstark argued in favor of a pre-Islamic Arabic Bible translation; A. Baumstark, "Das Problem eines vorislamischen christlich-kirchlichen Schrifttums in arabischer Sprache," *Islamica* 4 (1931): 562–75; Baumstark, "Eine frühislamische und eine vorislamische arabische Evangelienübersetzung aus dem Syrischen," *Atti del XIX Congresso Internazionale degli Orientalisti* (1935) (Rome: G. Bardi, 1938), 682–84. Baumstark's theories were refuted by G. Graf, *Geschichte der christlichen arabischen Literatur* (Rome: Biblioteca Apostolica Vaticana, 1947), 1:143–45. Guillaume, on the basis of Islamic sources, also argued for the existence of an Arabic Bible in the Prophet's time. See A. Guillaume, "The Version of the Gospels Used in Medina," *Al-Andalus* 15 (1950): 289–96. Cf. the more comprehensive approach of J. Blau, "Sind uns Reste arabischer Bibelübersetzungen erhalten geblieben?" *Le Muséon* 86 (1973): 67–72. Griffith again refuted this idea, arguing that the first Bible translation in Arabic was not before the late eighth century (likely among Melkites in Palestine). See S. H. Griffith, "The Gospel in Arabic: An Inquiry into Its Appearance in the First Abbāsid Century," *Oriens Christianus* 69 (1985): 126–67; see more recently H. Kachouh, "The Arabic Versions of the Gospels and Their Families," PhD diss., University of Birmingham, 2008, and again Griffith, *Bible in Arabic*, esp. chap. 1. Kachouh argues for a pre-Islamic date for the original behind a specific Gospel manuscript (Vat. Ar. 13). Griffith, in his later work, concedes an earlier date for Arabic translations of the Gospels (perhaps late seventh century), but not a pre-Islamic date.

137. As David Bertaina has reminded me, the liturgical life of the church itself was a key medium of evangelization as well.

138. Jack Tannous has pointed out to me that the Syriac word here rendered "readings" is *qeryānē*.

139. Forness, *Preaching Christology*, 159. For the original Syriac, see *Homiliae selectae Mar-Jacobi Sarugensis*, ed. P. Bedjan (Paris: Harrassowitz, 1905–1910), 3:581–82.

140. Forness, *Preaching Christology*, 161.

141. Forness, *Preaching Christology*, 161–62; Jacob of Serugh, *Homily on the Faith* in *Homiliae*, ed. Bedjan, 3:622.

142. T. Andræ, *Mohammed, sein Leben und sein Glaube* (Göttingen: Vandenhoeck & Ruprecht, 1932); English trans.: *Mohammed: The Man and His Faith*, trans. T. Menzel (New York: Charles Scribner's Sons, 1936), 92. On this tradition, see also H. Lammens, *L'Arabie occidentale avant l'Hégire: Chrétiens et juifs à la mecque à la veille de l'Hégire* (Paris: Dar Byblion, 2006; first published 1928), 21. Andræ's reference to Quss ibn Sa'ida might be problematic. The author of the *Encyclopaedia of Islam* article under this name writes, "It is not impossible that Ḳuss had relations with the Christians of Najrān, but it is wrong to take him, as has sometimes been done, as the bishop of that town." Ch. Pellat, "Ḳuss b. Sā'ida," *EI2*, 5:529. One might compare the perspective of Karl Ahrens, who argues that Muhammad was influenced by the sermon of a Christian hermit on the last judgment. See K. Ahrens, "Christliches im Qoran," *Zeitschrift der deutschen morgenländischen Gesellschaft* 84 (1930): 15–68, 148–90, esp. 60–65.

FOUR The Qur'an in Conversation with Christianity

1. Ayoub, "Nearest in Amity," 157.

2. "By depicting such common piety, the Qur'ān aims at establishing a fellowship of faith among the faithful of the two communities." Ayoub, "Nearest in Amity," 157.

3. *Rhetoric,* II:13; trans. W. Rhys Roberts.

4. Neuwirth, *Qur'an and Late Antiquity,* 116–17.

5. For example, it is found in the late first or early second-century Greek Christian text the *Didache,* 7:1–3.

6. Irenaeus, *The Demonstration of the Apostolic Preaching,* trans. Armitage Robinson (New York: Macmillan, 1920), 72.

7. Sinai, *The Qur'an,* 143. See also Neuenkirchen, "Eschatology." Neuenkirchen refers to Trinitarian introductions to lectionaries in Syriac liturgy.

8. For "proto-basmalah," see, for example, Lindstedt, *Muḥammad and His Followers,* 46–47, who also considers the possibility that this inscription is not pre-Islamic, but rather from one of the "early followers of Muhammad" (47).

9. "The invocation seeks to syncretize the two main monotheistic poles of Arabia by equating North Arabian *Allāh* with South Arabian *Raḥmān.*" Al-Jallad, "Pre-Islamic *Basmala,*" 18. Note also the studies of Manfred Kropp: "Tripartite, but Anti-Trinitarian Formulas in the Qur'ānic Corpus, Possibly Pre-Qur'ānic," in G. S. Reynolds, ed., *New Perspectives on the Qur'an* (London: Routledge, 2011), 247–64; he also discusses in this context Q 6:101. See also M. Kropp, "'Im Namen Gottes, (d.i.) des gnädigen (und) B/(b)armherzigen,' Die muslimische Basmalah: Neue Ansätze zu ihrer Erklärung," in M. Kropp and H. Kaufhold, eds., *Oriens Christianus: Hefte für die Kunde des christlichen Orients* 97 (2013/2014): 190–201.

10. Among the most typical is that *al-raḥmān* refers to divine mercy in this world, available to all, and *al-raḥīm* to divine mercy in the next world, available to only believers. This opinion is expressed by Ibn Kathīr (d. 774 AH/1373 CE), who reports: "[*Al-Raḥmān*] carries a broader scope of meanings pertaining to the mercy of Allah with His creation in both lives. Meanwhile [*al-raḥīm*] is exclusively for the believers." See Ibn Kathir, *Tafsīr,* trans. S. Al-Mubarakpuri (Riyadh: Dar-us-Salam, 2003), 1:67. There is no clear basis in the qur'anic text for this effort at disambiguating the two terms.

11. See further Sinai, *The Qur'an,* 143.

12. Ibn al-Jawzī, *Zād al-Masīr,* 1:16. Note the comment of Mahmoud Ayoub: "Most commentators have included the Jews among those who have 'incurred' divine wrath and the Christians among those who have 'gone astray.'" M. Ayoub, *The Qur'an and Its Interpreters* (Albany: SUNY Press, 1984), 1:49.

13. *The Noble Qur'an,* trans. M. T. al-Hilali and M. M. Khan (Medina: King Fahd Complex for the Printing of the Holy Qur'an, n.d.), 1–2. Earlier printings of the Hilali-Khan translation (before a revision under Saudi sponsorship) do not mention Jews and Christians explicitly in Q 1:7. For more, see the Global Qur'an blog post at https://gloqur.de/quran-translation-of-the-week-102-interpretation-of-the-meanings-of-the-noble-quran-in-the-english-language-by-al-hilali-and-khan-the-story-behind-the-first-saud/.

14. Hilali-Khan also report (in a separate note) the story of Zayd b. ʿAmr b. Nufayl (one of the faithful *ḥanīf*s mentioned by Ibn Isḥāq), on the authority of Ibn ʿUmar, a story that has Jews themselves admit that they are the object of divine anger: "Zayd . . . went to Shām . . . enquiring about a true religion to follow. He met a Jewish religious scholar and asked him about their religion. He said, 'I intend to embrace your religion, so tell me something about it.' The Jew said, 'You will not embrace our religion unless you receive your share of Allāh's Anger.' Zaid said, 'I do not run except from Allāh's anger, and I will never bear a bit of it if I have the power to avoid it. Can you tell me of some other religion?' He said, 'I do not know of any other religion except *Hanīf* (Islamic Monotheism).' Zaid enquired, 'What is *Ḥanīf?*' He said, '*Ḥanīf* is the religion of (the Prophet) Abraham, he was neither a Jew nor a Christian, and he used to worship none by Allāh (Alone)—Islamic Monotheism.' Then Zaid went out and met a Christian religious scholar and told him the same (as before). The Christian said, 'You will not embrace our religion unless you get a share of Allāh's Curse.' Zaid replied, 'I do not run except from Allāh's Curse, and I will never bear any of Allāh's Curse and His Anger if I have the power to avoid them.' The story ends with Zaid's embrace of the 'religion of Abraham.'" Hilali-Khan, trans., *Noble Qur'an,* 2, n. 1.

15. K. Mohammed, "Produce Your Proof: Muslim Exegesis, the Hadith, and the Jews," *Judaism* 53, no. 1–2 (2004): 3+, *Gale Academic OneFile,* https://link.gale.com/apps/doc/A126076034/AONE?u=googlescholar&sid=bookmark-AONE&xid=89c948a6.

16. Regarding the Hilali-Khan translation of Q 1:7 (and the role of the Saudi government in sponsoring certain translations), Mohammed ("Produce Your Proof") writes: "With its petro-riches, the Saudi Arabian government has become the most prolific supplier of free Qur'ans and Quran translations. It should be noted that the Kingdom does not allow the printing and publication of any document without the vetting of such document by a governmental body. The translation of the Qur'an that can be obtained from any Saudi Embassy, and is distributed to almost every Sunni mosque throughout the world is *Translation of the Meanings of The Noble Qur'an in the English Language,* translated by Muhammad Taqi-al-Din al-Hilali and Muhammad Muhsin Khan. In their translation published by the King Fahd Complex for the Printing of the Qur'an, they rely on footnotes to supply the same information as provided in the foregoing works by al-Tabari and Ibn Kathir, as well as the famed Andalusian exegete, al-Qurtubi (d. 1273). In the edition published by Darussalam Publishers in Riyadh (with a slight title change), the information is however supplied in the form of interpolations of the translated text and reads thus: 'Not the way of those who have earned Your anger (such as the Jews), nor of those who went astray (such as the Christians).'"

17. See esp. Reynolds, "'Killers of the Prophets.'"

18. On the reshaping of Jesus's image in the Qur'an generally (vis-à-vis Syriac Christian understandings of his divine omniscience), see now A. J. Hayes, "'The Treasury of Prophecy': The Role of Knowledge in Salvation History for the Qur'ān in the Light of Syriac Tradition," in *Syriac Theology: Past and Present,* ed. M. Aras, C. Rizk, and K. von Stosch (Paderborn: Brill Schöningh, 2023), 209–46.

19. The interpreters debate whether this is indeed Jesus speaking here. Some traditions attribute the speech to the angel Gabriel, who is "below" Mary in one way or another. See Ibn al-Jawzī, *Zād al-Masīr,* 5:221.

20. *The Protoevangelium of James,* trans. O. Cullman, in *New Testament Apocrypha,* ed. W. Schneemelcher and trans. R. Wilson (Cambridge: J. Clarke, 1991), 1:426–39.

21. Note that the miracle of a tree is already mentioned by the Byzantine Christian Historian Sozomen (d. 450) (*Ecclesiastical History,* 5:21). Sozomen speaks of a tree at Hermopolis that, when the holy family passed by after arriving in Egypt, lowered its branches and worshipped Christ.

22. *Gospel of Pseudo-Matthew,* in *New Testament Apocrypha,* 1:462–65.

23. Shoemaker, "Christmas in the Qur'an." See also the further details added by G. Dye, "Lieux saints communs, partagés ou confisqués: aux sources de quelques péricopes coraniques (Q 19: 16–33)," in I. Dépret and G. Dye, eds., *Partage du sacré: Transferts, dévotions mixtes, rivalités interconfessionnelles* (Brussels: E.M.E. and Intercommunications, 2012), 55–122.

24. Shoemaker (*Creating the Qur'an,* 254–55) argues that the connection to the Kathisma Church is a sign that this material in the Qur'an, at least, comes from postconquest Palestine. He writes, provocatively: "Indeed, it boggles the mind to imagine that somehow this distinctively Jerusalemite combination of Nativity traditions could have been widely known and understood by the hundred or so illiterate herdsmen in the remote desert village of Mecca (since this is alleged to be an early Meccan sura), particularly when we find no evidence of any knowledge of this particular configuration of traditions anywhere else in late ancient Christianity—other than the Kathisma" (255). While granting the point that there is no proof that this tradition was known in the Hijaz, I would respond only that, if this tradition had made it to Christians in the Hijaz (who anyway left us with no written records other than the occasional inscription), there likely would still be no record of it.

25. *Infancy Gospel of Thomas,* trans. M. R. James (Oxford: Clarendon, 1924), 2:1–5.

26. To this end as well one might note that whereas the Qur'an never has Moses refute the teachings of Jews, it does have Jesus refute the teachings of Christians. This is seen in Q 5:73, and then dramatically later in the same Sura where Jesus (perhaps after his ascension, if not on the day of resurrection) seems to wash his hands of them: "I only said to them what Thou didst command me: 'Serve God, my Lord and your Lord.' And I was a witness over them, while I remained among them; but when Thou didst take me to Thyself, Thou wast Thyself the watcher over them; Thou Thyself art witness of everything." Tarif Khalidi writes in this regard, "He is the only prophet in the Quran who is deliberately made to distance himself from the doctrines that his community is said to hold of him." T. Khalidi, *The Muslim Jesus* (Cambridge, MA: Harvard University Press, 2001), 12.

27. The Qur'an, of course, seems to do precisely this when it refers to the scripture of Jesus as *injīl,* which seems to be ultimately derived from Greek *euangelion.* See Jeffery, *Foreign Vocabulary,* 71–72; Ambros and Procházka, *Concise Dictionary,* 314.

28. On parables in the Qur'an generally, see A. H. M. Zahniser, "Parable," *EQ* 4:9–12. Ja'far Subḥānī, *al-Amthāl fī al-Qur'ān al-karīm: dirāsa mubassaṭa ḥawla al-amthāl al-wārida fī al-kitāb al-'azīz* (Beirut: Dār al-Aḍwā', 2000). Zahniser ("Parable," 4:9) notes that Arabic *mathal* involves a semantic range that covers a number of English terms "simile, similitude, example, parable, allegory, proverb, motto, apothegm, aphorism, fable and maxim." He adds that this is similar to other cognate Semitic terms such as Hebrew *māshāl* and Aramaic *matlā*.

29. Note esp. T. Lohmann, "Die Gleichnisreden Muhammeds im Koran," *Mitteilungen des Instituts für Orientforschung* 12 (1966): 75–118, 241–87.

30. See R. Paret, "Sure 57, 12 f. und das Gleichnis von den klugen und den törichten Jungfrauen," in *Festschrift für Wilhelm Eilers: Ein Dokument der internationalen Forschung zum 27. September 1966*, ed. Gernot Wiessner (Wiesbaden: Otto Harrassowitz, 1967), 387–90; repr. *Der Koran* (Darmstadt: WBG, 1975), 192–96.

31. A. Tarasenko, "Jesus and His Parables in the Context of Rabbinic Judaism," *Acta Patristica et Byzantina* 12 (2001): 179–97, at 186. For a standard take on Jesus's parables in the Gospels, see K. R. Snodgrass, "Parables," *Dictionary of Jesus and the Gospels*, ed. J. B. Green and S. McKnight (Downers Grove, IL: InterVarsity, 2013), 591–601. One might compare the approach of Nathan Eubank in "Merit and Anti-Judaism in Matthew's Parables Since Jülicher," in A. Runesson and D. M. Gurtner, eds., *Matthew Within Judaism: Israel and the Nations in the First Gospel* (Atlanta: SBL Press, 2020), 425–46. As Eubank adroitly notes, the recent history of scholarship on parables involves a great deal of assumptions about what a "simple Galilean" marked with eschatological convictions would have intended, and what later interpreters (including the evangelists themselves) have added to that, especially by way of allegorical interpretation. An anonymous reviewer of this work noted that Jesus's use of allegory, and his lessons on the meaning of allegory (e.g., Matt 13:36–43, etc.), if they are primitive accounts, would show that a simple Galilean could handle this sort of thing.

32. "The traditional character of rabbinic literature is the reason of the paradox that, notwithstanding the dates of redaction of the rabbinic complications, statements found in rabbinic literature are often indispensable *background* to the NT." M. Kister, "Parables and Proverbs in the Jesus-Tradition and Rabbinic Literature," *Journal for the Study of the New Testament* 41 (2018): 5–28, at 6. After noting that the Hebrew term (cognate with Arabic *mathal*) is *not* used in the Old Testament for a parable, A. Hultgren writes: "The parables of Jesus fit more precisely in form and content within the context of the various *meshalim* known from rabbinic sources." *The Parables of Jesus: A Commentary* (Grand Rapids: Eerdmans, 2000), 6. On Gospel parables, see the classic work of J. Jeremias, *The Parables of Jesus* (London: SCM Press, 1963).

33. "The fact that the parables of Jesus are not used for argumentation in the sense of the 'parables' of ancient philosophers, popular rhetoricians, or rabbinic masters is significant for the content of Jesus' parables. There is very little previous learning that Jesus' hearers need to bring to the occasion beyond what is gained through life experience. . . . They would have been familiar to anyone who had even a rudimentary

acquaintance with the Jewish heritage, an acquaintance that anyone of that time and place would gain from life experience." Hultgren, *Parables of Jesus,* 9.

34. On the relative consensus of dating the Palestinian Talmud to the fifth century CE and the Babylonian Talmud to the sixth century, see M. Amsler, *The Babylonian Talmud and Late Antique Book Culture* (Cambridge: Cambridge University Press, 2023).

35. On this, see H. Ben Shammai, "The Status of Parable and Simile in the Qur'ān and Early *Tafsīr:* Polemical, Exegetical and Theological Aspects," *JSAI* 30 (2005): 154–69, esp. 167–69.

36. One might contrast the approach of A. Neuwirth, who (while not ignoring the use of parables and Jewish and Christian tradition) sees the Qur'an's use of parables as a "new" homiletic strategy. See the section "Neue homiletische Instrumente: Gleichnisreden und Parabeln (*mathal*)," in *Der Koran als Text der Spätantike,* 498–509. She presents the Qur'an's use of parables as an original development closely linked to the historical community of believers' engagement with their nonbelieving opponents. She argues (*Qur'an and Late Antiquity,* 312) that the use of parables begins as "an object of dispute and a means of persuasion among believers and unbelievers" but "quickly wins the consensus of the community." She also notes that the parable in the Qur'an is "in one sense an element of mantic speech, in that God himself strikes the likenesses" (ibid.).

37. Neuwirth, *Qur'an and Late Antiquity,* 306. She also notes here how Matt 7:29 speaks of the crowds being amazed with how Jesus teaches "as one who had authority," just after he had delivered a series of parables.

38. Ibn al-Jawzī, *Zād al-Masīr,* 6:298.

39. An anonymous reviewer noted to me the difference of Mark 4:12, where Jesus explains that he teaches in parables "so that" (not "because") they see and do not perceive.

40. Saleh, "End of Hope," 110.

41. Sweat, *Theological Role,* 34–35.

42. On this, see also the later work of K. Ahrens, "Christliches im Qoran," *Zeitschrift der deutschen morgenländischen Gesellschaft* 84 (1930): 15–68, 148–90, esp. 60–65. Ahrens largely agrees with the perspective of Andræ, although he emphasizes that in both Syriac Christian literature and the Qur'an there is an emphasis on the lordship and the mercy of God. In particular Ahrens notes how the Qur'an frequently refers to God as lord (*rabb*) and the human as servant (*ʿabd*), and how early Christian theological tradition shares this vision of God and God's relationship to humanity. In addition, by referring to God's grace (*faḍl, niʿma*) and mercy (*raḥma*), the Qur'an also softens the "despotic" image of God: "Gott ist zwar stets der Herr *rabb* und der Mensch der Knecht *ʿabd,* aber auch in der syrisch-christlichen Frömmigkeit herrscht dieselbe Vorstellung (Andrae 129), und schon bei Justin und 1 Clem. wird Gott gern als *despotēs* bezeichnet; andererseits aber ist die Despotennatur Gottes auch im Qoran, jedenfalls im mekkanischen, durch manche Züge gemildert" (ibid., 61).

43. As Jack Tannous has pointed out to me, the apocalyptic setting in which the blessed are commended for feeding the poor, the orphan, and the prisoner has a clear subtext in Matt 25:31ff. It is quite possible that the expression "face of God" is an adapta-

tion of the presentation of Christ in Matthew 25: "for I was hungry and you gave me food, I was thirsty and you gave me drink, I was a stranger and you welcomed me. . . . Then the righteous will answer him, 'Lord, when did we see thee hungry and feed thee, or thirsty and give thee drink? And when did we see thee a stranger and welcome thee, or naked and clothe thee? And when did we see thee sick or in prison and visit thee?' And the King will answer them, 'Truly, I say to you, as you did it to one of the least of these my brethren, you did it to me'" (Matt 25:35, 37–40).

44. Andræ, *Origines de l'islam,* 98.

45. *Didascalia Apostolorum,* trans. R. H. Connolly (Oxford: Clarendon, 1929), 86.

46. Andræ, *Origines de l'islam,* 131.

47. Andræ, *Origines de l'islam,* 135.

48. Andræ, *Origines de l'islam,* 130.

49. Ephrem, *Hymns on Faith,* 76–77 (hymn 4). In a note Wickes explains, "The 'sea' (*yammâ*), because it is vast, full of mysterious life, and because it is from here that the pearl comes (see hymns 81–85), forms one of Ephrem's favorite symbols of the incomprehensibility of God. Ultimately, within Ephrem's use of the metaphor stands an a fortiori argument: if you cannot comprehend the sea, how can you comprehend God?" (ibid., 77, n. 36). *Yammā* is incidentally cognate with the common qur'anic term for sea, *yamm* (see Q 7:136; 20:39, 78, 97; 28:7, 40; 41:40).

50. On repentance in the Qur'an, see G. S. Reynolds and Amir Moghadam, "Repentance in the Qur'an, Hadith, and Ibn Qudāma's *Kitāb al-Tawwābīn,*" *JAOS* 141 (2021): 381–401; A. Khalil, *Repentance and the Return to God: Tawba in Early Sufism* (Albany: SUNY Press, 2018).

51. G. S. Reynolds, "Original Sin and the Qur'an," *Islamochristiana* 46 (2020): 197–218, at 216.

52. Sinai, *The Qur'an,* 162.

53. Sinai, *The Qur'an,* 166. On the particular connections between the Qur'an and the eschatological imagery of the Book of Revelation, see D. Brady, "The Book of Revelation and the Qur'an: Is There a Possible Literary Relationship?" *Journal of Semitic Studies* 23 (1978): 216–25. Although Brady does not discuss this point, it is important to note that the Book of Revelation is not part of the Peshitta translation of the New Testament, although it was translated into Syriac by the sixth century.

54. Sinai, *The Qur'an,* 167.

55. Jacob of Serugh, *Mēmrā on the Sleepers of Ephesus,* 30, lines 177–82.

56. See Bertaina, "Bodily Resurrection."

57. On this, see Bertaina, "Bodily Resurrection," 50.

58. For an analysis of this passage in conversation with Islamic tradition, see S. Saeed, "Fights and Flights: Two Underrated 'Alternatives' to Dominant Readings in Tafsīr," *JQS* 24 (2022): 46–88.

59. Aphrahat, *Demonstrations* 8. See Kuriakose Valavanolickal, Aphrahat: *Demonstrations* I (Kottayam: St. Ephrem Ecumenical Research Institute, 2005), 184. Quoted in Bertaina, "Bodily Resurrection," 51. Jack Tannous has noted to me that Aphrahat here is likely developing 1 Cor 15:36–38.

60. Aphrahat, *Demonstrations* 8.

61. On Origen's doctrine of the resurrection, see A. Kakavelaki, "The Resurrected Body, Will It Be of Flesh or Spiritual? Theological Discussions from the Time of the Apostle Paul up to the Sixth Century AD," *Scrinium* 11 (2015): 225–41, at 229–34.

62. Babai the Great, *Liber de unione,* 195. The translation is found in *QB,* 388, and quoted by Bertaina, "Bodily Resurrection," 52.

63. Sinai, *The Qur'an,* 70.

64. Sinai, *The Qur'an,* 72.

65. See P. Crone, "The Religion of the Qur'ānic Pagans: God and the Lesser Deities," *Arabica* 57 (2010): 151–200, at 188–89. Mentioned by Sinai, *The Qur'an,* 69.

66. Grasso, *Pre-Islamic Arabia,* 180.

67. Aphrahat, *Demonstrations* 8, quoted in Bertaina, "Bodily Resurrection," 51.

68. On this point, see esp. Reynolds, "On the Presentation."

69. See the description of John of Ephesus in Bertaina, "Bodily Resurrection," 52–65.

70. As mentioned above (quoting Sidney Griffith), the Seven Sleepers of Ephesus tale was likely a response to "Origenists," who doubted the resurrection of the body.

71. The Qur'an does of course refer to some pagan gods by name. In Qur'an 53 (vv. 19–21) it refers to three pagan goddesses—al-Lāt, al-'Uzza, and Manāt—and in Qur'an 71 to five gods from the days of Noah (which in fact are Arabian gods). These deities are attested to in different ways by pre-Islamic sources (Greek, Syriac, and otherwise) and inscriptions, as carefully discussed by Grasso (*Pre-Islamic Arabia,* 179–86). However, Grasso also notes,"There is no archaeological evidence for the veneration of polytheistic deities after the fourth century" (184). Consequently, the best explanation for the appearance of these deities is as part of the qur'anic mise-en-scène that presents the prophet opposing polytheistic opponents, and not as evidence for an ongoing polytheistic culture.

72. On this topic, see also my early discussion in *QBS,* 156–67.

73. All three occurrences of *barzakh* in the Qur'an seem to have the sense of "barrier," either between the blessed and the damned in the afterlife (Q 23:100; cf. Luke 16:26) or between the seas in this world (Q 25:53, 55:20). See now C. Lange, "Barzakh," *EI3*.

74. "Les martyrs forment dans le Coran l'unique exception au sort attribué aux morts." T. Andræ, *Origines de l'islam,* 167. Note also Q 36:26, where an unnamed believer is told to enter the garden. Although it is not stated explicitly, this passage seems to imply that he was killed by his unbelieving people and received an immediate reward as a grace of martyrdom.

75. Muqātil b. Sulaymān, *Tafsīr Muqātil,* 1:314, on Q 3:169.

76. Al-Ṭabarī, *Jāmiʿ al-bayān fī ta'wīl al-Qur'ān,* 2:39–40, on Q 2:154; Al-Zamakhsharī, *al-Kashf 'an ḥaqā'iq ghawāmiḍ al-tanzīl,* 1:429, on Q 3:169–71; Ibn Kathīr, *Tafsīr,* ed. Muḥammad Bayḍūn (Beirut: Dār al-Kutub al-'Ilmiyya, 1424/2004), 1:191, on Q 2:153–54.

77. When *shahīd* (pl. *shuhadā'*) appears in the Qur'ān (e.g., 3:140, 4:69, 39:69), it is not clear whether it carries the meaning of "martyr." Perhaps the most likely case is

Q 4:69: "Whosoever obeys God, and the Messenger—they are with those whom God has blessed, Prophets, just men, martyrs [*shuhadā'*], the righteous; good companions they!" In certain cases (Q 2:282, 24:4) the term can only have the primary meaning of "witness." Goldziher argued that *shahīd* acquired the secondary meaning of "martyr" in post-qur'anic literature (through Syriac Christian influence), but the case of Q 4:69 suggests to me that this meaning exists already in the Qur'an. See Ignác Goldziher, *Muhammedanische Studien* (Halle: Niemeyer, 1888–1890), 2:350–51, cited by E. Kohlberg, "Shahīd," *EI2*, 9:204a. See also W. Raven, "Martyr," *EQ*, 282a.

78. On this topic, see Dal Santo, "Saints' Inactivity." Dal Santo traces this teaching in the thought of Ephrem and Narsai (d. 500) and argues that Mar Ishai (d. perhaps in the 570s) seeks to reconcile this teaching with a cult around the postmortem activity of the saints in his treatise *On the Martyrs.*

79. See Andræ, *Origines de l'islam,* 161–62.

80. Olivier Carré writes the following, noting also the argument of Régis Blachère in regard to the "sleep of the soul" among the church fathers: "Pour ce qui est de 'l'élévation' corps et âme dans le Coran, R. Blachère ([*Le Coran,* Paris: Maisonneuve, 1949], 900, n. 163) la compare aux 'âmes mortes vivant devant Dieu' de certains écrits syriaques contemporains du Coran, expression contradictoire dans les termes et, je pense, compréhensible seulement si l'âme n'est pas séparable du corps." O. Carré, "Méthodes et débats, à propos du Coran sur quelques ondes française actuelles," *Arabica* 53 (2006): 353–81, at 363.

81. On this, see Andræ, *Origines de l'islam,* 162–63. Aphrahat (*Demonstrations,* 8:19) also taught that this period of sleep is restful for the believers, but for the unfaithful and sinners it is restless (a teaching that might be connected to the later Islamic teaching of the torture in the grave during *barzakh*): "For the servant, for whom his Lord is preparing stripes and bonds, while he is sleeping desires not to awake, for he knows that when the dawn shall have come and he shall awake, his Lord will scourge and bind him. But the good servant, to whom his Lord has promised gifts, looks expectantly for the time when dawn shall come and he shall receive presents from his Lord. And even though he is soundly sleeping, in his dream he sees something like what his Lord is about to give him, whatsoever He has promised him, and he rejoices in his dream, and exults, and is gladdened. As for the wicked, his sleep is not pleasant to him, for he imagines that lo! the dawn has come for him, and his heart is broken in his dream."

82. Aphrahat, *Demonstrations,* 8:18.

83. On this, see Andræ, *Origines de l'islam,* 166.

84. Andræ, *Origines de l'islam,* 168. Andræ explains earlier that the martyr has a clear vision of paradise even at the moment of his condemnation, while still living (see the account of Stephen's martyrdom in Acts 7:55–56). The martyr has no fear of hell: "Il contemple déjà l'invisible de ses propres yeux et marche dans le monde céleste. . . . Il n'est déjà maintenant plus sur terre; son corps s'attarde bien encore ici-bas, mais son esprit est déjà dans le monde céleste" (ibid., 121).

85. Mar Ishai, *Traités sur les martyrs,* 32; Andræ, *Origines de l'islam,* 168.

86. Cf. also Q 2:154; this passage is discussed in Dal Santo, "Saints' Inactivity," 287. Andræ (*Origines de l'islam,* 168) traces this teaching all the way back to the Latin

father Tertullian in his *De anima* and writes that according to Tertullian, "All souls, even the just, will proceed to hell or live in different degrees of an intermediate state [after death]. The only exception made is for the souls of the martyrs who will travel immediately to paradise."

87. On the importance of the *Didascalia* to the Qur'an's ritual laws, see H. Zellentin, *The Qur'ān's Legal Culture: The* Didascalia Apostolorum *as a Point of Departure* (Tübingen: Mohr Siebeck, 2013).

88. *Didascalia,* 84; italics in original.

89. *Didascalia,* 85–86; italics added.

90. Dal Santo ("Saints' Inactivity," 284–85) emphasizes the devotion to the martyrs in the liturgical calendar of the East Syrian Church (which celebrated a feast for the martyrs on Easter Friday) and in the thought of East Syrian theologians including Mar Ishai: "Thus, the holy fathers decreed that the Feast of the Martyrs should occur when it did 'so that,' Ishai affirmed, 'the proximity of the commemoration of the saints' sufferings should help us to understand that, just as the solemnity of their commemoration is close to the glorious resurrection of our Saviour, so they themselves are also close to Christ and participate in his benefits': 'My desire,' it is written, 'is to leave this world and be with Christ (Phil. 1.23).'"

91. G. Bassetti-Sani, *The Koran in the Light of Christ: A Christian Interpretation of the Sacred Book of Islam,* trans. W. R. Carroll and B. Dauphinee (Chicago: Franciscan Herald Press, 1978). Bassetti-Sani argues that the Qur'an is a type of "preparation of the Gospel" revealed to Muhammad by God for the sake of the pagan Arabs, and in order to refute the ideas of (what Bassetti-Sani sees as) the presence of Sadducee Judaism in his context. He writes: "God has placed the task of being the sure guide, leading mankind to the fullness of the truth, in the hands of the Church, which alone possesses fullness of the light—and even the Church does not arrive at this fullness all at once, nor is it always ready to give instant solutions to the problems of mankind. It should have been the task of the Church, through its sons, to assist the Muslims, starting with the Christian truths that are latent in the Koran and bringing them to light" (ibid., 148).

92. G. Tartar, *Connaitre Jesus-Christ: Lire le Coran à la lumière de l'Évangile* (Combs-la-Ville: Centre évangélique de témoignage et de dialogue, 1985). Tartar writes in the introduction, "J'ai étudié le Coran et l'Islam dans un esprit de foi, de piété et de recherche sincère de la 'Vérité' révélée; et je me serais converti, si j'étais parvenu à la conviction que l'Islam représente la vraie religion; mais je n'y ai trouvé rien qui dépasse l'enseignement de l'Evangile, le complète ou l'enrichit" (3). Cf. his earlier work *Le Coran rend témoignage à Jésus-Christ* (Paris: Témoignage évangélique et dialogue islamo-chrétien, 1980). Much earlier I. di Matteo developed a similar argument, in a more scholarly and sober tone, in *La divinità di Cristo e la dottrina della Trinità in Maometto e nei polemisti musulmani* (Rome: Pontifical Biblical Institute, 1938).

93. See Paul of Antioch, "*Risāla ilā aḥad al-muslimīn,*" in L. Cheikho, ed., *Vingt traités théologiques d'auteurs arabes chrétiens (IXe–XIIIe siècles)* (Beirut: Imprimerie Catholique, 1920), 15–26; trans.: "Lettre aux musulmans," trans. P. Khoury, *Paul d'Antioche* (Beirut: Imprimerie Catholique, 1964), 169–87. An English translation by Nafisa Abdel-

sadek, "Paul's Letter to the Muslims: English Translation from Arabic and French Source Documents," is available at https://www.researchgate.net/publication/268216125_Paul's_Letter_to_the_Muslims_English_Translation_from_Arabic_and_French_source_documents.

94. See ʿAbd al-Jabbār, *Critique of Christian Origins*, pt. 2, v. 88.

95. Boisliveau, *Coran par lui-même*. Boisliveau discusses in depth the relationship between the argumentative strategies of the Qur'an and its self-references, and argues that all of this suggests a highly sectarian environment. She also speaks of the logic implied by the Qur'an's "self-canonization": "le Coran vient de Dieu parce qu'il vient de Dieu" (297).

96. In our correspondence David Bertaina has added another point, namely that the very nature of qur'anic style, what he calls "liturgical psalmody," also points to a Christian milieu, where teachings were communicated in metric homilies (*mēmrē*) and monks were reciting the Psalms as part of their daily rituals. We have seen (Chapter 3) that the prayer life of monks indeed seems to have been of interest to the Qur'an's author.

Bibliography

Primary Sources

ʿAbd al-Jabbār. *The Critique of Christian Origins: A Parallel English–Arabic Text.* Edited and translated by Gabriel Said Reynolds and Samir Khalil Samir. Provo: Brigham Young University Press, 2009.

Anderson, Gary A., and Michael E. Stone. *A Synopsis of the Books of Adam and Eve.* Society of Biblical Literature Early Judaism and Its Literature 5. Atlanta: Scholars Press, 1994.

Bedjan, Paul. *Histoire complète de Joseph par Saint Ephrem: Poème en douze livres.* Paris: Harrassowitz, 1891.

Ephrem. *Hymns on Faith.* Translated by Jeffery Wickes. Washington, DC: Catholic University of America Press, 2015.

———. *Saint Ephrem's Commentary on Tatian's* Diatessaron. Translated by Carmel McCarthy. Oxford: Oxford University Press/University of Manchester, 1993.

Epiphanius of Salamis. *The* Panarion *of Epiphanius of Salamis, Book 1 (Sects 1–46).* Translated by Frank Williams. 2nd ed. Leiden: Brill, 2009.

Ibn Hishām. *Sīrat Rasūl Allāh.* Edited by F. Wüstenfeld. Göttingen: Dieterich, 1858–1860. English trans.: Ibn Isḥāq, *The Life of Muḥammad.* Translated by A. Guillaume. Oxford: Oxford University Press, 1955.

Jacob of Serugh. *Jacob of Sarug's Homily on the Veil on Moses' Face.* Translated by S. P. Brock. Piscataway, NJ: Gorgias, 2009.

Ibn al-Jawzī. *Zād al-Masīr.* Edited by Muḥammad Zuhayr al-Shāwīsh, Shuʿayb al-Arnaʾūṭ, and ʿAbd al-Qādir al-Arnaʾūṭ. Beirut: al-Maktab al-Islāmī, 1404.

Mar Ishai. *Traités sur les martyrs, Patrologia Orientalis* 7:1. Translated by Addaï Scher. Paris: Firmin-Didot, 1911.

Muqātil b. Sulaymān. *Tafsīr Muqātil.* Edited by ʿAbdallāh Muḥammad al-Shaḥāta. Beirut: Dār al-Turāth al-ʿArabī, 2002. Originally published Cairo: Muʾassasat al-Ḥalabī, n.d.

Al-Rāghib al-Iṣfahānī. *Mufradāt alfāẓ al-Qurʾān.* Ed. Ṣafwān ʿAdnān Dāwūdī. Damascus: Dār al-Qalam, 1433/2011.

Al-Ṭabarī, Abū Jaʿfar. *Jāmiʿ al-bayān fī taʾwīl al-Qurʾān.* Edited by Muḥammad Bayḍūn. Beirut: Dār al-Fikr, 1408/1988.

Al-Wāhidī, ʿAlī b. Aḥmad. *Asbāb al-Nuzūl.* Translated by Mokrane Guezzou. Amman: Royal Aal al-Bayt Institute for Islamic Thought, 2008.

Al-Zamakhsharī. *al-Kashf ʿan ḥaqāʾiq ghawāmiḍ al-tanzīl.* Edited by Muḥammad Ḥusayn Aḥmad. Cairo: Maṭbaʿat al-Istiqāma, 1365/1946.

Secondary Sources

Afasuruddin, Asma. *The First Muslims: History and Memory.* London: OneWorld, 2008.

Ali, Abdullah Yusuf. *The Holy Quran.* Lahore: Muḥammad Ashraf, 1938.

Al-Jallad, Ahmad. *The Damascus Psalm Fragment.* Chicago: Oriental Institute of the University of Chicago, 2020.

———. "The Linguistic Landscape of Pre-Islamic Arabia: Context for the Qurʾan." Pages 111–27 in *Oxford Handbook of Qurʾanic Studies.* Edited by Mustafa Shah and Muhammad Abdel Haleem. Oxford: Oxford University Press, 2020.

———. "The Pre-Islamic *Basmala:* Reflections on Its First Epigraphic Attestation and Its Original Significance." *JSAI* 52 (2022): 1–28.

Al-Jallad, Ahmad, and Ali Al-Manaser. "The Pre-Islamic Divine Name ʿsy and the Background of the Qurʾānic Jesus." *JIQSA* 6 (2021): 107–36.

Al-Jallad, Ahmad, and Hythem Sidky. "A Paleo-Arabic Inscription of a Companion of Muhammad." *JNES* 83 (2024): 1–14.

———. "A Paleo-Arabic Inscription on a Route North of Ṭāʾif." *Arabian Archaeology and Epigraphy* (2021): 1–14.

Ambros, Arne A., and Stephan Procházka. *A Concise Dictionary of Koranic Arabic.* Wiesbaden: Ludwig Reichert, 2004.

Amir-Moezzi, Mohammad Ali, and Guillaume Dye, eds. *Le Coran des historiens.* Paris: Les éditions du Cerf, 2019.

Anderson, Gary A. *The Genesis of Perfection: Adam and Eve in Jewish and Christian Imagination.* Louisville: Westminster John Knox, 2001.

Andræ, Tor. *Les origines de l'islam et le christianisme.* Translated by Jules Roche. Paris: Adrien–Maisonneuve, 1955. Originally published as "Der Ursprung des Islams und das Christentum." *Kyrkshistorisk årsskrift* 23 (1923), 149–206; 24 (1924), 213–25; 25 (1925), 45–112.

Anthony, Sean W. "Muḥammad, Menaḥem, and the Paraclete: New Light on Ibn Isḥāq's (d. 150/767) Arabic Version of John 15: 23–16:1." *BSOAS* 79 (2016): 255–78.

Archer, George. "The Hellhound of the Qurʾan: A Dog at the Gate of the Underworld." *JQS* 18, no. 3 (2016): 1–33.

Ayoub, Mahmoud. "Nearest in Amity: Christians in the Qur'an and Contemporary Exegetical Tradition." *Islam and Christian-Muslim Relations* 8 (1997): 145–64.

Azaiez, M., G. S. Reynolds, T. Tesei, and H. M. Zafer, eds. *The Qur'an Seminar Commentary: A Collaborative Study of 50 Qur'anic Passages/Le Qur'an Seminar: Commentaire Collaboratif de 50 Passages Coraniques.* Berlin: de Gruyter, 2016.

Azaiez, Mehdi. *Le contre-discours coranique.* Berlin: de Gruyter, 2015.

Al-Azmeh, Aziz. *The Emergence of Islam in Late Antiquity: Allāh and His People.* New York: Cambridge University Press, 2014.

Azzi, Joseph. *Le Prêtre et le prophète: Aux sources du Coran.* Translated by M. S. Garnier. Paris: Maisonneuve et Larose, 2001.

Bannister, Andrew G. *An Oral-Formulaic Study of the Qur'an.* Lanham, MD: Lexington Books, 2014.

Baumstark, Anton. "Eine altarabische Evangelienübersetzung aus dem Christlich-Palästinensischen." *Zeitschrift für Semitistik und verwandte Gebiete* 8, no. 3 (1932): 201–9.

Baynes, Leslie. "Enoch and Jubilees in the Canon of the Ethiopian Orthodox Church." Pages 799–818 (vol. 2) in *A Teacher for All Generations: Essays in Honor of James C. VanderKam,* edited by Eric F. Mason, Samuel I. Thomas, Alison Schofield, and Eugene Ulrich. Leiden: Koninklijke Brill NV, 2011.

Bell, Richard. *A Commentary on the Qur'an.* Edited by C. E. Bosworth and M. E. J. Richardson. Manchester: University of Manchester, 1991.

———. "Mohammed's Call." *Moslem World* 24 (1934): 13–19.

———. *The Origin of Islam in Its Christian Environment.* London: Macmillan, 1926.

Bertaina, David. "Bodily Resurrection in the Qur'ān and Syriac Anti-Tritheist Debate." *JIQSA* 3 (2018): 43–77.

Boisliveau, Anne-Sylvie. *Le Coran par lui-même: vocabulaire et argumentation du discours coranique auto référentiel.* Leiden: Koninklijke Brill NV, 2014.

Brock, Sebastian. "St. Ephrem the Syrian on Reading Scripture." *Downside Review* 125, no. 438 (2007): 37–50.

Brockelmann, Carl. "Allah und die Götzen: Der Ursprung des islamischen Monotheismus." *Archiv für Religionswissenschaft* 21, no. 1 (1922): 99–121.

———. "Iqāmat aṣ-ṣalat." Pages 314–20 in *Festschrift Eduard Sachau: Zum siebzigsten Geburtstage gewidmet von Freunden und Schülern,* edited by Gotthold Weil. Berlin: Georg Reimer, 1915.

Calder, Norman. "Tafsīr from Ṭabarī to Ibn Kathīr: Problems in the Description of a Genre, Illustrated with Reference to the Story of Abraham." Pages 101–40 in *Approaches to the Qur'ān,* edited by Gerald Hawting and Abdul-Kader A. Shareef. London: Routledge, 1993.

Cheikho, Louis. *al-Naṣrāniyya wa-adabuhā bayna'arab al-Jāhiliyya.* Beirut: Dār al-Mashriq, 1912–23). French trans.: *Le Christianisme et la littérature chrétienne en Arabie avant l'Islam.* Beirut: Imprimerie Catholique, 1923; reprint: Piscataway, NJ: Gorgias Press, 2012.

———. *Shu'arā' al-naṣrāniyya qabl al-Islām.* Beirut: Dār al-Mashriq, 1890/1999.

Clivaz, Claire, and Sara Schulthess. "On the Source and Rewriting of 1 Corinthians 2.9 in Christian, Jewish and Islamic Traditions (1 Clem 34.8; GosJud 47.10–13; A Ḥadīth Qudsī)." *New Testament Studies* 61, no. 2 (2015): 183–200.

Cole, Juan. *Muhammad: Prophet of Peace amid the Clash of Empires*. New York: Nation Books, 2018.

Cook, L. Stephen. *On the Question of the Cessation of Prophecy in Ancient Judaism*. Tübingen: Mohr Siebeck, 2011.

Cragg, Kenneth. *Jesus and the Muslim: An Exploration*. London: Allen & Unwin, 1985.

Dal Santo, Matthew. "The Saints' Inactivity Post Mortem: Soul Sleep and the Cult of Saints East of the Euphrates." Pages 237–320 in *Debating the Saints' Cults in the Age of Gregory the Great*, edited by M. Dal Santo. Oxford: Oxford University Press, 2012.

Debié, Muriel. "Les controverses miaphysites en Arabie et le Coran." Pages 137–56 in *Les controverses religieuses en syriaque*, edited by Flavia Ruani. Paris: Geuthner, 2016.

de Blois, François. "Elchasai–Manes–Muḥammad: Manichäismus und Islam in religionshistorischen Vergleich." *Der Islam: Journal of Culture and History of the Middle East* 81, no. 1 (2004): 31–48.

———. "*Naṣrānī* and *Ḥanīf*: Studies on the Religious Vocabulary of Christianity and Islam." *BSOAS* 65, no. 1 (2002): 1–30.

de Premare, Alfred Louis. "'Comme il est écrit': L'histoire d'un texte." *Studia Islamica* 70 (1989): 27–56.

Del Río Sánchez, Francisco, ed. *Jewish Christianity and the Origins of Islam: Papers Presented at the Colloquium Held in Washington DC, October 29–31, 2015 (8th ASME Conference)*. Turnhout: Brepols, 2018.

Dictionnaire du Coran. Edited by M. A. Amir-Moezzi. Paris: Laffont, 2007.

Dmitriev, Kirill. "An Early Christian Arabic Account of the Creation of the World." Pages 349–87 in *The Qur'ān in Context: Historical and Literary Investigations into the Qur'ānic Milieu*, edited by Angelika Neuwirth, Nicolai Sinai, and Michael Marx. Leiden: Koninklijke Brill NV, 2010.

Donner, Fred. *Muhammad and the Believers at the Origins of Islam*. Cambridge, MA: Harvard University Press, 2010.

Droge, Arthur. *The Qur'an: A New Annotated Translation*. Sheffield: Equinox, 2013.

Durie, Mark. *The Qur'an and Its Biblical Reflexes: Investigations into the Genesis of a Religion*. Lanham, MD: Lexington Books, 2018.

El-Badawi, Emran Iqbal. *Queens and Prophets: How Arabian Noblewomen and Holy Men Shaped Paganism, Christianity and Islam*. London: OneWorld Academic, 2022.

———. *The Qur'ān and the Aramaic Gospel Traditions*. Abingdon: Routledge, 2014.

Fiema, Zbigniew T., Ahmad Al-Jallad, Michael C. A. Macdonald, and Laïla Nehmé. "*Provincia Arabia:* Nabataea, the Emergence of Arabic as a Written Language, and Graeco-Arabica." Pages 373–433 in *Arabs and Empires Before Islam*, edited by Greg Fisher. Oxford: Oxford University Press, 2015.

Fisher, Greg, and Philip Wood. "Arabs and Christianity." Pages 276–372 in *Arabs and Empires Before Islam*, edited by Greg Fisher. Oxford: Oxford University Press, 2015.

Forness, Philip Michael. *Preaching Christology in the Roman Near East: A Study of Jacob of Serugh*. Oxford: Oxford University Press, 2018.

Gallez, Édouard-Marie. *Le messie et son prophète: Aux origines de l'Islam*. Versailles: Éditions de Paris, 2005.

Geiger, Abraham. *Was hat Mohammed aus dem Judenthume aufgenommen*. Leipzig: Kaufmann, 1902 (reprint of Bonn: Baaden, 1833). English trans.: F. M. Young, *Judaism and Islam*. Madras: Delhi Mission, 1896.

Gibb, Hamilton A. R. "Pre-Islamic Monotheism in Arabia." *Harvard Theological Review* 55 (1962): 269–80.

Gnilka, Joachim. *Die Nazarener und der Koran: Eine Spurensuche*. Freiburg: Herder, 2007.

Goldziher, Ignác. "Die Ǵinnen der Dichter." *Zeitschrift der deutschen morgenländischen Gesellschaft* 45 (1891): 685–90.

Goudarzi, Mohsen. "Unearthing Abraham's Altar: The Cultic Dimensions of *Dīn*, *Islām*, and *Ḥanīf* in the Qur'an." *JNES* 82, no. 1 (2023): 77–102.

Grasso, Valentina. *Pre-Islamic Arabia: Societies, Politics, Cults and Identities During Late Antiquity*. Cambridge: Cambridge University Press, 2023.

Griffith, Sidney. "Arguing from Scripture: The Bible in the Christian/Muslim Encounter in the Middle Ages." Pages 29–58 in *Scripture and Pluralism: Reading the Bible in the Religiously Plural Worlds of the Middle Ages and Renaissance*, edited by Thomas Heffernan and Thomas E. Burman. Leiden: Brill, 2005.

———. *The Bible in Arabic: The Scriptures of the "People of the Book" in the Language of Islam*. Princeton: Princeton University Press, 2013.

———. "Christian Lore and the Arabic Qur'ān: The 'Companions of the Cave' in *Sūrat al-Kahf* and in Syriac Christian Tradition." *QHC*, 109–37.

———. "*Al-Naṣārā* in the Qur'ān: A Hermeneutical Reflection." Pages 301–22 in *New Perspectives on the Qur'ān: The Qur'ān in Its Historical Context 2*, edited by Gabriel Said Reynolds. Abingdon: Routledge, 2011.

Günther, Sebastian. "Muḥammad, the Illiterate Prophet: An Islamic Creed in the Qur'an and Qur'anic Exegesis." *JQS* 4 (2002): 1–26.

Hainthaler, Theresia. "'Adī ibn Zayd al-'Ibādī: The Christian Poet of al-Ḥīra and His Poem No. 3 Written in Jail." *Parole de l'Orient* 30 (2005): 157–72.

Haleem, Muhammad Abdel. *Understanding the Qur'an: Themes and Style*. London: I. B. Tauris, 1999.

Hawting, G. R. *The Idea of Idolatry and the Emergence of Islam: From Polemic to History*. Cambridge: Cambridge University Press, 1999.

———. "Were There Prophets in the Jahiliyya?" Pages 186–212 in *Islam and Its Past: Jahiliyya, Late Antiquity and the Qur'an*, edited by Carol Bakhos and Michael Cook. Oxford: Oxford University Press, 2017.

Heidemann, Stefan. "The Evolving Representation of the Early Islamic Empire and Its Religion on Coin Imagery." Pages 149–96 in *The Qur'ān in Context: Historical and Literary Investigations into the Qur'ānic Milieu*, edited by Angelika Neuwirth, Nicolai Sinai, and Michael Marx. Leiden: Brill, 2007.

Hirschberg, J. W. *Jüdische und christliche Lehren im vor- und frühislamischen Arabien: Ein Beitrag zur Entstehungsgeschichte des Islams.* Krakow: Nakladem Pollskiej Akademii Umiejetnosci, 1939.

Hirschfeld, Hartwig. *New Researches into the Composition and Exegesis of the Qoran.* London: Royal Asiatic Society, 1902.

Hodgson, Marshall G. S. *The Venture of Islam: Conscience and History in a World Civilization,* Vol. 1 of *The Classical Age of Islam.* 2nd ed. Chicago: University of Chicago Press, 1974.

Hoffman, Thomas. *The Poetic Qur'ān: Studies on Qur'ān Poeticity.* Wiesbaden: Harrassowitz, 2007.

Horovitz, Joseph. "'Adi ibn Zeyd, the Poet of Hira." *Islamic Culture: The Hyderabad Quarterly Review* 4 (1930): 31–69.

Hoyland, Robert. "'*Arabī* and *a'jamī* in the Qur'ān: The Language of Revelation in Muḥammad's Ḥijāz." Pages 105–15 in *Scripts and Scripture: Writing and Religion in Arabia Circa 500–700 CE,* edited by F. Donner and R. Hasselbach-Andee. Chicago: Oriental Institute, 2022.

———. *Arabia and the Arabs: From the Bronze Age to the Coming of Islam.* London: Routledge, 2001.

———. "Epigraphy and the Emergence of Arab Identity." Pages 219–42 in *From Al-Andalus to Khurasan: Documents from the Medieval Muslim World,* edited by Petra M. Sijpesteijn, Lennart Sundelin, Sofía Torallas Tovar, and Amalia Zomeño. Leiden: Brill, 2006.

———. "The Language of the Qur'an and a Near Eastern Rip van Winkel." Pages 17–43 in *A Life with the Prophet? Examining Hadith, Sira and Qur'an,* edited by Albrecht Fuess and Stefan Weninger. Berlin: EBVerlag, 2017.

Huart, M. Clément. "Une nouvelle source du Qorân." *Journal Asiatique* 10 (1904): 125–67.

Hughes, Aaron W. *Abrahamic Religions: On the Uses and Abuses of History.* New York: Oxford University Press, 2012.

Hurgronje, C. Snouck. *Mohammedanism: Lectures on Its Origin, Its Religious and Political Growth, and Its Present State.* New York: G. P. Putnam's Sons, 1916.

Hussain, Saqib. "Adam and the Names." *BSOAS,* forthcoming.

Jeffery, Arthur. *The Foreign Vocabulary of the Qur'ān.* Leiden: Brill, 2007.

Jones, Alan. "The Oral and the Written: Some Thoughts About the Quranic Text." *The Arabist: Budapest Studies in Arabic* 17 (1996): 57–66.

Kashouh, Hikmat. *The Arabic Versions of the Gospels: The Manuscripts and Their Families.* Berlin: de Gruyter, 2012.

Kermani, Navid. *God Is Beautiful: The Aesthetic Experience of the Quran.* Translated by Tony Crawford. Cambridge: Polity, 2015.

Khalidi, Tarif. *The Qur'ān: A New Translation.* London: Penguin Classics, 2008.

Kister, M. J. "'Labbayka, Allāhumma, Labbayka . . .': On a Monotheistic Aspect of a Jāhiliyya Practice." *JSAI* 2, no. 1 (1980): 33–57.

———. "'*Al-Taḥannuth*': An Inquiry into the Meaning of a Term." *BSOAS* 31, no. 2 (1968): 223–36.

Kulik, Alexander. *Retroverting Slavonic Pseudepigrapha: Towards the Original of the* Apocalypse of Abraham. Atlanta: Society of Biblical Literature, 2004.

Lammens, Henri. "Les chrétiens à la Mecque à la veille de l'hégire." *Bulletin de l'institut français d'archéologie orientale* 14 (1918): 191–230.

———. "Qoran et tradition: Comment fut composée la vie de Mahomet." *Recherches de Science Religieuse* 1 (1910): 25–51. English trans.: "The Koran and Tradition: How the Life of Muhammad Was Composed." Pages 169–87 in *The Quest for the Historical Muhammad,* translated by Ibn Warraq. Amherst: Prometheus, 2000.

Lane, Edward. *An Arabic-English Lexicon.* London: Williams and Norgate, 1863–1893.

Lange, Christian. "'What No Eye Has Seen and No Ear Has Heard': Towards a Sensory History of Early Islam." *JSAI* 51 (2021): 245–92.

Lecker, Michael. "Muḥammad." Pages 157–66 in *The Islamic World,* edited by Andrew Rippin. Abingdon: Routledge, 2008.

Levenson, Jon D. *Inheriting Abraham: The Legacy of the Patriarch in Judaism, Christianity, and Islam.* Princeton: Princeton University Press, 2012.

Licht, Jacob. *Storytelling in the Bible.* Jerusalem: Magnes, 1978.

Lindstedt, Ilkka. *Muḥammad and His Followers in Context: The Religious Map of Late Antique Arabia.* Leiden: Brill, 2024.

Loreto, Romolo. "Results from the 2009–2016 Excavation Seasons in the Historical Centre of Dūmat al-Jandal, Ancient Adummatu." *Proceedings of the Seminar for Arabian Studies* 48 (2018): 151–64.

Loynes, Simon P. *Revelation in the Qur'an: A Semantic Study of the Roots n-z-l and w-ḥ-y.* Leiden: Brill, 2021.

Madigan, Daniel. *The Qur'ān's Self-Image: Writing and Authority in Islam's Scripture.* Princeton: Princeton University Press, 2001.

Margoliouth, D. S. "The Origins of Arabic Poetry." *Journal of the Royal Asiatic Society of Great Britain and Ireland* 3 (1925): 417–49.

Massignon, Louis. "Les 'sept dormants' apocalypse de l'Islam." *Analecta Bollandiana* 68 (1950): 245–60.

Melchert, Christopher. "'God Created Adam in His Image.'" *JQS* 13 (2011): 113–24.

Miller, Nathaniel. *The Emergence of Arabic Poetry: From Regional Identities to Islamic Canonization.* Philadelphia: University of Pennsylvania Press, 2024.

Minov, Sergey. *Memory and Identity in the Syriac* Cave of Treasures: *Rewriting the Bible in Sasanian Iran.* Leiden: Brill, 2011.

———. "Satan's Refusal to Worship Adam: A Jewish Motif and Its Reception in Syriac Christian Tradition." Pages 230–71 in *Tradition, Transmission, and Transformation from Second Temple Literature Through Judaism and Christianity in Late Antiquity,* edited by Menahem Kister, Hillel I. Newman, Michael Segal, and Ruth A. Clements. Leiden: Brill, 2015.

Mir, Mustansir. "The Qur'anic Story of Joseph: Plot, Themes, and Characters." *Muslim World* 76 (1986): 1–15.

Monroe, James T. "Oral Composition in Pre-Islamic Poetry." *Journal of Arabic Literature* 3 (1972): 1–53.

Montgomery, James E. "The Empty Ḥijāz." Pages 39–97 in *Arabic Theology, Arabic Philosophy: From the Many to the One. Essays in Celebration of Richard M. Frank*, edited by James E. Montgomery. Leuven: Peeters, 2006.

Nasr, Seyyed Hossein, Caner K. Dagli, Maria Massi Dakake, Joseph E. B. Lumbard, and Mohammed Rustom, eds. *The Study Quran: A New Translation and Commentary.* New York: HarperOne, 2015.

Nehmé, Laïla. "New Dated Inscriptions (Nabataean and Pre-Islamic Arabic) from a Site near al-Jawf, Ancient Dūmah, Saudi Arabia." *Arabian Epigraphic Notes* 3 (2017): 121–64.

Nehmé, Laila, ed. *The Darb al-Bakrah: A Caravan Route in North West Arabia Discovered by Ali I. al-Ghabban: Catalogue of the Inscriptions.* Riyadh: Saudi Commission for Tourism and National Heritage, 2018.

Neuenkirchen, Paul. "Eschatology, Responsories and Rubrics in Eastern Christian Liturgies and in the Qur'an: Some Preliminary Remarks." Pages 131–46 in *Early Islam: The Sectarian Milieu of Late Antiquity?*, edited by G. Dye. Brussels: Éditions de l'Université de Bruxelles, 2023.

Neuwirth, Angelika. *The Qur'an and Late Antiquity: A Shared Heritage.* Translated by S. Wilder. Oxford: Oxford University Press, 2019. Originally published as *Der Koran als Text der Spätantike. Ein europäischer Zugang.* Berlin: Verlag der Weltreligionen, 2010.

Nöldeke, Theodor. "Arabs (Ancient)." Pages 659–73 in *Encyclopedia of Religion and Ethics*, vol. 1, edited by James Hastings, John A. Selbie, and Louis H. Gray. New York: Charles Scribner's Sons, 1967.

———. *Geschichte des Qorāns*, 1st ed. Göttingen: Verlag der Dieterichschen Buchhandlung, 1860; 2nd ed., Nöldeke's revised work titled *Über den Ursprung des Qorāns*, including F. Schwally, *Die Sammlung des Qorāns*, edited and revised by F. Schwally. Leipzig: T. Weicher, 1909, 1919; 2nd ed. including G. Bergsträsser and O. Pretzl, *Die Geschichte des Koran-texts.* Leipzig: T. Weicher, 1938; reprinted in 1 vol., Hildesheim: Olms, 1970. English trans.: *History of the Qur'ān.* Edited and translated by Wolfgang H. Behn. Leiden: Brill, 2013.

Obermann, Julian. "Koran and Agada: The Events at Mount Sinai." *American Journal of Semitic Languages and Literatures* 58 (1941): 23–48.

Paret, Rudi. *Der Koran. Übersetzung.* Stuttgart: Kohlhammer, 1962.

Parrinder, Geoffrey. *Jesus in the Qur'ān.* London: Faber & Faber, 1965.

Pohlmann, Karl-Friedrich. *Die Entstehung des Korans. Neue Erkenntnisse aus Sicht der historisch-kritischen Bibelwissenschaft.* Darmstadt: Wissenschaftliche Buchgesellschaft, 2013.

Rahman, Fazlur. *Major Themes in the Qur'an.* 2nd ed. Chicago: University of Chicago Press, 2009.

Reissner, H. G. "The Ummī Prophet and the Banu Israil of the Qur'ān." *Muslim World* 39 (1949): 276–81.

Retsö, Jan. *The Arabs in Antiquity: Their History from the Assyrians to the Umayyads.* London: Routledge, 2003.

Reynolds, Gabriel Said. "Biblical Turns of Phrase in the Quran." Pages 45–69 in *Light upon Light: Essays in Islamic Thought and History in Honor of Gerhard Bowering*, edited by James E. Montgomery. Leiden: Brill, 2019.

———. "A Flawed Prophet? Noah in the Qur'ān and Qur'anic Commentary." Pages 260–73 in *Islamic Studies Today: Essays in Honor of Andrew Rippin*, edited by Majid Daneshgar and Walid Saleh. Leiden: Brill, 2016.

———. "Intratextuality, Doublets, and Orality in the Qur'an, with Attention to Suras 61 and 66." Pages 513–42 in *Unlocking the Medinan Qur'an*, edited by Nicolai Sinai (Leiden: Brill, 2022).

———. "Moses, Son of Pharaoh: A Study of Qur'ān 26 and Its Exegesis." Pages 289–301 in *Exegetical Crossroads: Understanding Scripture in Judaism, Christianity and Islam in the Pre-Modern Orient*, edited by Georges Tamer, Regina Grundmann, Assaad Elias Kattan, and Karl Pinggéra. Berlin: de Gruyter, 2018.

———. "The Muslim Jesus: Dead or Alive?" *BSOAS* 72 (2009): 237–58.

———. "Noah's Lost Son in the Qur'ān." *Arabica* 64 (2017): 129–48.

———. "On the Presentation of Christianity in the Qur'ān and the Many Aspects of Qur'anic Rhetoric." *Al-Bayān: Journal of Qur'ān and Ḥadīth Studies* 12, no. 1 (2014): 42–54.

———. "On the Qur'ān and the Theme of the Jews as 'Killers of the Prophets.'" *Al-Bayān: Journal of Qur'ān and Hadith Studies* 10 (2012): 9–34.

———. "On the Qur'anic Accusation of Scriptural Falsification." *JAOS* 130 (2010): 189–202.

———. "Le problème de la chronologie du Coran." *Arabica* 58 (2011): 477–502.

———. *The Qur'ān and Its Biblical Subtext*. Abingdon: Routledge, 2010.

———. *The Qur'ān and the Bible: Text and Commentary*. New Haven: Yale University Press, 2018.

———, ed. *The Qur'ān in Its Historical Context*. London: Routledge, 2008.

———. "Their Very Words? A Preliminary Evaluation of Reported Speech in the Qur'an." *JNES* 82 (2023): 1–14.

Reynolds, G. S., M. Klar, H. Sidky, and M. Sirry, eds. *Yale Dictionary of the Qur'an*. New Haven: Yale University Press, forthcoming.

Rippin, A. "Reading the Qur'ān with Richard Bell." *JAOS* 112 (1992): 639–47.

Robin, Christian. "*Al-'Ilāh* et *Allāh*: Les deux noms de Dieu chez les Arabes chrétiens de Najrān au 6e siècle de l'ère chrétienne." *Hawliyāt* 19 (2020): 57–109.

Robin, Christian, Alī Ibrāhīm al-Ghabbān, and Sa'id Fāyiz Al-Sa'īd. "Inscriptions antiques de la région de Najrān (Arabie saoudite méridionale): nouveaux jalons pour l'histoire de l'écriture, de la langue et du calendrier arabe." *Comptes rendus des séances de l'Académie des Inscriptions et Belles-Lettres* (2014): 1033–1128.

Rodinson, Maxime. *Mohammed*. Translated by Anne Carter. New York: Pantheon, 1971.

Roncaglia, Martiniano. "Éléments Ébionites et Elkésaites dans le Coran." *Proche Orient Chrétien* 21 (1971): 101–26.

Rubin, Uri. "*Ḥanīfiyya* and Ka'ba: An Inquiry in the Arabian Pre-Islamic Background of the *Dīn Ibrāhīm*." *JSAI* 13 (1990): 85–112.

Rudolph, Wilhelm. *Die Abhängigkeit des Qorans von Judentum und Christentum.* Stuttgart: W. Kohlhammer, 1922.

Saleh, Walid. "End of Hope: Suras 10–15, Despair and a Way Out of Mecca." Pages 105–23 in *Qur'anic Studies Today,* edited by Angelika Neuwirth and Michael Sells. London: Routledge, 2016.

Schenzle, Ruben. "If God Is King, Is Man His Vicegerent? Considering *Ḫalīfa* in Regard to Ancient Kingship." Pages 132–48 in *New Approaches to Human Dignity in the Context of Qur'ānic Anthropology,* edited by Rüdiger Braun and Hüseyin I. Çiçek. Newcastle upon Tyne: Cambridge Scholars Publishing, 2017.

Schoeps, Hans Joachim. *Theologie und Geschichte des Judenchristentums.* Tübingen: Mohr (Paul Siebeck), 1949.

Segovia, Carlos. "Abraha's Christological Formula *rḥmnn w-msıḥ-hw* and Its Relevance for the Study of Islam's Origins." *Oriens Christianus* 98 (2015): 52–63.

Seppälä, Serafim. "Reminiscences of Icons in the Qur'an?" *Islam and Christian-Muslim Relations* 22 (2011): 3–21.

Shahîd, Irfan. *Byzantium and the Arabs in the Fourth Century.* Washington, DC: Dumbarton Oaks, 2006.

Shoemaker, Stephen. "Christmas in the Qur'an: The Qur'anic Account of Jesus' Nativity and Palestinian Local Tradition." *JSAI* 28 (2003): 11–39.

———. *Creating the Qur'an: A Historical-Critical Study.* Berkeley: University of California Press, 2022.

———. *A Prophet Has Appeared: The Rise of Islam Through Christian and Jewish Eyes.* Berkeley: University of California Press, 2021.

Sinai, Nicolai. "The Christian Elephant in the Meccan Room: Dye, Tesei, and Shoemaker on the Date of the Qur'ān." *JIQSA* 9 (2024): 1–64.

———. *Key Terms of the Qur'an: A Critical Dictionary.* Princeton: Princeton University Press, 2023.

———. *The Qur'an: A Historical-Critical Introduction.* Edinburgh: Edinburgh University Press, 2017.

———. *Rain-Giver, Bone-Breaker, Score-Settler: Allāh in Pre-Quranic Poetry.* New Haven: American Oriental Society, 2019.

———. "Religious Poetry from the Quranic Milieu: Umayya b. Abī l-Ṣalt on the Fate of the Thamūd." *BSOAS* 74 (2011): 397–416.

Sokoloff, Michael. *A Syriac Lexicon: A Translation from the Latin, Correction, Expansion, and Update of C. Brockelmann's* Lexicon Syriacum. Winona Lake, IN: Eisenbrauns, 2009.

Speer, Robert E. "The Attitude of the Evangelist Toward the Muslim and His Religion." Pages 217–51 in *Lucknow, 1911: Being Papers Read and Discussions on the Training of Missionaries, and Literature for Muslims at the General Conference on Missions to Muslims Held at Lucknow, Jan. 23–28, 1911,* edited by E. M. Wherry. London: Christian Literature Society for India, 1911.

Speyer, Heinrich. *Die biblischen Erzählungen im Qoran.* Gräfenhainichen: Schulze, 1931; reprint: Hildesheim: Olms, 1961.

Sprenger, Aloys. *Das Leben und die Lehre des Moḥammad.* Berlin: Nicolai, 1861.

Sweat, Laura. *The Theological Role of Paradox in the Gospel of Mark.* London: T&T Clark, 2013.

Tannous, Jack B. "Arabic as Christian Language and Arabic as the Language of Christians." Pages 1–94 in *Medieval Encounters: Arabic-Speaking Christians and Islam,* edited by Ayman S. Ibrahim. Piscataway, NJ: Gorgias, 2022.

———. *The Making of the Medieval Middle East: Religion, Society, and Simple Believers.* Princeton: Princeton University Press, 2018.

Trimingham, J. Spencer. *Christianity Among the Arabs in Pre-Islamic Times.* London: Longman, 1979.

van Putten, Marijn. *Quranic Arabic: From Its Hijazi Origins to Its Classical Reading Traditions.* Leiden: Brill, 2022.

Van Roey, Albert, and Pauline Allen, eds. and trans. *Monophysite Texts of the Sixth Century.* Orientalia Lovaniensia Analecta 56. Leuven: Peeters, 1994.

Villeneuve, François. "The Greek Inscriptions at al-ʿArniyyāt and Umm Jadhāyidh." Pages 285–92 in *The Darb al-Bakrah: A Caravan Route in North West Arabia Discovered by Ali I. al-Ghabban. Catalogue of the Inscriptions,* edited by Ayman S. Ibrahim. Riyadh: Saudi Commission for Tourism and National Heritage, 2018.

Wansbrough, John. *Quranic Studies: Sources and Methods of Scriptural Interpretation.* Amherst: Prometheus Books, 2004.

Watt, W. Montgomery. "Belief in a 'High God' in Pre-Islamic Mecca." *Journal of Semitic Studies* 16 (1971): 35–40.

———. *Muhammad at Mecca.* London: Oxford University Press, 1960.

———. "The Qur'ān and Belief in a 'High God.'" *Der Islam* 56 (1979): 205–11.

Webb, Peter. *Imagining the Arabs: Arab Identity and the Rise of Islam.* Edinburgh: Edinburgh University Press, 2016.

Weil, Gustav. *The Bible, the Koran, and the Talmud; or, Biblical Legends of the Musselmans: Compiled from Arabic Sources and Compared with Jewish Traditions.* New York: Harper and Brothers, 1846.

Wellhausen, Julius. *Reste arabischen Heidentums: Gesammelt und erläutert.* Berlin: Georg Reimer, 1887.

Wherry, E. M., ed. *Lucknow, 1911: Being Papers Read and Discussions on the Training of Missionaries, and Literature for Muslims at the General Conference on Missions to Muslims Held at Lucknow, Jan. 23–28, 1911.* London: Christian Literature Society for India, 1911.

Wild, Stefan, ed. *Self-Referentiality in the Qur'ān.* Wiesbaden: Harrassowitz, 2006.

Witztum, Joseph Benzion. "Ibn Isḥāq and the Pentateuch in Arabic." *Jerusalem Studies in Arabic and Islam* 40 (2013): 1–71.

———. "The Syriac Milieu of the Quran: The Recasting of Biblical Narratives." PhD diss., Princeton University, 2011.

Youssef, Ahmed. *Le moine de Mahomet: L'entourage judéo-chrétien à La Mecque au VIe siècle.* Monaco: Rocher, 2008.

Zellentin, Holger M. *Law Beyond Israel: From the Bible to the Qur'an*. Oxford Studies in Abrahamic Religions. Oxford: Oxford University Press, 2022.

Zwemer, S. M. *Arabia: The Cradle of Islam. Studies in the Geography, People, and Politics of the Peninsula with an Account of Islam and Mission-Work*. Edinburgh: Oliphant Anderson and Ferrier, 1900.

Index of the Qur'an, the Bible, and Other Ancient Sources

Qur'an

Bible: Old Testament

Other Ancient Sources

General Index

Arabic surnames beginning with "al-" or "Al-" are alphabetized according to the following word.